New Media Campaigns and the Managed Citizen

The political campaign is one of the most important organizations in a democracy, and whether issue- or candidate-specific, it is one of the least understood organizations in contemporary political life. This book is a critical assessment of the role that information technologies have come to play in contemporary campaigns. With evidence from ethnographic immersion, survey data, and social network analysis, Philip Howard examines the evolving act of political campaigning and the changing organization of political campaigns over the last five election cycles, from 1996 to 2004. Over this time, both grassroots and elite political campaigns have gone online, built multimedia strategies, and constructed complex relational databases. The contemporary political campaign adopts digital technologies that improve reach and fund-raising and at the same time adapts its organizational behavior. The new system of producing political culture has immense implications for the meaning of citizenship and the basis of representation.

Philip N. Howard is an assistant professor in the Communications Department at the University of Washington. He has published a co-edited collection entitled *Society Online: The Internet in Context* (2003) as well as articles in *New Media & Society, American Behavioral Scientist,* and the *Annals of the American Academy of Political and Social Science.* Howard has been a Fellow at the Pew Internet and American Life Project in Washington, D.C., and the Stanhope Centre for Communications Policy Research in London.

COMMUNICATION, SOCIETY, AND POLITICS

Editors

W. Lance Bennett, *University of Washington*

Robert M. Entman, *North Carolina State University*

Editorial Advisory Board

Larry M. Bartels, *Princeton University*

Jay G. Blumler, *Emeritus, University of Leeds*

Daniel Dayan, *Centre National de la Recherche Scientifique, Paris*

Doris A. Graber, *University of Illinois at Chicago*

Paolo Mancini, *Università di Perugia*

Pippa Norris, *Kennedy School of Government, Harvard University*

Barbara Pfetsch, *Wissenschaftszentrum Berlin für Sozialforschung*

Philip Schlesinger, *University of Stirling*

Gadi Wolfsfeld, *Hebrew University of Jerusalem*

Politics and relations among individuals in societies across the world are being transformed by new technologies for targeting individuals and sophisticated methods for shaping personalized messages. The new technologies challenge boundaries of many kinds – among news, information, entertainment, and advertising; among media, with the arrival of the World Wide Web; and even among nations. *Communication, Society, and Politics* probes the political and social impacts of these new communication systems in national, comparative, and global perspective.

Titles in the series:

C. Edwin Baker, *Media, Markets, and Democracy*

W. Lance Bennett and Robert M. Entman, eds., *Mediated Politics: Communication in the Future of Democracy*

Bruce Bimber, *Information and American Democracy: Technology in the Evolution of Political Power*

Murray Edelman, *The Politics of Misinformation*

Frank Esser and Barbara Pfetsch, eds., *Comparing Political Communication: Theories, Cases, and Challenges*

(continued on page following index)

For Gina Neff, my nectar

New Media Campaigns and the Managed Citizen

Philip N. Howard
University of Washington

CAMBRIDGE
UNIVERSITY PRESS

CAMBRIDGE UNIVERSITY PRESS
Cambridge, New York, Melbourne, Madrid, Cape Town, Singapore, São Paulo

Cambridge University Press
40 West 20th Street, New York, NY 10011-4211, USA

www.cambridge.org
Information on this title: www.cambridge.org/9780521847490

First published 2006

Printed in the United States of America

A catalog record for this publication is available from the British Library.

Library of Congress Cataloging in Publication Data
Howard, Philip N.
New media campaigns and the managed citizen / Philip N. Howard.
p. cm. – (Communication, society, and politics)
Includes bibliographical references and index.
ISBN 0-521-84749-4 (hardback) – ISBN 0-521-61227-6 (pbk.)
1. Internet in political campaigns – United States. 2. Communication in politics –
United States – Technological innovations. 3. Political campaigns – United States –
Technological innovations. 4. Mass media – Political aspects – United States.
5. Information technology – Political aspects – United States. I. Title. II. Series.
JK2281.H69 2006
324.7′3′0973–dc22 2005008088

ISBN-13 978-0-521-84749-0 hardback
ISBN-10 0-521-84749-4 hardback

ISBN-13 978-0-521-61227-2 paperback
ISBN-10 0-521-61227-6 paperback

Contents

Tables and Figures

TABLES

FIGURES

Acknowledgments

In the summer of 2003 I was invited to be a Research Fellow at the Stanhope Centre for Communications Policy Research in London, and I worked in an office that looked onto the Speaker's Corner of Hyde Park. Speaker's Corner is one of the oldest living institutions for free speech, an institution used at different times by Marcus Garvey, George Orwell, Vladimir Lenin, and Karl Marx. One of the other academics in residence at Stanhope was Christian Sandvig, and he decided it would be worthwhile to try to bring a wireless internet connection, coined Wi-Fi, to Speaker's Corner. In contrast with the oldest institution of free speech, Wi-Fi is one of the newest technologies for free speech, used by political activists and digerati and espoused as a politically liberating technology. Both the institution of Speaker's Corner and the technology of Wi-Fi support wireless communication.

But Sandvig had problems bringing Wi-Fi to Speaker's Corner. The equipment had to be ordered online and shipped from overseas, and the United Kingdom had very strict regulations about what kind of power and reach his equipment could have. The equipment was difficult to assemble, and eventually the antenna had to be perched atop telephone books and a series of poles held together with duct tape. Could today's free speech technology be for anyone other than a devoted hobbyist?

Dr. Sandvig had a program on his laptop that would reveal Wi-Fi field strength by making the sounds of someone banging on a piano keyboard with their elbows. The stronger the Wi-Fi signal, the higher the pitch of the piano sounds. He had hoped to be able to project the field as far as the sausage stand in Hyde Park, so that the customers could eat and use the internet. Ideally, the proprietors were to rename their establishment Wi-Fi Dogs. But it didn't quite work. A section of Speaker's Corner was covered by Wi-Fi, but the antenna projected the Wi-Fi field in a plane, descending from the third floor of Stanhope House on the other side of Bayswater Road, down to the ground of the park across the street. This meant that one's Wi-Fi card had to be at the right altitude to get a signal. If you were on the second level of a passing double-decker bus, you could get a good signal. In the park, a particular row of maple trees had a good signal. One of the highlights of that summer was perching on chairs at the edge of the rooftop, playing with antenna angles while Sandvig skirted trees in the English sun. Unappreciative roller bladers glared at him as he held up a laptop making piano sounds and testing the field of reception.

There is always a difference among technological dreams, organizational logistics, and institutional impact. Sometimes I wonder whether Wi-Fi is a myth, but Sandvig insists he can find Wi-Fi fields when he needs them. That summer, the exciting new technology that was going to revolutionize our political lives was Wi-Fi. It had previously been chat, e-mail, Usenet, and the internet, and if you went further back the same excitement had brewed over television, radio, the post office, and Greek pottery shards. That summer, two questions crystallized in my mind: Why is our political imagination so rife with images and rhetoric about how new technologies fix democratic institutions? More specifically, how are information technologies being used in contemporary campaign politics?

It is usually best to describe technological innovation in terms of evolution, rather than revolution, and the same caution should be used to describe institutional innovation. As viscerally exciting as a technology may be, it is the structure, function, and change in social institutions that is of most interest to social scientists. The rhetoric and excitement of technological innovation, especially when it comes to new media innovations, has obscured some of the fundamentally interesting changes in the shape and character of our political institutions. New media have not revolutionized our political institutions, but our political institutions have evolved significantly over the last decade. Too many scholars have downplayed these changes because they want to see direct causal connections between technological innovation and changing media habits. I suspect they will be waiting for a while, but I am certain that they are missing the important aspects of institutional innovations that have occurred, have left a clear trail of evidence over the last decade, and must be evaluated in both a scholarly and normative manner.

Communities of friends and colleagues often overlap. The people in these communities make my choice of profession worthwhile, and they are the main reason for attending academic conferences. Critiques by these friends and colleagues – Lance Bennett, Larry Bogad, Minna Bromberg, Steve Jones, Gina Neff, Stephanie Nolen, Monroe Price, Christian Sandvig, Michael Schudson, David Silver, Jennifer Stromer-Galley, and Barry Wellman – kept me motivated yet on guard. Several of my colleagues at the University of Washington, including David Domke, Kirsten Foot, John Gastil, Patricia Moy, and Keith Stamm, have also given valuable feedback on chapters. As chairs of my home department, Jerry Baldasty and Tony Giffard provided both intellectual and institutional support for me to get this book done. Several faculty at Northwestern University provided important feedback and guidance in the early stages of this research. Wendy Griswold, Charlie Moskos, Allan Schnaiberg, James Schwoch, and Charles Ragin have all generously given both vocational and vacational support. Brian Uzzi and Art Stinchcombe at Northwestern, and Jim Witte at Clemson University, were particularly helpful with methods strategy. Perhaps most important, two political consultants read the manuscript through in its entirety. They, and most of my other informants, accepted my promise of anonymity and must be thanked anonymously.

I am grateful to Lee Rainie and the Pew Internet & American Life Project for financial support during my fieldwork and for access to the project's high-quality survey data, and I am grateful to Dan Packel for research assistance. Eunice Chen, Nancy Dosemann, and Patricia Humphrey provided fabulous administrative support for this research. Several students at the University of Washington and other colleagues provided invaluable assistance with copyediting and fact checking: Diane Beall, Danielle Endres, Maria Garrido, and Tema Milstein. Several of this book's graphics are the product of Paul Ford's creative intellect. The University of Washington has been a generous institution.

Steve Jones has been an important mentor and friend. In our edited book, *Society Online*, he cogently argued for making it a convention to lowercase the "i" of "Internet," and I have done so in this book. Also supportive are the kind communities at three particular cafes: Stuzzico at Marble Arch in London, Vivace at Capitol Hill in Seattle, and Solstice at the University District in Seattle. Once again, Francisco Zarate's friendship and generosity allowed me to hide in Argentina while finishing a manuscript. I hope this friendship lasts a long time because it allows me repeatedly to take advantage of his hospitality.

Some of the ethnographic evidence presented in this book was also analyzed in Philip N. Howard, "Digitizing the Social Contract: Producing

American Political Culture in the Age of New Media," *Communication Review* 6 (September 2003): 213–245, and Philip N. Howard and Tema J. Milstein, "Spiders, Spam, and Spyware: New Media and the Market for Political Information," in Mia Consalvo, ed., *Internet Studies 1.0* (New York: Peter Lang, 2003). Table I.1 in the Introduction appeared in Philip N. Howard, "Deep Democracy, Thin Citizenship: The Production of Political Culture in a Digital Age," *Annals of the American Academy of Political and Social Science* 597 (2005). An earlier version of the discussion about network ethnography methods, which here appears in the Appendix, appeared in Philip N. Howard, "Network Ethnography and the Hypermedia Organization: New Media, New Organizations, New Methods," *New Media & Society* 4(4) (November 2002): 550–574. Technical definitions appear in the index and glossary, and some of them are reprinted with permission from Webopedia (http://www.webopedia.com, copyright 2004 Jupitermedia Corporation, all rights reserved).

Ultimately, I am grateful to the political campaign consultants who gave generously of their time and insight, allowing an outsider with questions to follow them from conventions and planning meetings, to happy hours, victory dinners, and sullen campaign take-downs. That professional political consultants play a significant role in our political culture is not the story of this book. This book is about how they construct technologies for mediating the relationships between voters and candidates, citizens and democratic institutions. Through this work, political consultants specializing in information technology reify many of the ignoble traits of competitive politics, while encoding many of their noble aspirations for better communication between citizens and political leaders. The goal of this book is not to embarrass them but to illustrate that they are doing some things wrong and that it is incumbent on the rest of us to make our expectations clear through public oversight. I take them seriously, I treat them critically, and I remain grateful for their help.

In 1998, Al Hammond casually sketched out a possibility for my doctoral research on my napkin, and he was kind enough to let me keep the napkin. Its pictograms probably have as much explanatory power as my dissertation did, but this book has moved significantly beyond both the napkin and my doctoral work. As part of my obligations to my respondents, I have melted my tapes and destroyed the code pad that identifies respondents with interview notes. If anyone wants to critique my arguments or subpoena my evidence, I still have my soiled napkin filed in my research filing cabinet under "N" and can defer to it as needed. Photos and other data from this research are online at www.managedcitizen.org.

Lew Bateman and Bob Entman helped me to develop my theoretical hooks, and Stephanie Sakson managed me and the manuscript with grace.

Speaker's Corner may have been the first barometer of public opinion in a modernizing nation-state. For many centuries, England was the world's wealthiest, most advanced democracy, where Kings and Parliaments relied on surveys of the activity at Speaker's Corner for their construction of public opinion. Today, the United States is the world's wealthiest, most advanced democracy. Public opinion is constructed in different ways through communication technologies, and in this book I analyze how political campaigns use new information technologies to construct public opinion.

La Ricoleta, Buenos Aires

Prologue: The Flows of Information in Competitive Politics

On the first night of the 2000 Democratic National Convention, Los Angeles is pungently warm from the day's heat, but the climate inside the convention hall is cool and dry.

In the first hours of the meeting, runners in red jackets move along the aisles of the convention floor, distributing placards. During Jesse Jackson's rousing appeal for party unity, the convention floor is a sea of blue placards, clear visual consensus that everyone present is fervently behind the Gore-Lieberman team. Then the giant digital screen, towering over the stage, fills with stirring images of average families living and loving happily after eight years of prosperity under a Democratic President.

During the two minutes of video, runners move up the aisles of the New York delegation and distribute black signs proclaiming "NY loves Hillary" in white script. As Hillary Clinton takes the stage and television cameras swivel to capture the roar from New York's delegates, their delegation is marked by a distinct, united sea of black posters. After she speaks, the runners replace placards with the same efficiency.

Every important speaker is met with an impressively coordinated turnover in delegate placards. The display is for the benefit of prime-time viewers. Some runners are charged with planting signs designed to appear as if they were made at home on the kitchen table: "Nurses for Gore," "Firemen for Gore," and "Wichita for Gore." The constant re-arrangement of signs leaves delegates uncertain about what they are holding and waving at the cameras. It takes just two minutes to reconstruct the appearance of consensus among delegates, a unity that is presented to the national cameras. No interpretive labor is required of delegates. Little interpretive labor is required of viewers.

For months before the convention, the party Web site celebrated "the most open and accessible and interactive convention in the history of politics." Streaming video let curious viewers take in different parts of the convention, from the makeup room behind the podium, to a bird's-eye view of the delegations. Visitors to the Web site were invited to help redraft the party's 1996 policy platform. The convention chairman, Joe Andrew, began the invitation by writing, "Don't be surprised if the ideas you and other Democrats have shared are included in the Platform adopted this summer at our Convention." When a Web visitor sent in a submission, the Web site responded with a personalized response from Al Gore. It is not clear that any online submissions made it into the official party platform.

At 7 o'clock the arena lights dim and a hush descends on the audience. Cameras swing into action and aim at strategic parts of the stage, particular delegations, and of course the podium itself.

The stage is empty, but the giant screen above flickers to life, showing the long hallway of cinderblock walls and storage rooms below the convention floor.

Bill Clinton springs out of one of the doorways into view on screen. Delegates jump to their feet and cheer. A camera moves ahead of him, as he walks to give his last address to DNC delegates. The scandal-ridden two-term sitting President looks radiant with energy, and the camera precedes him as he makes his way up through the labyrinth of underground passages.

The crowd sees Clinton begin to react to their cheers, which are now loud enough to echo down into the basement chambers. The audience can see him smile and quicken his pace. As if a Baptist minister approaching the pulpit, he shakes out his tensions in his arms, stretches his neck, jogging behind the camera. The audience loves this, and as the delegates respond to his maneuvers, he, in turn, responds. Clearly, he feels the crowd returning his energy, amplified in their cheers.

Suddenly, Clinton is no longer a preacher warming up for an energetic sermon; now he is a prizefighter, head down, jabbing and dancing lightly to the left and right. He throws punches at imaginary opponents. The crowd is fevered now, some people punching the air with fists, matching Clinton's rhythm. He is doing fancy footwork, every pace bringing him up to the stage level and the sound of frenzied delegates.

The camera shows him rounding a corner, then another, and then bounding up a few final stairs. As he gets closer to the entrance, he can hear the crowd roar and his punches get faster, harder, his feet move more quickly. With a burst of spotlights he is on the stage and the crowd reaches a new height of collective, ecstatic, effervescence. Our attention moves from the larger-than-life, projected image of Clinton to the genuine article on stage.

On television and online, the spectacle is streamed around the world to anyone who will watch, party faithful and detractors alike. Data on their real-time reaction are fed back to campaign strategists.

Near the convention, Francie is getting ready at the Independent Media Center (IMC). She is twenty-three, petite, and dressed in black and green army fatigues bought at a secondhand store. Francie is angry at her country, disgusted by its blind faith in an environmentally unsustainable economy. Francie believes in a carbon tax that would discourage polluters and create a revenue stream for research into green technologies. She doesn't believe that the mainstream media do justice to environmental issues, so she has volunteered with the IMC.

The IMC is set up in an old hotel ballroom with no air conditioning. There is electricity, however, and activists have taken over the main floor of the hotel, laying wires to power the battery of technologies that they will use to organize the logistics of their protest and broadcast their own counter-convention.

Under crumbling plaster beams and flickering chandeliers the IMC has built a large bank of computers, a small video filming area, and several almost-soundproof radio booths. Off the decrepit ballroom are a kitchen and a meditation room. Snarls of wire run everywhere, taking the news and views of convention protester activity out to the world. The room is hot, crowded, and tangy with ozone from all the electronics.

Francie is wired up. She gets instructions from a centralized dispatcher through her headphones. The dispatcher monitors police frequencies, tracks police movements, and records confrontations. Through her own cell phone she maintains occasional text communication with two friends who have also come for the protests but been assigned to other parts of the city. She has worked out an exit strategy with her friends, just in case she gets into trouble or disagrees with instructions from the dispatcher.

She has to be careful. At the Republican National Convention, John Sellers, director of the Berkeley-based Ruckus Society, was arrested and charged with several misdemeanors, including conspiracy, reckless endangerment, obstruction of justice, and possession of instruments of crime. While he had provided training on nonviolent direct action techniques to many protesters, the police credited him with master-minding the week of protests. He was held on a million dollars' bail. When he was picked up, they noted his "instruments of crime": his cell phone and Palm Pilot.

Francie is equipped to broadcast video and has agreed to bear witness and record confrontations between protesters and police. She can stream small chunks of video content through her commercial provider and has set up a system to both archive and forward video to the data storage server maintained offsite by the protester organization. Two wireless Web cams are strapped to her baseball hat. She has a couple of battery packs in her pants pockets, two small bottles of water around her waist, and a GPS device on her wrist. Her shift on the streets is going to be five hours long, and even though the equipment does not weigh much, she is already tired from the heat.

The dispatcher sends her to the corner of Figueroa and 8th Street. She climbs up into the well-manicured flower bed of an office complex. From here she can see the entire intersection: police lined in riot gear to protect an entrance to the convention grounds, cohorts of activists moving freely, and a circle of Anarchists drumming in the middle of the street.

The drumming intensifies as the circle evolves into a phalanx. Dressed in black, pounding drums and shaking fists, the Anarchists get ready to rush at the police line – not with the intention of breaking through, but planning to stop short and provoke a violent reaction from the police. Most of the activists are there for peaceful protest or civil disobedience, and they dislike this provocative Anarchist strategy. The streets start to clear and the air gets tense in anticipation of what is to come.

Most of the activists are on the sidewalks now or crowding in flower beds, chanting "Peace-ful Pro-test! Peace-ful Pro-test!" in response to Anarchist maneuvers. The Anarchists stomp in heavy boots as they move in formation at the police line. Francie's camera records whatever she turns her head to see.

Twenty feet from the police line, the rhythmic drumming goes into double time, and the Anarchists rush forward, howling and shaking their fists. The phalanx stops just short of the barricade, with protesters and police face to face. But someone throws a punch and the truncheons come out. A second later the tear gas canisters rain down. Frantically, the activists scramble for a way out of the intersection.

Francie flees, but some roads have been blocked off and her retreat becomes a route into a police blockade. Police close all exits from the street and several hundred protesters are trapped. Francie knows it will take several hours to arrest and release everyone, one by one, so she texts with her friends about what happened.

Sitting on the curb, she uploads her video data.

It is almost 9 o'clock, and in another part of the city, Lance swears and shouts to his son: "Nathan, it WANTS you again!" Lance puts down the remote control because it has stopped working. On top of the television sits a black box, and on top of the little box a red light is flashing. Even though the family is not watching coverage of the convention, they are about to play a small part in the election season.

In exchange for free access to the internet, the family has agreed to make themselves available for surveys whenever the internet provider summons them. Nathan has had two weeks to answer these questions, but he has not done so and the TV signal is being blocked.

Nathan pads into the room and takes the keyboard off a shelf to begin the survey. The screen specifically asks for him and lists other directions about how to prepare for the survey.

"The instructions say you are supposed to leave," he says without looking at his father. Nathan knows this is one occasion when his father will actually leave the room. He is expecting another commercial survey. But this one is different: It is about politics. Nathan sits up. He likes to think about politics, but hasn't really been motivated to get involved. When the service was first installed, the provider asked general questions of each family member. More recently, the family was being asked about detergents, but now the screen asks, "Do you support the idea of a minimum wage?"

From this basic query grows a series of more complex questions that probe the nuances of Nathan's opinion. His knowledge of the issue is taxed, but he is alone, so clicks through the "pro" and "con" arguments without feeling self-conscious. For some of the questions, the company has provided background information so that he can teach himself about the issues. He is careful about forming his preferences.

The surveyors promise to send his opinions to "the policy makers who count," but he doesn't know much more about what the survey company does with his answers. Nathan weighs options and answers. He returns to the basement without telling his father he is done.

Lance peeks in a few minutes later and is happy to see the TV signal is back on. He is not watching coverage of Bill Clinton's speech nor is he watching news about the clash of ideologies on the streets of Los Angeles. He is watching something else and isn't interested in politics.

He eases into the couch for the remainder of the night, satisfied that his remote control works again.

Amanda and I arrive at the Velvet Lounge and she offers to show me how to work the room "DC style." She teaches me the trick of holding business cards inside the left sleeve with the fourth finger of my left hand so that left thumb, index and middle finger can hold my Manhattan, and the right hand can be free and dry to shake hands with people. We can keep our business cards discreetly hidden but easy to produce without rummaging through pockets or switching drink hands. She has also developed a technique for smoothly giving and receiving business cards at the same time with the same hand but I cannot master this in time to start meeting her friends at the monthly NPHaHo (Net Politics Happy Hour) event. From the White House Webmaster and the head of the President's favorite polling firm to the coordinator of an online newsletter for log cabin Republicans and a lobbyist for the American Pharmaceuticals Association, about sixty campaign consultants have come to talk about politics online. In the atmosphere of bluesy music, dark red walls, and wrought-iron candelabras, representatives from the Sierra Club, Christian Coalition, National Association for the Advancement of Colored People, National Rifle Association, American Civil Liberties Union, League of Women Voters, and other groups toast the future of the political internet. These organizations may be adversaries, but in this room individuals are not really representing their organizations – they identify with a higher calling and a subversive community. Many in the NPHaHo group are devoted to "e-politics," designing new media technologies for political communication. They share a commitment to making democracy more direct and deliberative and represent this community agenda in the diverse organizations that employ them.

In the 1996, 2000, and 2004 campaign seasons, a community of political consultants specializing in information technology built the tools that allowed convention delegates to nominate their candidate for President, that allowed activists to coordinate civil disobedience and protests, and that allowed citizens to express their policy preferences about the minimum wage. Major political parties, candidates, and lobbyists relied on strategic advice from companies such as Mindshare.com, Aristotle.com, and PoliticsOnline.com. Election.com designed the Web-based voting system used by delegates to register their votes, while SpeakOut.com provided the 360-degree Web cam of the convention floor with gavel-to-gavel coverage of the proceedings, instant polling and voter reaction to convention events, and chat room commentary on news developments. Grassroots.com provided services to people who wanted to start their own online protest movements, and Voter.com provided specialized election news and a matching service to help citizens find compatible politicians. Vote.com collected survey data on public opinion and sent the results to elected officials; InterSurvey collected household survey data through WebTV services; HarrisInteractive maintained an online polling panel of almost a million people; and Capitol Advantage built the interactive color-coded maps that pundits and news services around the country used to (mis)predict the distribution of electoral college votes on election night.

Here in Washington, D.C., within the safe velvet confines of the bar, they have philosophized about their work, fantasized about potential projects, and fed the collective imagination about how new information technologies can be used to help enrich our democratic experience. When the coalition has dispersed for the evening, Amanda and I leave the Velvet Lounge and she sums up the event from her insider's point of view. "There's a mini Constitutional Congress going on right now," she says. "Whatever American democracy looks like in fifteen or twenty years, it will have been designed by us."

Introduction: The Hypermedia Campaign

A fter the 2000 election, exit polls revealed that a third of the electorate had used the internet to learn about the campaigns. After the 2004 election, surveys revealed that over half the electorate had gone online to get news or information about the campaigns.[1] Yet the growing number of citizens who use the internet in their political lives may not realize that they are being fed highly personalized information. In the weeks before the 2000 election, when "Elaine" – a conservative, middle-aged voter living in Clemson, South Carolina – logged onto her favorite Republican Web site, she saw headlines about the commitment of Republican candidates to the Second Amendment right to bear arms and pro-life arguments against abortion. When "Lois," a middle-aged Republican voter living in Manhattan, logged onto the same site, she was never shown those headlines. Designers of the Republican Web site knew that even though Lois was conservative on many issues, their statistical models suggested she would support some form of gun control and a woman's right to choose. The Webmasters were right, but neither Elaine nor Lois suspected that, as members of the same political party, they were receiving significantly different political information during the campaign season. In fact, they assumed the opposite – that everyone in their political party received the same content.

Information technologies have played a role in campaign organization of the major parties since the 1970s, but it is only over the last decade that adopting new technologies also became an occasion for organizational restructuring within political parties and campaigns. The result of this

[1] Exit poll data from 2000 reported in CNN *Election 2000 Exit Polls* CNN, 2000 (cited 2003), available from http://www.cnn.com/ELECTION/2000/epolls/US/P000.html. Post-election 2004 figure from author's calculations using data from the Pew Internet and American Life Project.

I

restructuring is the *hypermedia campaign,* an agile political organization defined by its capacity for innovatively adopting digital technologies for express political purposes and its capacity for innovatively adapting its organizational structure to conform to new communicative practices. In other words, it is not simply that political campaigns employ digital information technologies in their communications strategies. Integrating such technologies becomes an occasion for organizational adaptation, effecting organizational goals and relationships among professional staff, political leadership, volunteers, financial contributors, citizens, and other political campaigns. Political hypermedia are the conjoined superstructure of fast, high-capacity hardware and software communication tools that let people transmit, interact with, and filter data. First, political hypermedia are structured literally over and above traditional media in a network of satellites, relay stations, and data bases that coordinate the retrieval and delivery of public and private content. Second, these media operate at greater speeds and with greater amounts of content than do traditional media. Third, they permit simulations of offline interaction, speedy circulation of social signs and meanings, rapid decomposition and recomposition of messages, and increased transience of socially significant symbols. The rising prominence of hypermedia campaigns has been marked by three trends.

First, a service class of professional political technocrats with special expertise in information technology (IT) arose. Like pollsters, TV ad managers, and other campaign strategists, the consultants specializing in IT collected information about competing candidates and prospective voters for the campaign and projected information about the campaign to the electorate. Unlike these other campaign managers, however, the consultants specializing in IT also *built* new communication technologies for citizens and candidates. Second, the political consulting industry replaced mass-media tools with targeted media tools, ranging from fax and computer-generated direct mail to e-mail and Web site content, which allowed the industry to tailor messages to specific audiences. The hypermedia campaign builds a targeted-media strategy. It not only produces political content for mass consumption over broadcast technologies, it also produces political content for private consumption over networked technologies. Third, the engineers of political hypermedia made technical decisions about political hypermedia that constrained subsequent decisions about the production and consumption of political content. The hypermedia campaign took advantage of the norms and values entrenched in technology when designer's choices – embedded with attitudes about how democracy should work – were turned into code. In this sense, the code in software has become embedded with the normative choices of designers. The tools of a political campaign and the choices that campaign managers make about manipulating data, ideas, and people reflect their own political norms. Some campaigns choose to obstruct real learning about political issues, manipulate their membership, and prevent too much interactivity. Other campaigns allow a range of interactive tools, adapt their organizational behavior to allow members to both produce and consume political content, and give such members the capacity to seed their own campaigns.

Political communications technologies have become so advanced that it is possible for campaign managers to send significantly different messages to potential supporters. Citizens experienced with computing technologies will sort through the manipulative messages and find content more sophisticated than ever before. Richly detailed political information is increasingly available on the internet, in the form of direct correspondence from political leaders, policy options from diverse voices, and records of government activity. At the same time, political campaigns in the United States are increasingly manipulative, as managers find new ways to distribute propaganda, mine data, mask political interests, and mislead people unfamiliar with computing technologies.

One of the most lucid cases for periodizing political campaign styles is made by historian Robert Dinkin in *Campaigning in America*. He labels the period between the 1950s and the last election he analyzed, the 1988 campaign year, as the "Mass Media Age." This was a period in which the power of influence of the grassroots organization of political parties increased in comparison to the party elites and political consultants, the television attained dominance as the most costly and most popular conduit for political information, and truly national political campaigns came to exist (Dinkin 1989). But I argue that the hypermedia campaign has succeeded the mass media campaign, such that the 1988 campaign season was the beginning of an important transition in the organization of political information in the United States. This introduction provides a historical background to the role of information technology in political campaigning. The first step in my argument, however, is to define the relationship between political culture and communication technology and offer a theoretical framework for how this relationship should be studied.

Throughout these chapters I explore four different kinds of code. First, there is the software code for Web sites, relational databases, and content distribution systems that has become the primary medium through which we now produce and consume political content. Second, there is the normative code of political campaign managers that shapes decisions about technology design and campaign strategy, a normative code that they encrypt in the information architecture that other citizens use but do not always understand. Third, there is the language-based conceptual system for encoding and organizing political information, which provides a structure consisting of political objects, events, processes, and memory. Analytically framing political life through inputs and outputs tends to privilege the consumption of political information over the production of political information. Contemporary theory treats culture as competing discursive strategies. Rather than providing standardized values, culture provides resources for interpreting and approaching problems and provides different resources in different ways to different subcultures. These cultural resources take the form of discourse, such as talk, media, text, and, as analyzed here, the hardware and software of information technologies. Finally, there are the encrypted informational systems that few people understand and to which few have access. This is the secret language of lobbyists' relational databases and private data-mining services that code labels about who we are and what our public policy preferences are likely to be.

The range of tools for producing and consuming political information has greatly expanded over the last decade. Of course, most politicians produce Web sites with content about their goals and aspirations. But more and more citizens use a sophisticated tool kit for interrogating the work and ideology of political representatives. Some look for news or information about politics or the campaign, go online to get news or information about the elections, or participate in online discussions or "chats" about the elections. Others register their own opinions by participating in electronic polls, get information about a candidate's voting record, or learn when and where to vote.

A growing number of people send and receive e-mail supporting or opposing a candidate for office and contribute money to a candidate running for public office through his or her Web site. They explore these Web sites for details about candidates' positions on the issues, send e-mails with campaign and election jokes, and send friends and relatives information about "getting out the vote." They research political endorsements or ratings of candidates by favored organizations. They visit Web sites that provide information about specific issues or policies of interest, such as the environment, gun control, abortion, or health care reform. They also visit partisan sites, such as those run by the political parties, a candidate, or a campaign, and compare points of view with nonpartisan sites. Not everyone learns about politics in these ways, but a growing proportion of the public does (Howard 2005).

The short history of political life online includes both discouraging and inspiring chapters. Information technologies enable the major political parties and lobbyists to hone their skills for manipulating public opinion. However, voters are turning to ever more diverse resources for their political news, often preferring interactive political media over television news. Campaign managers themselves say they like to use technologies such as the internet to create informational feedback loops between candidates and constituents. Whenever information-gathering technologies diffuse – whether they are computer-assisted telephone interview systems, Nielsen television ratings, or the internet – these technologies are used to help politicians calibrate their messages. However, the feedback loops for interactive information technologies, or *hypermedia*, are different enough from those in the mass media campaign manager's tool kit that they warrant specific and critical treatment.

THE EVOLUTION OF HYPERMEDIA CAMPAIGNS
IN THE UNITED STATES

Between the 1988 and 2004 presidential campaign seasons, the political internet emerged as a critical component of U.S. campaign strategies. The proportion of people using the internet to collect news or to research policy alternatives increased significantly as the technology diffused. From inside candidate and issue campaigns, the internet and related tools allowed a number of campaigns to make significant advances in fund-raising, volunteer coordination, logistics, intelligence on voters, and opposition research. As journalists began to cover these campaigns, they produced stories about the new digital democracy, hypermedia campaigns, and cyber-activism. Internet technologies, headlines declared, were revolutionizing political life. Just as the new economy had become a fast-paced, interactive system in which traditional economic elites had to battle with young, creative start-ups for the attention of the information-savvy consumer, politics was becoming a fast-paced, interactive system in which traditional political elites had to engage with new actors offering creative policy options for the information-savvy citizen.

Political information technologies develop in stages, in concordance with the size of campaign budgets. This means that most of the innovation in political campaign strategy occurs under immense dead-line pressures, at the height of campaign seasons, and when money is flowing to strategists whose professional standing will change when their issue or candidate wins or losses. Presidential campaigns are the biggest, most consistent spenders on new media tools. Lobbyists also spend significant funds during a presidential election year or in years when their key issues are addressed by legislation. Candidate campaigns at the congressional or state level put financial resources toward innovative communication strategies in two-year election cycles.

POLITICAL COMPUTING

Computers have been used to process political information since the early 1970s, though the classic text on the political consulting industry labels the consultants and firms themselves as the "new campaign technology" (Sabato 1981). An analyst with the AFL-CIO's Data Processing Department, which in 1973 registered almost nine million names in its computer memory bank, advertised his enthusiasm for the political applications of the computer:

> In sheer speed the computer is awesome. In sorting information, the computer can read 350,000 numbers per second off a disc. When information is going out, the computer performs equally prodigious feats: in one hour, it can turn out 30,000 of the 3 × 5 cards [of member profiles], 66,000 lines on a listing or 75,000 mail labels. A lot of volunteers have to do a lot of typing to match that.
> (Hardesty 1976)

Even though the computer was a new, powerful tool to the political campaigns of the 1970s, we can read this analyst's statement and immediately identify what has changed over the last couple of elections. Not only are billions of numbers per second read on contemporary computer disks, but this is done on personal computers, not large organizational computers. There are no more 3 × 5 data cards, and a political consultant is just as likely to send 7,500,000 e-mails as 75,000 postal letters. So it is not sufficient to say that computers have long had a role in political life; over the years they have become personal, networked, and evolved significantly from the elaborate, card-sorting, computing devices of thirty years ago.

By the mid-1980s, the Republican National Committee had built an extensive private intranet for research into President Reagan's Democratic opponents. Already, intelligence collected by all fifty state party headquarters, all fifty state campaign headquarters, and aides in 208 broadcast markets could be accessed from Air Force One. Republican leaders could then catch inconsistencies in Democratic statements and produce their own instant parry (Johnson-Cartee and Copeland 1997). Some public policy officials were beginning to use computers to model scenarios, and it was found that the process of modeling was itself an important process of negotiation between the stakeholders in public policy debates. The concreteness of computer models forced stakeholders to share and classify their expectations openly, turning the act of computer modeling into an act of consensus building (Dutton and Kraemer 1985). At the time, social scientists were most interested in how computers were used by political parties and grassroots movements, but the lobbyists used computers most adroitly. Beginning in the 1970s, they were the first to use computers to produce form letters from constituents to political leaders. At one time, the handwritten letter of grievance from a constituent would capture the attention of Capitol Hill staff. The flood of form letters, even though addressed and signed by constituents, strained staffing resources (Frantzich 1982). However, lobbyists sought bigger, more efficient campaign stunts, and computer technology allowed strategists to manage their intelligence on voters and politicians with greater alacrity. By the end of the 1980s, a number of scholars had published instructive books about how political campaign consultants could and should use computer technologies to manage voter lists with spreadsheets and permanent data records, to test campaign messages with videotaped speeches and electronically recorded feedback from focus groups, and to take instant polls from specific samples of the population (Luntz 1988; Tehranian 1990).

1988

In terms of campaign communication technologies, 1988 was the year that the Democratic and Republican National Committees discovered the fax machine. The major presidential and lobbyist campaigns had staff devoted to using this new technology – people who would maintain call lists for "blastfaxing" and who would sort the faxes the organization received. Many of the hypermedia technologies we use today, from cellular phones to the internet, had been designed in prototype but not hit the commercial market. But even prototype technologies, conceived by engineers aware of technical possibilities, inspired others to conceive of organizational and institutional possibilities (Arterton 1987; Sabato 1988; McLean 1989). Although the national party committees and well-financed lobbyists had had access to computing technologies since the early 1970s, by the end of the 1980s researchers found small communities of urban activists, scientists working for peace, and small public bureaucracies using computer technologies to improve their political communication strategies and organizational efficiency (Downing 1989; Huff et al. 1989).

1990

By the 1990 campaign season, e-mail had become a commercially viable communication tool and was immediately classified as an empowering technology for the citizen-activist (Ganly 1991). The term "narrowcasting" was coined to describe the strategy of hitting voters with direct *postal* mail using computers and relational databases to tailor printed political messages to the addressee. Campaign professionals later used the word to describe the process of sending e-mails to particular people or the process of customizing Web pages for particular interests. Online discussion groups clearly allowed people to build ties across traditional socioeconomic boundaries, to build empathy with other members sharing grievances, and to draw new participants into civic life (Wittig and Schmitz 1996).

1992

By the 1992 campaign season, not only was e-mail available to activists and intelligentsia, but satellite dishes allowed political messages to be broadcast directly into local markets. The major presidential campaigns learned from the strategies of activists who maintained e-mail lists and bulletin boards for their members. At the time, the networked infrastructure was found in dense urban areas, such as New York City, and on the nation's university campuses. While activist and computer-literate members of these communities had lively discussion groups, the content of Bush, Clinton, and Perot campaign discussion groups did not vary much from the content already sent out in fax releases. Campaign managers were very careful to make their discussion groups more like announcement lists (Diamond et al. 1993; Myers 1993). Some lists evolved into fora for smart debate, but this rarely happened to lists closely supervised by campaigns with an integrated communications strategy (Kirp 1992; Ronfeldt 1992; Hacker et al. 1996). In 1992, however, the excitement about new media had less to do with the internet and more to do with direct satellite transmission of Perot's thirty-second infomercials into local television markets. These electronic informational services allowed community journalists to tailor content for their neighborhoods, reporting as if they were on the campaign trail, asking questions, and keeping on top of campaign subterfuge. Insiders called these kinds of technologies "soft" formats because they allowed politicians to get messages to voters without using the hierarchical news dissemination technologies of traditional broadcast and newspaper journalists. Direct, decentralized, and networked technologies allowed access to the media environments people actually used in their daily lives: cable news services, call-in radio shows, MTV, late-night talk shows, small-town newspapers and online computer services (Diamond et al. 1993; West 1993).

As the White House Press Secretary Dee Dee Myers said of the 1992 campaign, "Through the proliferation of computer modems, faxes, e-mail, interactive satellites, and other new modes of communication, several rounds of charges and countercharges are often exchanged in time for the evening news" (Myers 1993, 181). In her opinion, the ever more fast-paced interaction between campaigns was not a result of a particular communication tool but a result of multiple, networked technologies that formed a new system for collecting and distributing political information.

1994

In 1994, future California senator Dianne Feinstein, a Democrat, was the first candidate to build a Web site for her constituency office. A year later, Democratic Senator Ted Kennedy, of Massachusetts, was the first sitting senator to develop an official Web site. But while most political offices and campaigns were equipped with stand-alone computers, networking was far from standard in political organization (Casey 1996). Since new media technologies were increasingly part of the public reality and fantasy about how to make democracy efficient, academics began to philosophize about what citizenship might mean in an electronic polity (Friedland 1996; Graber 1996; Grossman 1996). What would it be like if we could all vote online? Speculation about online elections and the rise of articulate grassroots movements equipped with information-rich media was grounded in the assumption that accessible political information seeds vigorous deliberative democracy (Huckfeldt 1995; Sachs 1995; Glass 1996; Groper 1996). After the 1994 campaign season, the first naysayers argued that the digital divide prevented important rural, poor, and minority populations from participating in digital discourse, and that those who were participating were portioning themselves in groups of like-minded thinkers (Kling 1996).

1996

The 1996 presidential campaign season was important to the development of political hypermedia for two reasons. First, the truly networked quality of political hypermedia took shape, with satellite networks, cell phone networks, and the internet all becoming conduits for political information. For example, with Clinton and Gore approaching the Chicago Democratic Convention on different trains, DNC campaign managers set up the first moving-train interview feeds with a system of helicopter and satellite relay stations that allowed both candidates to communicate with supporters and journalists from different parts of the country while en route to the event. The White House and congressional e-mail infrastructure had been developed during Clinton's first term in office and, though distinct from the campaign communications infrastructure, was adeptly used by the incumbents to communicate both with journalists and directly with the public (Browning 1996; Casey 1996; Tedesco et al. 1998). Second, political hypermedia tools were developed for measuring and manipulating public opinion. The first examples of negative online advertising appeared, and researchers acknowledged that online discussion groups were not necessarily more honest, fair, or respectful than political debate offline. But research also found that in comparison with other media, the internet seemed to have a constructive role in political debate (Klotz 1998a,b). Academic research began to make tentative claims about the relationship between having an effective Web site and getting more votes (D'Alessio 1997; Rash 1997; Johnson et al. 1999). However, these findings may have had more to do with the strong correlation among being a voter, highly educated, and using the internet, a correlation that has weakened over time.

Institutional resistance from political parties to online campaigning disappeared in the 1996 campaign, as the national political organizations became very active in using the internet for contacting voters. Comparatively, nontraditional, alternative political actors were more dependent on e-mail, as the larger organizations could afford a full battery of television, radio, mail, and telephone communications (Bimber 1998a).

Several important texts appeared on new media and politics, but they did more by way of positing advantages and imagining problems than methodically assessing evidence of what was still a relatively new phenomenon (Selnow 1998; Willock 1998). Analysis of how citizens used the internet expanded beyond activists' internet use. Those people who were found browsing the internet for content or discussing social problems on Usenet seemed to have a unique and noble set of political norms, and they were given different labels: digital citizens, netizens, or digerati (Hauben 1997; Hill and Hughes 1997). Some argued that these norms were a result of internet use and were bound to spread as the rest of the population went online. Others thought these norms were going to dissolve as the rest of the public went online. Many argued that the important impact of new media was in allowing both campaigns and citizens to bypass the institution of established media interests (Johnson et al. 1999). Technologies such as the internet provided decentralized media for exchanging information and a fundamentally different way of distributing political information from the centralized systems of mass communications media (Selnow 1998). One of the best examples of this was the Library of Congress's THOMAS server system, which presented many government documents, speeches, committee minutes, and reports for public access online, a system that was up and running during the 1996 campaign.

But an important thesis was developed in response to the 1996 campaign, an argument that challenged scholarly enthusiasm for a digital deliberative democracy by asking for real evidence that political deliberation online was actually different from deliberation offline. Did the new media technologies actually have an effect on the Realpolitik of campaign strategies and games (Margolis et al. 1997; Margolis 2000)? Several scholars argued that when political campaigns developed an online instantiation, it was only a symbolic gesture at participating in a popular medium and not a substantive commitment to interactivity, an accusation that would be repeated in the analysis of the role of new media in the 2000 and 2004 presidential campaigns (Klinenberg and Perrin 2000; Stromer-Galley 2000; Puopolo 2001; Warnick and Endres 2004). However, many new media technologies, such as the internet, were serving both as a tool for organizing public opinion and as a tool for surveilling private lives (Howard 2003, 2005). The shape and character of this political campaigning online receives more attention in later chapters.

1998

Over two-thirds of the candidates for congressional seats in this election had established Web sites, driven by campaign managers hoping to capitalize on small online donations (Dulio et al. 1999). Outside this more widespread use of Web sites for campaign communications, 1998 was also a big year for the political internet because Congress released the Starr Report online. Over 400 pages of procedural melodrama and pornographic presidential details were quickly and easily accessible to the concerned public. In addition, campaign managers began to meet and share stories about organizing hypermedia campaigns and for the first time produced tangible numbers about the impact of online campaign advertising strategy on visibility (Faucheux 1998; Jagoda and Nyhan 1999). However, the online campaign still took on a relatively limited form. First, campaign Web sites were called "brochureware" because they merely reproduced content derived from print sources. Second, the Web sites themselves were rarely used as organizational tools for the campaign itself, with content specifically for coordinating campaign staff, candidate schedules, and volunteer resources. Third, campaign Web sites were not yet used as data-mining tools. Although some have cogently argued that the internet was constructed, from the very beginning, as a tool for the surveillance of users, political Web sites aggressively collected data on users only after the 2000 campaign (Elmer 2004).

In 1999, Jesse Ventura won the governorship of Minnesota as the first candidate to win an elected office with an e-mail–dependant communications strategy. Whereas PeaceNet activists and people with access through universities founded the political internet, it was now becoming a tool for the average citizen. Scholars observed that the internet was becoming a community-building tool, not just a tool for advancing radical political agendas. Indeed, it was a localizing tool for overcoming collective action problems and engaging with local, state, or federal agencies on day-to-day questions of policy and practice (Hill 1998; Klein 1999; Mele 1999; Tambini 1999; McGrath 2000). Scholars, however, still had difficulty finding a distinct media effect, such as changes in voter turnout or political sophistication or even a stable population of engaged citizens and policy makers committed to deliberative processes online (Hurwitz 1999; Kamarck 1999). The THOMAS system for distributing information about the legislative process was online, but not all government agencies had such an interactive internet presence and the new media ideal of transparent government was far from being met.

Moreover, the internet was not just a place for community building and finding information on political campaigns. It was also a place for political manipulation. Political consultants began customizing their political content in earnest. The number of citizens online was sufficient; the penetration of new media technologies was sufficient; and campaign budgets were big enough to begin building the relational databases needed to target messages online. Where political deliberation was occurring, it was rarely inclusive and constructive (Milbank

1999; Wilhelm 2000). Online activists seemed to have the same political profile as the offline population and were perhaps even more likely to stick by major party candidates (Hill 1998). The political internet business was recast as an aspect of the larger internet industry bubble, with similar cults of personality for leaders within the industry and financial hyperbole for investors (Morris 1999; Ransell 1999).

2000

The important advance in the 2000 campaign season was that new media became as crucial for internal organization as they were for external publicity. Both candidates for party nomination and the ultimate nominees devoted significant resources to their Web site content, with variation in informational breadth, depth, interactivity, readability, and negativity (Benoit and Benoit 2000). Complex relational databases allowed campaign staff to model public reactions, predict voter turnout, manage financial and personnel resources, and adapt communications strategy on an hourly basis at the neighborhood level. In the campaign season of 2000, the big political parties and lobbyists raised the stature of new media strategists within their campaigns. Web site managers became chief information officers and were given access to campaign war rooms; significant portions of the budget for traditional media buys were reapportioned to develop new media applications. The presidential nominating conventions were broadcasted on the Web. Democratic Senator Bill Bradley, a challenger to Al Gore for the Democratic nomination, was the first to raise one million dollars online. In one day of the primary season, Senator John McCain, a challenger to George W. Bush for the Republican nomination, raised half a million dollars online. By this election, the Republican National Committee claimed to have a million activists online, and nearly four-fifths of major party candidates for the Senate maintained Web sites (Jagoda 2000; Puopolo 2001).

The Green Party presidential candidate benefited from a system of vote swapping, coordinated online. The Nader campaign's goal was to earn 4 percent of the electorate's support and the opportunity for federal matching funds in a subsequent election, whereas the Gore campaign's goal was to win more electoral college delegates than the Bush campaign. Gore supporters agreed to vote for Nader in districts where Gore was sure to win, and Nader supporters agreed to vote for Gore in districts where Gore's victory was uncertain. Almost 30,000 people agreed to swap votes, including some 1,400 Florida-based Nader supporters who agreed to vote for Gore. In 2000, political hypermedia were deeply integrated within campaigns. They were used for unique content not found in other media, purposefully as an organizational tool, and aggressively for data mining.

Survey research compared the role of the political internet in 1996 with that in 2000 and found a significant growth in the number of people who were participating in online discussion groups, researching candidates and policy options, and following political news online (Rice and Katz 2003). Of course, such citizens also received increasingly sophisticated political messages. Political marketing strategies were on the rise, whereby political parties mimicked the branding and retailing strategies developed in the commercial marketplace (Scammell 2000). Some survey research suggested that the political hypermedia were particularly engaging for young people who were comfortable with technology and less likely to consume political news through other media (Delli Carpini 2000). It appeared there was marked enthusiasm for voting online; statistical models suggested that familiarity with internet technologies was a greater predictor of participation in an online vote than a "sense of duty" (Bainbridge 2003; Stromer-Galley 2003). Interestingly, some scholars wrote about new aspects to grassroots campaigns, arguing that many activists had become transnational activists, no longer merely citizens but "rooted cosmopolitans" (Tarrow 2001).

2002

This was the year that many electoral districts, embarrassed by their logistical bungles in counting ballots in the 2000 election, invested heavily in digital equipment for recording votes. Although touch-screen polling stations were not sharing data over the internet, some were networked within polling stations. Miami-Dade County, the epicenter of electoral drama in 2000, invested almost $25 million in 7,200 touch-screen machines. Around the country, almost 20 percent of registered voters used an electronic voting system (McNulty and Truslow 2003). In terms of the political research the public conducted online, the internet portal America Online reported that more than 30 million voters had accessed their political content online since the 2000 election. Services such as MeetUp.com, MoveOn.org, and blogs were used by millions of people to research political options and express political opinions. At this point, social scientists were finding that important political decisions had been made about the information architecture of many search engines, privileging some information sources over others while excluding other information sources altogether (Introna and Nissenbum 2000).

Voter News Service had provided the data used by journalists to predict incorrectly the electoral outcome of the 2000 election, but was unable to improve its data collection techniques in time for subsequent elections. Pollsters still recorded a modest rise in the proportion of people going online for political news, but scholars who dug deeper into such data insisted that there was no "internet revolution" because users seemed to prefer the Web sites of the *New York Times, Wall Street Journal,* CNN, and other Web sites purporting to offer news, such as the Drudge Report and National Rifle Association. The tiny minority of people using the internet for politics comprised the more engaged segment of society anyway, not people "newly enraptured with politics" by new media options (Norris 2000b; Kohut and Rainie 2003). Similar survey data revealed that the public clearly wanted to be able to vote online, and assumed that it was only a matter of time before the technology for direct democracy arrived at their doorsteps (Bainbridge 2003; Stromer-Galley 2003).

The amount of political information online had been growing since the early 1990s, and by the 2002 election the average citizen could find genuinely user-friendly, intelligible databases of knowledge, not just quantities of unsorted, raw information. One could look up the top ten polluters in a neighborhood and click through to read about the sources of pollution, the definition of pollutants, and the political avenues for protesting pollution. One could track the records of specific politicians, matching political statements with voting records, funding contributions, and political affiliations. If citizens did not trust the quality of this information, often culled directly from the records of government agencies such as the Federal Election Commission and the Library of Congress, they went directly to the campaign Web sites of candidates and incumbents for the candidates' messages. The information was available, though people with different search skills experienced measurable levels of frustration and failure in finding government information online (Hargittai 2003).

By 2002, however, there were several major problems with the way political business was being done on the nation's information architecture. The BBC discovered that Florida's Republican secretary of state had removed 57,000 voters from the state's voter rolls before the 2000 election, using faulty data from a privately held firm in Atlanta, ChoicePoint's subsidiary Database Technologies. It turns out that 95 percent of the individuals listed in the data file were actually innocent of a crime, and 54 percent of the individuals on the list were African American (Palast 2003). On average, 30 percent of African Americans in Florida came out on election day, voting nine-to-one in favor of Gore. On average, 40 percent of whites and Latinos in Florida came out on election day, voting evenly for Gore and Bush. Even with the conservative assumption that only 5 percent of the correctly identified felons were African American, this administrative decision cost Gore well over 6,000 votes.[2] The data file had other kinds of errors. Whereas a criminal conviction date was provided for most people in the data file, a small number of people had no confirmed conviction dates, and a small number of people had conviction dates in the future. Of course, to know the real impact of this mistake a correct list of Florida voters who should have been excluded from the rolls is needed, but no such list has been produced.

These kinds of electronic mistakes occurred before the counting mistakes for the polling districts, the transmission mistakes by the polling stations trying to get data to the media, the exit poll mistakes by Election Data Services trying to anticipate outcomes, the display mistakes by the data firm responsible for color-coding the distribution of electoral college votes as the results came in, and the interpretive mistakes by television newsroom journalists trying to get data to the viewers. Bush's margin of victory of 577 votes in this electoral college district provides an important lesson: Data quality affects political outcomes.

2004

In this election year, campaigns – and scholars – discovered blogs. In particular, Howard Dean's presidential campaign made strategic use of blogs, encouraging people to write up their thoughts on politics within the informational architecture provided by the Dean campaign.

---

[2] This is a conservative estimate of net number of votes that would have been cast for Gore if the innocent people denied voting privileges had been allowed to vote. If 57,000 people were removed from the voter rolls, 54 percent of whom were African American and 95 percent of whom were innocent of a crime, then 54,150 people were unfairly denied a vote. If the 5 percent of correctly identified felons were all African American, then 49 percent of the total sample were African American and denied the vote (27,930 people), and 46 percent of the total sample were of other races and denied the vote (26,220 people). Assuming that turnout rates reflected those across Florida, 30 percent of the disenfranchised African Americans would have voted (8,379 people) and 40 percent of the other disenfranchised Floridians would have voted (10,488 people). Assuming that voter preferences reflected those across the state, 90 percent of African American voters would have voted for Gore (7,541 people) and 10 percent would have voted for Bush (838 people). Assuming that the other disenfranchised Floridians would have voted evenly for Gore and Bush (5,244 people for each candidate), we can estimate that 6,082 people would have voted for Bush, and 12,783 would have voted for Gore, giving Gore a net advantage of 6,703 votes.

The campaign released configurable, open-source software for setting up community politics Web sites in support of its candidate.[3] Dean led his competitors for the Democratic nomination in donations, most of which came online. The Dean campaign also took advantage of MeetUp.com's technology, which allowed community groups to easily form, discuss online, and then meet in person to continue discussion. But in this campaign season the people designing electronic voting technologies revealed that they had their own strong political affiliations and were not independent purveyors of public technologies either in terms of intellectual property law or in political affiliation. The president of Deibold, a manufacturer of automatic teller machines and paperless touch-screen voting stations, invited wealthy Republican donors to a fund-raising dinner at his home in Columbus, writing, "I am committed to helping Ohio deliver its electoral votes to the president next year." That the president of a voting technology company would be committed to electing a Republican president while also committed to building voting technologies for citizens was an obvious conflict of interest. Less clear was the conflict of private and public interests in the way Deibold and other companies were building electronic voting equipment. On one hand, voting is supposed to be a civic act, discretely done in the public sphere. On the other hand, the companies building the technologies had claimed that that the software code and hardware mechanisms were proprietary. These software systems were not inscrutable, however, and close examination discovered inadequate cryptography, leaked software code, data without protective passwords, and unanswered questions about ways and means of manipulating electronic ballots (Warner 2003).

The presidential candidates relied heavily on internet technologies to both get messages out and organize volunteers. The Republican National Committee had its Voter Vault, while the Democratic National Committee had its Datamart. Both parties had consultants develop tools for their armies of neighborhood volunteers, tools that would distribute data on voters in the neighborhood and allow volunteers to upload new information on these voters. Citizens who provided Bush or Kerry with e-mail addresses were sent an e-mail message every day, so that the news of the day could be spun in some way. Experiments revealed that when citizens expressed conservative or liberal policy preferences and their state of residence to either Republicans or Democrats, the major political

---

[3] General Wesley Clark was the only candidate for the Democratic nomination for President to encourage this activity without regulation by campaign managers.

parties were able to tailor content to reflect both ideological and regional interests. One of the more controversial political nonprofit groups, America Coming Together (ACT), used handheld computing technology in its door-to-door canvassing in Ohio. After interviewing prospective voters revealed policy interests, the ACT canvassers were able to show short, strategically chosen digital videos on topics of interest. The most complex relational databases of the day provided clues about which states and districts to devote coveted campaign resources to and which states and districts to leave to local organizers.

Candidate Web sites provided basic issue positions while avoiding both direct and indirect forms of dialogue, and only the intensity of the campaign battle seemed to drive up the quality and quantity of political information on these sites (Stromer-Galley 2000; Xenos and Foot 2005). A decade before, campaigns had begun distributing prepared interview responses by satellite, called "video actualities," to local television markets. This was a way for campaigns to both manage questions and provide answers. Local journalists would splice in their questions to create the impression that they were interrogating political candidates, where in fact the answers were canned and the journalist had limited creative freedom in phrasing questions without making the interview seem nonsensical. In 2004, campaigns, government agencies, and many large corporations developed other kinds of electronic press kits to help journalists interpret public policy and prepare the news. While these actors aggressively helped to shape news production, some of the public began to treating the Web sites of these actors as direct sources of news. In particular, the Web sites of political candidates had a direct agenda-setting influence on both the public and journalists (Ku, Kaid, and Pfau 2003).

INFORMATION TECHNOLOGY IN CAMPAIGNS AND ELECTIONS

Two kinds of data reveal how important information technologies have become to the system of political communication in the United States. Survey data reveal that citizens increasingly use information technologies such as the internet to learn about political campaigns, follow the news, and engage in political activities by volunteering, donating funds, or researching public policy options. Survey data about how campaigns increasingly use information technology in their communications strategy reveal that, at least at the national level, almost every political campaign fielded by major party candidates and most minor party candidates must now have a Web site. Sometimes the Web site is a basic statement of a candidate's political ideas, but increasingly Web sites offer interactive ways of participating and also serve as internal logistical tools for campaign operations. These dual trends in political communication, from citizens and campaigns, must be acknowledged as a prelude to the key research questions taken up in subsequent chapters.

Perhaps two singular events mark the importance of the internet in the modern public sphere in the United States, two events that both occurred on September 11. On September 11, 1998, the Starr Report was released to a public hungry for details, clogging e-mail traffic and crashing servers with political and pornographic content. On September 11, 2001, the internet became an important conduit for immediate news coverage of what was happening, but also for finding loved ones after the terrorist attacks and for collective expressions of grief. Many campaigns began developing political applications for new media technology, and the amount of political content available over hypermedia grew, as did the number of people using hypermedia to explore political content. Table I.1 reveals patterns in the rise of the internet as a political communication tool over the last five election cycles. It shows that the online population has come to look much more like the offline population, with notable changes in how the internet is used in politics. Since the internet is now well embedded in the everyday lives of many in the United States, it is sensible to present data about particular online activities not as percentages of a sample of internet users but as percentages of a sample of the total adult population (Howard et al. 2001). This allows for easier comparison of trends about how the internet is used as medium for political information. More important, this allows for more meaningful generalizations about patterns of cultural consumption for the entire country and theory building about the role of the internet in the larger public sphere. The table reveals several important trends up to the 2004 elections, in which the internet was available to most of the population, and a significant portion of that population chose to learn about politics over the internet. These survey questions were fielded in the month leading up to each election period since 1996.

Over this period, the portion of the public reporting to have read a daily newspaper dropped from about 50 percent to below 40 percent. The proportion of people listening to news radio also declined substantially. The proportion of people who had ever gone online rose from 23 percent in 1996 to 59 percent in 2004. By 2004, some 31 percent of the population reported going online on a daily basis for news, approaching the

Table I.1A: *Comparative Media Use, 1996–2004, Percentage*

Comparative media use	1996	1998	2000	2002	2004	Change
Yesterday, did you get a chance to read a daily newspaper, or not? Answered "yes."	50[a]	47[a]	40	39	38	−12
[How did you get most of your news about the election campaigns?] Answered "radio."[b]	44	41	17	13	16	−28
Did you watch the news or a news program on television yesterday, or not? Answered "yes."	59[a]	65	64	61	62	3
Do you ever go online to access the internet or World Wide Web or to send and receive e-mail? Answered "yes."	23[c]	41	54	61	59	36
Yesterday, did you go online? Answered "yes."	–	–	30	35	36	6
Do you ever get news online? Answered "yes."	–	–	12	41	69	57
Yesterday, did you get news online? Answered "yes."	–	–	12	17	31	19
Do you ever look online for news or information about politics or the campaign? Answered "yes."	4	6	16	24	57	53
Yesterday, did you look online for news or information about politics or the campaign? Answered "yes."	7	9	9	8	17	10
Total weighted N	4,360	3,184	13,343	2,745	4,542	

Source: The author's calculations using data from the Pew Center for the People and the Press and the Pew Internet and American Life Project.

Notes: Wherever I could not repeat Pew calculations from raw data, I report the findings from original press releases available at www.pewinternet.org and www.people-press.org. I have made every effort to extract comparable data from their regular post-election surveys even though changing research agenda made some lines of questioning inconsistent.

[a] This question was fielded in April of that year.

[b] For 1996 and 1998, radio use is based on the number of people who reported listening to news on the radio in the previous day. For 2000 and 2002, this was extracted from a multiple response question, "How did you get most of your news about the

Table I.1A (*Footnote continued*)

election campaigns in your state and district? From television, from newspapers, from radio or from magazines or from the internet?" Two responses were solicited, and I created a separate "radio" variable if either response was for radio. A tiny fraction of respondents chose "magazine," so this category is not used in this analysis.

[c] This question was fielded in July 1996.

[d] In 2000, this question was prefaced by "Thinking about yesterday. . . . "

[e] In 1996, this question was worded "Has any of the information you have received online about the 1996 elections influenced your choice of candidates?"

[f] This question was fielded in October 1996.

[g] Each year, respondents were queried about whether they participated in some of the popular online political activities of that election season. Since this list changed (grew longer) over time, this figure is the proportion of people having completed at least 25 percent of the activities suggested by the interviewer that year: looking for news or information about politics or the campaign; having gone online to get news or information about the elections; participating in on-line discussions or "chat" groups about the elections; registering their own opinions by participating in an electronic poll; getting information about a candidate's voting record; getting information about when and where to vote; sending e-mail supporting or opposing a candidate for office; receiving e-mail supporting or opposing a candidate for office; contributing money to a candidate running for public office through his or her Web site; looking for more information about candidates' positions on the issues; getting or sending e-mail with jokes about the campaigns and elections; getting or sending information about getting people out to vote; finding out about endorsements or ratings of candidates by organizations or groups; visiting Web sites that provide information about specific issues or policies that interested the respondent, such as the environment, gun control, abortion, or health care reform; visiting partisan sites, such as those run by the political parties, a candidate, or a campaign; visiting non-partisan sites, such as those run by the League of Women Voters; participating in online discussions, signing petitions online, or donating money online; subscribing to candidate or party e-mail notices; volunteering online for campaign service; learning about ballot initiatives or races for presidential, Senate, House, governor, or local offices; finding out how candidates are doing in the public polls; checking the accuracy of politician's claims with online sources; watching political video clips online; following election returns online.

[h] In 2004, this question was worded, "When you go online, do you ever encounter or come across news and information about the 2004 elections when you may have been going online for a purpose other than to get the news?" This is the percent responding "yes."

Table I.1B: *Information about Politics and Campaigns Online, 1996–2004, Percentage*

Information about politics and campaigns online	1996	1998	2000	2002	2004	Change
Have you gone/Did you ever go online to get news or information about the [current] elections?	6	6	10	13	30	24
Did you go to a Web site looking to read the news, or did you just happen to see some political news while you were doing something else? Responded "looking to read the news"	–	12	7^d	9	–	–3
…Responded "just happened to see the news."	12	20	5^d	15	30^h	18
Were you following up on news that you FIRST heard about someplace else, or were you going online to learn what was in the news? Responded "following up."	–	17	3^d	4	–	–13
…Responded "going online to learn."	–	9	4^d	5	–	–4
How often do you go online to get news about the elections? At least weekly.	2	4	13	8	23	10
How important has the internet been in terms of providing you with information to help you decide how to vote? Responded "very or somewhat important."	–	14	–	20	24	6
Has/Did any of the information you have received online about the [elections] made/make you decide to vote for or against a particular candidate? Responded "yes."	2^e	3	8	5	8	6
Do you ever visit Web sites that provide information about specific issues or policies that interest you such as the environment, gun control, abortion, or health care reform? Responded "yes."	–	11	–	24	21	10
Total weighted *N*	4,360	3,184	13,343	2,745	4,542	

Source and notes: See Table I.1A.

Table I.1C: *Civic Engagement, 1996–2004, Percentage*

Civic engagement	1996	1998	2000	2002	2004	Change
Some people seem to follow what's going on in government and public affairs most of the time, whether there's an election or not. Others aren't that interested. Would you say you follow what's going on in government and public affairs? Responded "most of the time."	52	46	–	49	54	2
Some people go online for campaign news because they are very interested in politics and enjoy following it. Others don't enjoy politics, but they keep up with it because they feel it's their duty to be well-informed. Which view comes closer to your own? Of those who go online, responded "enjoy politics."	38^f	29	–	31	–	–7
... Of those who go online, responded "feel duty."	59^f	57	–	66	–	7
When you go online to get information about the elections, do you ever do any of the following things? Responded doing at least 25% of the offered options.^{g}	–	6	5	16	22	16
Have you ever signed up for an electronic newsletter from a journalism or political organization that e-mails the latest news about politics and elections? Responded "yes."	–	7	–	6	6	–1
Total weighted N	4,360	3,184	13,343	2,745	4,542	

Source and notes: See Table I.1A.

proportion of the population that read a daily newspaper. The proportion of people who especially went online for political or campaign news grew from 4 percent in the 1996 elections to 57 percent in the 2004 elections. The portion of adults who look for news or information about politics on a *daily* basis during campaign periods was 17 percent in the 2004 elections. However, respondents were also asked whether they had ever gone online to look for news or information about that specific election period, and the population who responded positively grew from 6 percent in 1996 to 30 percent in 2004.

An important demographic transition has taken place in the online population over the last decade, which explains many changes in the ways people use the internet for political communication. Some of the activities popular a decade ago reflected the demographics of the online population of that time. Early internet users tended to be male and white, as well as younger, more educated, wealthier, more technically sophisticated, and more ideologically conservative than the general population. Subsequently, as more people gained internet access, the demographics and interests of internet users came to reflect those of the country at large (Howard et al. 2001). In terms of internet access, many of the digital divide categories disappeared, and gender, race, income, education, and age became less reliable predictors of who was using the internet. In terms of internet content, there were important deficits in the kinds of information women and racial minorities found personally relevant and accessible. In the early years of the political internet, the average user was deeply interested in public life and eager to use the technology as a means of democratic engagement. By the turn of the century, such users were in the minority, but this is not to say that the average internet user was apolitical.

Given the structure and presentation of content online, it is important to distinguish between users who intentionally research political information and those who casually stumble across such information. Those who intentionally go online for political information probably have a greater interest in politics than those who remember seeing a political news story while looking for some other kind of information. The proportion of people who deliberately look for news online has declined somewhat over time, as has the proportion of people who go online to follow up on news they heard offline, the proportion of people who report finding political news while doing something else online. Most telling, by the 2004 campaign, a quarter of the adult population said the internet was "somewhat" or "very important" in helping them decide how to vote. A small but growing group reported that something they learned online made them decide to vote for or against a particular candidate, and in 2004, a fifth of the population reported having visited a

Web site about specific issues, such as the environment, abortion rights, or health care.

Even though television is still the dominant medium for election news, those who have used the internet for political information report different reasons for preferring the internet as a medium (Howard 2005). They find the information more convenient, feel that other media do not provide enough news, find information not available elsewhere, and find that online news sources reflect their personal interests. They augment their understanding of current events and their knowledge of records of political candidates or deepen their understanding of particular issues by visiting the Web sites of national and local news organizations, commercial online services, and government, candidate, or issue-oriented Web sites.

The sequence of Pew surveys also allows some comparison of changing political norms over time. For obvious reasons, presidential campaigns catch more public attention than midterm elections. Over time, about half of the sample says they "follow what's going on in government and public affairs most of the time." When asked why they are motivated to go online for campaign news, the proportion of people who say they do it because they "enjoy politics" has declined, while the proportion believing it "their duty" increased between 1998 and 2002. The September 11 terrorist attacks in 2001 might have had an affect on people's sense of duty, but the question on motivation was not fielded in 2000, so this attribution is tentative.

According to the survey data, the four most commonly used media for information about politics are television news programs, radio, newspaper, and the internet. Increasingly, the cultural content of one medium includes references to content available on other media, most often the internet. The internet, additionally, allows users to help produce political information through blogs, personal campaign sites, and other forms of content creation. Comparative data on the production of political content online are difficult to come by, especially when it comes to personal web pages and blogs. Table I.2 reveals the growing number of campaigns for the Senate, the House of Representatives, and governor that produced campaign Web sites.

Overall, the proportion of political candidates for elected office producing a campaign Web site has grown significantly over the last five election seasons. Interestingly, candidates from the two major political parties are more likely to have campaign Web sites than minor party

Table I.2A: *Candidates with Campaign Web Sites, U.S. Senate Races,*
1996–2004, Percentage

Parties	Candidates and Web sites	1996	1998	2000	2002	2004	Change
All	Number of candidates sampled	126	140	117	126	159	–
	Number of candidates with Web sites	59	73	88	92	113	–
	Percentage of candidates with Web sites	47	52	75	73	71	+24
Major	Number of major party candidates	72	68	65	69	77	–
	Number of major party candidates with Web sites	48	49	59	62	71	–
	Percentage of major party candidates with Web sites	67	72	91	90	92	+25
	Percentage of major party incumbent candidates with Web sites	–	70	85	90	100	+30
	Percentage of major party challenger candidates with Web sites	–	74	95	90	88	+14
	Percentage of major party candidates with Web sites, competitive races	–	100	100	97	81	–19
Minor	Number of minor party candidates	54	72	52	56	82	–
	Number of minor party candidates with Web sites	11	24	29	28	42	–
	Percentage of minor party candidates with Web sites	20	33	55	55	51	+31

candidates. Campaign Web sites may be a way for minor party candidates to present their ideas to the public, but this evidence suggests that overall, minor party candidates have been slower to produce campaign Web sites than their better-funded competitors from the Democratic and Republican parties. Almost all of the major party candidates for Senate and governor produced a campaign Web site, especially if they were a challenger candidate. If a race was especially competitive – with

Table I.2B: *Candidates with Campaign Web Sites, U.S. House Races, 1996–2004, Percentage*

Parties	Candidates and Websites	1996	1998	2000	2002	2004	Change
All	Number of candidates sampled	1,380	1,075	1,265	1,123	1,209	
	Number of candidates with Web sites	222	377	696	640	824	
	Percentage of candidates with Web sites	16	35	55	57	68	+52
Major	Number of major party candidates	851	780	824	769	832	
	Number of major party candidates with Web sites	189	274	542	543	675	
	Percentage of major party candidates with Web sites	22	35	66	74	81	+59
	Percentage of major party incumbent candidates with Web sites	–	19	53	72	76	+57
	Percentage of major party challenger candidates with Web sites	–	52	77	75	86	+34
	Percentage of major party candidates with Web sites, competitive races	–	57	95	97	91	+34
Minor	Number of minor party candidates	529	295	441	359	377	
	Number of minor party candidates with Web sites	33	103	154	144	149	
	Percentage of minor party candidates with Web sites	8	34	35	40	40	+32

the outcome an even bet in the month before the election – the candidates in the race were almost certain to have produced a campaign Web site. Today, the vast majority of campaigns for Senate, House of Representatives, or governor produce a campaign Web site. More important, campaigns increasingly have at their disposal – either through affiliation with parties and lobbyists or through direct purchase from consultants – technologies for using personal information about voters.

Table I.2C: *Candidates with Campaign Web Sites, Gubernatorial Races,*
1996–2004, Percentage

Parties	Candidates and Web sites	1996	1998	2000	2002	2004	Change
All	Number of candidates sampled	37	151	28	162	44	
	Number of candidates with Web sites	–	104	23	121	30	
	Percentage of candidates with Web sites	–	75	82	75	68	−7
Major	Number of major party candidates	22	73	20	72	23	
	Number of major party candidates with Web sites	–	69	19	68	21	
	Percentage of major party candidates with Web sites	–	95	95	95	91	−4
	Percentage of major party incumbent candidates with Web sites	–	84	83	96	78	−6
	Percentage of major party challenger candidates with Web sites	–	100	100	95	100	0
	Percentage of major party candidates with Web sites, competitive races	–	96	–	96	68	−28
Minor	Number of minor party candidates	15	78	8	90	21	
	Number of minor party candidates with Web sites	–	35	4	50	9	
	Percentage of minor party candidates with Web sites	–	44	50	55	43	−1

Sources: 2004 from CampaignAudit.org. 1996–2002 compiled from multiple sources. In each year, projects managed to sample upward of 90% of the total number of candidates (Kamarck 1999; D'Alessio 2000; Schneider 2001; Foot and Schneider 2002; Kamarck 2002; Congressional Quarterly 2003).
Notes: Kamarck (1999) defines competitive races being "in play or an even bet" in the October/November 1998 issue of *Campaigns and Elections* magazine. Kamarck explains that there were no governors' races in 2000 that were classified by the Annenberg Public Policy Center as toss-up races. The 2002 data calculated from Foot and Schneider (2002). In 2002 and 2004 a race was judged competitive if the Cook Political Report labeled the electorate in that district as either leaning toward a candidate or a toss-up. In 2002 and 2004, some political organizations produced multiple Web sites advocating candidates for office, so the definition of candidate campaign Web site used by Foot and Schneider is also used here: A candidate Web site is content at a specific domain name that was clearly produced or sponsored by the official candidate campaign organization.

This is a book about the people who develop and deploy these technologies and the emerging practices that are transforming patterns of political communication.

OUTLINE OF THE BOOK

Chapter 1 argues that the many different formats for political information – Web sites, e-mail, databases, and news – now provide a material schema within which we construct political lives. Networked information technologies provide the structure for the contemporary system of political communication, a system that transforms important aspects of the democratic process. This chapter expands on the concept of political hypermedia and critiques the use of the traditional analytical frame of "media effects" in studying the role of information technologies in political life. Core concepts of deliberative democracy theory and cultural sociology inform a better analytical frame, one that is grounded in the experience of campaign managers and that treats these technologies as both a product of and container for political content.

Chapter 1 also introduces the community of political managers who work primarily at the national level of campaign organization in the United States. These IT professionals work not only for candidates from the Republican and Democratic parties, but also for independent campaigns and grassroots movements with alternative perspectives on issues on the national agenda. Based on observations of political hypermedia projects developed between 1999 and 2003, I construct the analytical frame that many campaign consultants subscribe to when they manage the production and consumption of political information.

I introduce two pseudonymous organizations in chapter 2: a political data-mining company called DataBank.com and a political action committee called Astroturf-Lobby.org. A decade ago, only the wealthier lobbyists and presidential campaigns could afford the services of DataBank.com, but now the firm also sells detailed relational databases to the country's nascent grassroots movements and individuals eager to start a small campaign of their own. Political data became a marketable product, something that could be sold to grassroots movements, elite campaigns, or corporate lobbyists. "We invite gun owners to join the NRA and women who use contraceptives to join NOW," says one consultant. "And then we sell guns to NRA members and condoms to NOW members." Astroturf-Lobby.org also merges voting records, credit card purchase histories, and social science survey data, but whereas DataBank.com sells its services to anybody, Astroturf-Lobby.org prefers to help conservative affinity groups. Both organizations help aggrieved clients to campaign for legislative relief by finding and activating a sympathetic public. Both organizations also provide key logistical and intelligence services to candidate campaigns around the country, in doing so, the organizations play a major role in managing the production of political culture in the United States.

Whereas chapter 2 analyzes the generation of political information through hypermedia, chapter 3 analyzes how political information is consumed through hypermedia. Here I introduce two pseudonymous organizations, Voting.com and GrassrootsActivist.org, both of which specialize in helping "political information consumers" learn about politics. While these two organizations are compared for their approaches to the consumption of political information, they are contrasted for their motivations. Both firms developed a number of innovative applications: e-mail forms that allowed citizens to send their political opinions to the relevant elected officials, searchable databases that would tell voters which candidate's platforms would most closely match their personal political preferences, and applications that helped elected officials process the deluge of constituent e-mail. I discuss two important aspects of the structure of political consumption: shopping for candidates and the rise of issue publics. In conclusion, I explore the connection between the production and consumption of political information in the marketplace of political ideas.

How has the organization of campaigning evolved? In chapter 4, I discuss the norms and organizational behavior of the e-politics community. Over the past decade, this small group of professionals has brought IT to the country's major political parties, lobbyists, and government offices through political propaganda Web sites, high-tech campaign logistics, and wired advance-team planning. I present evidence about the community's culture: shared features of identity, common personal and professional goals, a distinct policy project, and an ideology about information grounded in the language of technology, marketplace, and direct democracy. The e-politics community has a shared understanding of cause-and-effect relationships and common goals about how to shape political life with information technology. Whereas pollsters, spin masters, and logistics experts tend to be partisan, if not wedded to particular Presidents and presidential hopefuls, the architects of political hypermedia serve competing political masters. These consultants claim to work for a higher goal – a more transparent, accountable system of representation through technology – by wiring up a digital democracy. I draw from several areas of the social sciences: theories about epistemic communities from political science, theories about communities of practice from sociology, and theories about knowledge networks from management.

Also in chapter 4, I respond to recent studies of campaign organization that posit the growing role of professional pollsters and professional fund-raisers by exploring the role of information technology officers in the nation's more prominent candidate and issue-positioned campaigns. Large political campaign organizations have rarely been treated ethnographically, and little is known about their internal organization. Political campaigns, whether they are advancing a candidate or an issue position, have always had to be flexible and adaptable organizations. While pollsters supply campaigns with important information about the electorate and fund-raising professionals generate revenue, information technology experts have also had significant influence on campaign organization. Information technology experts build their political values into the tools and technologies of modern campaigns, with direct implications for the organization and process of campaigning. The transformed campaign – a hypermedia campaign – is the result of the important technological and organizational innovations that have occurred in the last decade. This campaign works with small feedback loops between candidate and constituent, low information waste, and unobtrusive ways of collecting data. People and organizations are tied up in multiple, overlapping affiliations, yet have many neutral "thinking grounds," both physical and virtual. These structures of affiliations also have to be full of people who are comfortable in collaborative relationships and not afraid of or restricted by the communication technology at hand.

Chapter 5 discusses the meaning of citizenship and representation in a digital democracy. Knowing what we now know about the complexities of the hypermedia design processes, the context in which political consultants work, and the kinds of content campaign managers produce, what can we do to build a healthy digital democracy? I return to the analytical frame revealed in chapter 1, to compare how the process of producing and consuming political information has changed over the last decade. The social contract is renewed whenever citizens vote or engage in political activities, but imperfect information prevents them from understanding their roles, their leadership choices, or their leader's choice. Imperfect information also prevents leaders from understanding the policy preferences of citizens. To solve the problem of imperfect information, several companies set out to design communication tools that would better help candidates and campaigns produce content. The production of political campaigns through internet technologies is a process of tailoring content not for mass consumption but for private consumption. The parallels with e-commerce are obvious; "mass customization," "broadcast individualism," and "direct marketing" are all terms that now apply to the production of political icons, arguments, and actors. However, the use of political hypermedia for these kinds of strategies changes the meaning of citizenship. I develop three theories about what citizenship and franchise mean in the wired democracy. An important task in scholarly argument is addressing negative hypotheses and counterfactual evidence. Are the hypermedia campaigns and forms of citizenship I observe and analyze really that new? If we looked beyond the particular evidence presented here, and imagined the universe of cases, all types of political campaigns, and all forms of citizenship in the public sphere, would the analysis be the same? Chapter 5, the conclusion, is devoted to answering the first question by building theory about the differences between mass media and hypermedia systems of political communication and about the roles of thin, shadow, and privatized citizenship. The Appendix addresses the second question by explaining my sampling choices in social network analysis, survey, interview, and ethnographic methods.

ONE

Political Communication and Information Technology

H ow does the culture of competitive political campaigning influence the design of new information technologies, and how do such technologies shape systems of political communication? In the Introduction, I surveyed the evidence about how the sources of political information and means of political engagement have changed over the last decade. I described the ways communication technologies have been used to produce and consume political content, referring variously to news, Web sites, e-mail, and other formats for political information. In this chapter I argue that these hypermedia are components of a new system of political communication formed around online petitions, digital news sources, candidate Web sites, relational databases, and more. I review some of the different ways of studying the role of technology in politics. I make a theoretical argument for moving beyond media effects to a more balanced approach that considers the role of campaign managers and technology engineers in both the production and consumption of political content. I introduce this community of designers and end the chapter with a discussion of how they frame their own work as brokers of information between campaigns and citizens.

Political culture includes more than abstract values and ideologies. Political culture is also defined by the material aspects of information technologies which provide very concrete schema that pattern our values and ideologies and, consequently, our voting behavior and public policy opinions. At least as important in understanding how media stimuli effect public opinion is understanding where those stimuli come from and how those stimuli may change with new technologies of political communication. Networked information technologies increasingly alter our habits of learning political information and our abilities to express and convey opinions to leaders; our contemporary habits of political learning and means of political expression define this new system of political communication.

POLITICS IN CODE

Between the 1996 and 2004 presidential campaigns, hypermedia technologies were deeply integrated in almost all campaign organizations and advertising strategies. The managers of political information technologies helped to improve the campaign's organizational efficiency, from internal communications between advance teams, pollsters, and speech writers to external communications with journalists, regulatory agencies such as the Federal Communications Commission (FCC) and Federal Election Commission (FEC), other campaigns, and the public. However, information management with new media technologies was still a specialized skill set in 2000, and the political managers with this skill set formed a community that cut across many organizational and ideological boundaries. Some of these specialized campaign managers had met online or had been working on hypermedia projects for a few years, but most met for the first time at the summer political conventions of 2000. By the summer conventions of 2004, the hot-shot new media campaign consultants were highly valued and highly placed within wealthy candidate and special interest campaigns.

Whereas only a few hours of convention speech-making are broadcast on television each night, almost all of the interesting cultural content produced at the conventions of 2000 and 2004 was channeled through technologies built by the e-politics community. They created dynamic Web sites, assembled comprehensive intranets or extranets, designed e-commerce solutions, and dabbled in graphic design where necessary. They took out-of-the-box applications and customized them, did strategic technology consulting, internet marketing, and Web site hosting. They designed interactive multimedia tools to help campaigns generate political messages and project them to the right voters. They also created tools to help voters simplify and analyze the political messages they consume.

Democrats, Republicans, and protesters produced an immense amount of carefully crafted content in political conventions, content that was designed to fit within their multimedia tools. More impressive was the filtering that occurred, especially concerning the programmatic content of the DNC and RNC. For delegates, there were no meaningful breakout sessions, policy debates, tense late-night deals, concessions, or consensus building – such activities are really for candidates and party elites. Convention activities are totally scripted, demanding little substantive engagement from either delegates and demanding little interpretive labor from observers. Television cameras broadcast simple messages of unanimity through delegates holding up scripted placards they did not produce themselves.

In 1948, Philadelphia was the location for the first televised political convention, so in 2000, campaign managers often forecasted the internet's impact on modern politics by referencing television's impact on political communication. Some technologies, such as internet relay chats, or "chat," were supposed to have an important impact by allowing more people to discuss politics, either within their communities or directly with politicians and policymakers. But practically, as Larry Purpuro, the RNC deputy chief of staff and Webmaster in 2000, explained, "Anybody involved in a campaign, regardless of their ideology, is always concerned about control. Chat is difficult to control." Still, the Republican Party's 2000 convention Web site claimed that they were hosting the "most interactive and broadly participatory political convention in history." However, most of the major news organizations registered fewer users the week of the convention. Pseudo.com's highly publicized 360-degree Web cam, which was supposed to bring the public right onto the 2000 Republican convention floor, was canceled for the 2000 Democratic National Convention. Instead, the company donated their Web cam equipment to the Smithsonian. That summer, both Republicans and Democrats offered a special space for political internet businesses at their conventions: The Democrats in Los Angeles called theirs "Internet Avenue" to distinguish it from the Republican's "Internet Alley" in Philadelphia. On Internet Avenue, the Pew Charitable Trusts sponsored "Democracy Row," where the e-politics community could interact directly with internet businesses, nonprofits, and academics advertising their projects. They traded business cards, project proposals, and organizational propaganda. Project Vote Smart distributed material boldly asking: "Will you govern or be governed?"

Members of the e-politics community found the conventions of 2000 and 2004 important because they could meet face to face, discuss their projects, and plan collaborations. They saw each other's business projects, but the political conventions become a community event for the consultants who manage political communication. The conventions helped political campaign managers with specialized skills in hypermedia to form their sense of common culture, collective project, and shared ideology.

Between the conventions, and Independent Media Centers, I met many of the people who constitute the e-politics community. At both conventions, Michael Cornfield from George Washington University and several faculty from the Annenberg School of Communication at the University of Pennsylvania provided commentary and added legitimacy to start-up endeavors. Doug Bailey was there to represent Freedom Channel, a service for streaming political actualities online. Voter.com displayed literature about its online citizen-candidate matching services. Its voter info-booths, which stood like ubiquitous bank machines, provided political information by touch screen. Mindshare and Issue Dynamics, two consultancies with expertise in using hypermedia for issue-specific lobbyists, discretely looked for clients and made new connections. Aristotle, a company well known for its data-mining techniques, sold access to its voter profiles. The representatives of social entrepreneurship funds from the Markle Foundation and Pew Charitable Trusts looked for investment opportunities. Grassroots.com advertised its services to activist organizations.

All in all, this cadre of political campaign managers who specialize in new media information technologies was defined by two important attributes: a set of shared norms about how technology should be used in political life and a collective project aimed at encoding those norms into the structure of political communication.

DIGITAL DEMOCRACY IN THEORY AND PRACTICE

Our theories and speculations about digital democracy, however, are more advanced than our ability to measure such an abstract institution. There has been much written that explores the philosophical, theoretical, and cultural implications of how a digital democracy could take shape. Often such works study discourse to clarify and qualify the concepts of "politics online," "electronic democracy," and "virtual state" (Tehranian 1990; Friedland 1996; Hacker 1996; Hague and Loader 1999; Tambini 1999; Barney 2000; Everard 2000; Sunstein 2001). For the most part, the arguments of these texts were composed in anticipation of evidence about cultural change. In other words, they helped us map out the range of possible futures. Several are summaries and analyses of rhetorical claims or well-articulated hypothetical scenarios based on what is known and possible in computer-mediated communication systems. In political science, for example, theorists have taken up the possible role of internet technologies in public deliberation. Critical thinkers warn that we need to be aware that our definitions of digital democracy affect our expectations of it and that electronic technology may make it easier to create aggregated and categorical identities rather than appreciating particular and personal identities (Calhoun 1998; Bowker and Star 1999). Others argue the opposite: that political hypermedia technologies allow for narrowcasting and too much particular content shaped for particular people. Of course, these discursive studies map out the structured relationship between the terms that we use to define and act on our political reality. Most of these kinds of studies give us a set of conditions for improving democracy with the internet: Technologies have to be designed from the bottom up to serve deliberative, democratic institutions and must be both interactive and accessible. Despite all the principled discussion on how internet technologies "can" be designed to improve democratic discourse with the right regulatory, economic, or experiential context, there are few studies on how – or if – this is being done.

A number of studies use survey and experimental methods to explore how people learn through computer-mediated communication and whether they are learning much about politics. Although empirical, several experiments and small projects have demonstrated that internet technologies have immense *potential* for helping grass-roots activism (Arterton 1987; Downing 1989, 1991; McGrath 2000) or other forms of engagement in practice. But there is a significant difference between experimenting with particular technology systems such as e-mail or Usenet in a controlled environment and understanding deeper institutional change across a society (Groper 1996; Hill and Hughes 1997). The few pieces that are grounded in lived experience were conducted before internet technologies were part of the mainstream political process or are speculative and anecdotal exercises in futurism (Toffler 1985, 1990; Toffler and Toffler 1995; Graber 1996; Gray 2001). While there exist several edited collections that compile distinct case studies, there has been no large study of the internet's effect on political communication that uses a systematic cultural method (Alexander and Pal 1998; Davis and Owen 1998; Dijk and Hacker 2000; Ferdinand 2001; Moll and Shade 2001; Kamarck and Nye 2002). There are a number of trade books about new media in political field sites, but it is important to move beyond impressive media stunts and particular communications technologies that capture the imagination of commentators (Miles 2001; Rheingold 2002).

Technologies and social organizations evolve together, so an analytical frame that treats a media effect as something that happens a posteriori, a social outcome or effect of a technological input or cause, is likely to provide limited explanatory power and miss important evidence about the evolution. The search for the net effects of new media must move beyond technology diffusion questions to an examination of how technology and democratic institutions are growing together through technical and political decisions that simultaneously shape organizational constraints and capacities. So far, much of our study of information technology and political communication has been of media consumption patterns, using large-scale survey methods. Such surveys miss the nuances of cultural change, and simple media consumptions patterns are only part of the character of a political communication system. Political communication systems, particularly those used by candidate and issue campaigns, are formed by complex technical, cultural, political, and economic influences (Williams and Williams 2003).

Our social imagination about the positive impact of hypermedia on political culture has been fueled by corporate efforts to brand the digital democracy. Through advertising campaigns, corporate identities – such as Microsoft or Accenture Consulting – can be associated with the advancement of a healthy public sphere and deliberative democracy. Visually, such advertisements overlay historical documents such as the Magna Carta or Declaration of Independence with the pixilated, contemporary interface of the computer screen.

For example, the advertisement "Democracy.com" from Accenture Consulting asks, "Will the internet give government back to the people?" and lets us discretely know that "now it gets interesting." Surveys of our expectations for digital democracy reveal a deeply held conviction that purposefully designed technologies can cause institutional transparency and public deliberation:

> The general public will have ready access to government information and services over their computers. The internet will be an agent for democracy, as each community has an electronic town hall. Voting will be done online via personal computer. Internet-based voting will dramatically strengthen democracy. The selection of leaders will be done via electronic media, without paper ballots or voting booths. Citizens will vote from home by computer on daily and weekly issues which are raised by their elected representatives. (Bainbridge 2003, 320)

In the last few years, a several "how to" books on cyber-activism and the "launch of a new democracy" have appeared, with titles such as *Cybercitizen* and *Teach Yourself E-Politics* (Hayward 2000; Kush 2000, 2004). Several academic projects produced source books to help journalists use new media technologies for researching political stories, and think-tanks published out their own reports (Project Vote Smart 2005).

Practitioners, especially in the political consulting industry, began to take hypermedia very seriously. Pundits covered the arrival of electronic democracy, bringing celebrity to a new breed of political consultants – those who could write Hypertext Markup Language (Ganly 1991; Wright 1995; Heclo 1999; Milbank 1999; Ransell 1999; Shapiro 1999; Lewis 2001). Conference proceedings, strategy books, industry research reports, seminars from political consultants, think tanks, and major management consultants help prepare political campaigns for the using new information technologies (Faucheux 1998; Jagoda and Nyhan 1999; Multiple 1999; Walch 1999; Clift 2000; Jagoda 2000; Accenture 2001; Ireland and Nash 2001). Many of these publications read as if a small part of the consulting industry was trying to teach campaign staff – and the wider public – what to dream about and expect from the new wired democracy. The summer before the 2000 campaign season, *USA Today* declared: "Getting on line is so simple a 'kid with an attitude' can organize a political force" (Drinkard 1999). The dreams were big, but there was also some distance between what was hoped for in a digital democracy, what was technically possible, and what actually occurred.

Each of the major e-politics firms helped generate publicity for its own projects through the publication of books predicting political revolution through information technology. Dick Morris, who founded Vote.com, wrote a book of the same name (1999). Dan Bennett and Pam Fielding, through their parent company, e-Advocates, published *The Net Effect: How Cyberadvocacy Is Changing the Political Landscape*, which included a foreword by Senator John D. Rockefeller IV (1999). Elaine Kamarck, one of Vice President Al Gore's chief technology strategists during his 2000 presidential campaign, co-edited two collection of essays, *Democracy.com* and *Governance.com* (Kamarck and Nye 1999, 2002). Ted Kennedy was the first U.S. Senator to have a Web site, and his site designer, Chris Casey, wrote *The Hill on the Net* (1996) about the institutional resistance he experienced as the House Democrats' main information technology expert.

We had punditry about the potential for digital democracy, rich commercial and cultural rhetoric about the convergence of new media and politics, and a small industry of specialized campaign consultants devoted to making this convergence happen. With such a wide range of actors building digital democracy in theory and practice, how could I investigate changes in our complex system of political communication? To make this study rigorous, I developed special techniques for sampling and studying political campaigns in the multifaceted domestic political landscape of the United States.

A NETWORK ETHNOGRAPHY OF HYPERMEDIA CAMPAIGNS

Computers have helped to manage political data since the early 1970s, and the most widely recognized (and suffered) consequence of this innovation was direct mail correspondence with constituents, one of the first forms of targeted political campaigning through media. But what is the emerging role of the new information technologies, digital and networked, in our system of political communication? I designed a *network ethnography* of national political campaigns and campaign staff in the United States. The Appendix provides the details of my methodological choices, but in short this process involved collecting both qualitative evidence through ethnographic emersion and quantitative evidence through surveys and social network analysis. Social network analysis was not the goal of this research but the means to a richer, theoretically revealing, multimethod inquiry.

My research questions took me into a professional community that specializes in building new media tools for explicit political use. This community outfits political campaign staff with new tools for organizing volunteers and collecting donations, builds and analyzes extensive databases on voter preferences and behavior, and projects political ideology through new media by designing, operating, and interlinking technology. It builds private intranets, publicly accessible Web sites, and delivery systems for actualities, logistical information, and campaign propaganda. Members often call themselves the e-politics community, but they work for many different kinds of organizations across the country. This situation presented a profound methodological challenge: How could I delve into the cultural dynamics of this particular, powerful community while contextualizing my observations within the system of relations among other political actors, such as parties, lobbyists, and the news media?

This field site was not a traditional professional community, since it was defined by multiple overlapping ties of very different kinds.

Individuals in the community occupied different positions in several companies, nongovernmental agencies, academic centers, government agencies, news media, and nonprofit organizations, such as political parties and community groups. Some worked in sole proprietorships or for politicians or firms on contract. Others worked for some of the more traditional businesses – such as polling or public relations agencies – that were trying to add to the range of products and services they offer the country's political leaders, parties, and lobbyists. Many worked for the few midsized firms that actually describe themselves as being in the business of e-politics. Members of the community had relatively complex formal, semiformal, and informal relationships that quickly became difficult to track because the field site was more of an occupational than organizational category. Members of the group felt they were engaged in the same sort of work, identified with their work, and maintained social relationships relevant to both work and leisure. Many did not have equivalent or comparable organizational roles; rather, they constituted a knowledge-based community of practice. Despite the diversity of formal organizational affiliations, I believed that this group shared principle and causal beliefs, patterns of reasoning about how politics should and should not work, an understanding of the value of technology in politics and commitment to this marriage, and, consequently, a common policy agenda. For many members, the primary basis of affiliation was the project of digitizing democratic institutions, not loyalty to their formal employers.

After only a few interviews, it became clear that the organizational culture of campaign consultants was well formed. They were consistently producing technologies that simultaneously violate public privacy norms and empowered citizens for independent political action. Repeat decisions and consistent patterns of campaign strategy showed that the way of producing political information through new media tools was well entrenched. To understand the production and consumption of contemporary political information, network ethnography allowed me to study the practice of digital democracy in the field itself, using a systematic cultural method. Inspired by other qualitative studies of small groups participating in democratic exercises, I spent the 2000 election year with the e-politics community, attending conferences and the national party conventions, volunteering with their projects, and conducting interviews around the country. Inspired by books such as Jane Mansbridge's *Beyond Adversary Democracy* (1983), Nina Eliasoph's *Avoiding Politics* (1998), and Herbst's *Reading Public Opinion* (1998), I sought insight into political culture and sought to generate rich theoretical explanations of how it gets structured. Network ethnography allowed me to extract rich data through ethnographic experience, while systematizing my selection of field sites.

Qualitative methods are desirable for rendering rich data on social interaction, but alone are ill equipped for studying the community life of these specialized new media campaign consultants. Social network analysis is desirable for rendering an overarching sketch of social interaction, but alone is ill equipped for giving detail on incommensurate yet meaningful relationships. I developed a system of network ethnography, a synergistic research design that uses the strengths of each approach to make up for the weaknesses of the other. Combined network ethnography allowed me to study the norms, rules, and patterns of behavior of a key group within the larger context of other political actors in the United States. Network ethnography used social network analysis to justify case selection for ethnography, facilitating the qualitative study of the varied individuals and organizational forms in this particular epistemic community.

In concrete terms, the arguments in this book are supported by several kinds of evidence. Three kinds of evidence are used in chapters 2 and 3: my analysis of participant observations of eighteen political hypermedia projects from major national political consulting firms, PACs, candidate campaigns, and political parties between 1999 and 2003; my ethnographic emersion with consultants during the 2000 presidential campaign season; and my analysis of fifty-two in-depth interviews with political campaign managers. Projects and interview subjects were chosen strategically after several iterations of social network analysis, an analysis of all formal conferences about democracy and technology in the United States between 1995 and 2000. Fortunately, I had the universe of cases to work with – conference records on some 765 experts in political information technologies who participated in twenty-six conferences over the five-year period – about how new media technology was being used in campaign strategy. Since this is evidence from a systematic ethnography, corporate and individual identities are masked to respect the confidentiality promised to subjects. Thus, I report words and describe situations accurately, but in chapters 2 and 3 I ascribe campaign managers' words and organizational situations to pseudonyms.

POLITICAL CONSULTANTS AS A CULTURAL INDUSTRY

Despite the diversity in political affiliations, many campaign managers adhere to a set of norms, rules, and patterns of behavior and have a well-defined set of professional objectives. They are members of competing firms, state organizations, parties, and charities and may argue on different sides of specific public policy questions, but they share a broad vision of how to conduct democratic deliberations with new communication tools. John Phillips, co-founder of Aristotle consulting, described the boundaries of this community:

> We're all like-minded in thinking that technology can play a role in politics, that's what makes it a community. It's not about your particular issue or your particular party. We have a shared interest in utilizing technology for everybody's greater good. I still hope my message will be more convincing than theirs.   (Phillips 2000)

Phil Noble, a consultant from South Carolina who founded Politicsonline.com, emphasized the aspects of the group that makes it a community:

> What defines our community is a common language, a common interest and a common pursuit. We share the language of the internet, a professional vernacular, and a common set of basic experiences. We are working in the field of internet and politics. We all know each other, communicate with each other and learn from each other. We aren't geographically contiguous, but that's not so important.   (Noble 2000)

But sometimes consultants also share the experience of social stigma because of their work. We perceive their work to be about concocting or manipulating public opinion. Journalists expose (or sometimes cover up) suspicious connections between lobbyists and politicians, academics expose (or sometimes contribute to) campaign propaganda, and citizens expose (or sometimes deepen) their own ignorance by consistently supporting candidates and political parties by taking informational shortcuts. Campaign managers are the masters of spinning political information. Some think that political campaign consultants will do this kind of work for the highest bidder and that unethical behavior is a feature of this professional cohort. Similarly, Vaughan's analysis of how NASA engineers manage information concludes that "actions are not necessarily the outcome of intent, conscious choice or planning, even though the outcomes may, to some extent, be predictable" (Vaughan 1996, 403). We might expect that political campaign managers will do unscrupulous things to win. But the day-to-day work of political campaigning does not involve obvious decisions about deviating from public or private expectations of ethical behavior in a democratic competition between people or ideas. Campaign strategies with new information technologies may be innovative or deviant, may risk public wrath, or may be part of the struggle to keep up with political opponents already using unethical strategies.

Shared Goals and Projects

Most political consultants specializing in information technology call what they do "e-politics," or the business of applying new media technology to politics. They put content online, they do opposition research, and they build and use tools for campaign logistics. These tools help take donations, organize volunteers and gather intelligence on voters. The professional consultants who are experts in political hypermedia may join a firm, political party, governmental, or nonprofit organization, but the community itself is part of a large, professional cohort. They are, in this way, an epistemic community of shared goals, identities, and fundamental, ideological principles about how politics should be organized (Haas 1992; Knorr-Cetina 1999).

E-politics companies put out a significant amount of propaganda advertising their products, services, and goals to financiers, campaign clients, and voters. Even though these print propaganda, speeches, and private sales pitches are designed to entice prospective clients, they are good statements about how community members feel the new media information communication technologies should be used: to provide citizens with interactive opportunities, to document campaign positions, to use links to establish a networked community, to commit to a privacy policy no matter how weak, to disclose sponsorship, and to make arguments by contrasting opposing views. They are familiar with the particular advantages of e-mail lists, for example: "You can send exactly the messages you want, to precisely the lists you want," as one consultant said.

People in e-politics agree on set of best practices about campaigning online and will passionately argue that new media communication tools are going to raise the quality of political discourse, as one senator's aide explains:

> That means manipulation, distortion, sensationalism, and any of the other moral shortcuts which persist in such "stealth media"

as direct mail and phone calls won't work well on the internet. Indeed they may explode in the campaign's face. Don't ever put something online which you couldn't live with having circulated throughout your district in the last hours of a campaign.... In short, we firmly believe that the internet raises the ethical bar for victory. The standards that have governed mass media campaigns will not suffice online.

Here the aide reveals what the community sees as the principal ailment of democratic culture in the United States: the traditional media system. This technical system affords the basest behavior from political campaigns. However, campaigns face new kinds of political risks when their content is arranged and resequenced in unintended ways. It is hard to prepare and manage the appearance of all campaign material before the public in the way possible with television material. Aspiring politicians are cautioned to put as little spin on their material as possible because, as another consultant said, "If there's a false claim or a syrupy after-taste to your positive message, you'll have a harder time of it now that the internet is here."

Along with a shared definition of what ails modern democracy, they share a vision of the cure, arguing that new communication technology can vastly reduce the transaction costs of political participation. Some see themselves as democratic warriors. Noble, for example, believes that new information technologies are making it possible for him and his colleagues to overhaul political organizations:

Seeds of revolution have been sown: media, fundraising, communications backbone of campaigns, instant response and local action. We are rewriting the rules of political engagement in this country.   (Noble 2000)

Tim Vickey of George W. Bush's 2000 campaign team managed many of the new media technologies used, and like the others in his professional community, he saw his work as improving the quality of democratic deliberation:

We're never going to completely eliminate the popularity contest. But we're expanding it beyond just sound bites, so people are going to have to digest it a little more, which brings the public back into democracy.   (Jagoda 2000)

Dick Morris, once a senior adviser to President Clinton, had to leave D.C. politics in 1996 after a sexual scandal and started Vote.com as a way of channeling public rancor at political elites. He, too, believed the interactive aspect of information technologies would challenge the complacency of unresponsive politicians:

> Anybody who thinks that getting a communication from a voter in your district is spam – that guy is pork. Roast pork unless he changes his point of view. (Morris 2000)

People in the e-politics community acknowledge that technology does not affect the public incentive to participate but expect that new media technologies will reduce the high "transaction costs" of getting involved in electoral politics. They assume that citizens are political and genuinely interested in the specific issues that affect them, but that staying informed on a topic, following the issues through the political process, and competing with vocal lobby groups takes too much time and money. The traditional way to deal with these transaction costs was to subscribe to political umbrella groups such as parties and formal lobby groups, which help individuals sort through political communication.

The primary source of identity is devotion to the e-politics project. Whereas many pollsters and professional campaign consultants are associated with a political party or ideology, many of the new media consultants are more committed to their professional goals. Mike Cornfield, director of the Democracy Online project and a high-profile member of the community, describes its political dimension:

> The online politics community is bi-partisan at this point. . . . The community defines itself against political professionals who rely on television and direct mail and off-line methods, and what unites them across partisan lines is their commitment to develop politics online. (Cornfield 2000)

This is in sharp contrast to other kinds of political professionals, whose party affiliation defines their client base and professional network for most of their career. In fact, Noble articulates that members of the community ascribe to norms they read as resident in the internet architecture itself:

> The values they share are inherent to the internet: in terms of dispersed information, the concept of openness, and the sense of exploration. Those are not political values, and only in loosest sense

are they social values. If there is a value, it is that everyone is a small
"d" democrat.   (Noble 2000)

According to e-Advocates' Pam Fielding, who has worked with both
Republicans and Democrats, "Very few of us are ideologically committed.
We don't want to make institutional commitments. We are all freelancers
in a way." Few members of the e-politics community are tied to the big
political parties. They enjoy the freelance work, which gives them the
option to leave politics altogether and to market other kinds of products
with other kinds of consumer campaigns. This may be an added blow
to political parties who not only have to compete for voters and donors,
but also increasingly have to compete or pay for the allegiance of the new
political hypermedia consultants.

Most of the individuals in this community are men under thirty who
graduated in political science and love being involved in the new economy. More important, most have worked with one another on projects
or appeared together in conference panels. They regularly met for happy
hour, and several marriages within the community help solidify identity.
The e-politics community is primarily made of Generation X-ers who
grew up with computers, feel comfortable trying out new technologies,
and constantly check their e-mail. Laura Dove, a Republican Quaker and
one of the first people to work on e-politics, feels that people with her
expertise are getting more power after every successful campaign: "Most
of the people in the community are actually middle management. In
ten or twenty years, they'll be in charge." This attitude bemuses older
political consultants, such as Noble, who quipped, "The amusement of
youth is that they can remake the world."

The offices of some companies can feel more like fraternity houses,
with foosball tables, mini-basketball courts, and dance floors. In D.C.,
there is a regular poker game among the some of the male consultants.
As a response, several women who are part of the core group created a
lunch meeting for professional women in the community. Other women,
such as Lynn Reed, instead expect to be treated like one of the guys:

> I've adopted the personal skill set to deal with the male politics
> world. I expect them to treat me as one of the guys. On the other
> hand, I attended an EMILY's List training session in 1994, and I
> wouldn't be where I am today without that support. (Reed 2001)

In fact, most of the women in the group feel that they have benefited in some way from women-only clubs, organizations, and other

47

forms of gender-specific support outside the community. These include technology-centered groups such as Women's International Net and the D.C. chapters of Webwomen and Webgrrls. This demographic sameness could be problematic for the choices encoded into e-politics software. However, some of the most inventive groups in designing political hypermedia have been those who hope to use the technology to reach and activate communities without a voice. For example, the League of Women Voters has developed rich reference databases for voters who want to research candidates, parties, and policy options.

Us/Them, In/Out

Because the group is a professional community, its identity is partly defined by its members' relationships with other political professionals, especially journalists, pollsters, and traditional political consultants. Vickey described a kind of territorial competition between this community and other political consultants:

> The fundraisers and the media people see us as threatening their turf. Part of this has to do with the way the money flows. Online campaigns mean smaller budgets for TV ads, quick and effective fundraising, and easy campaign communications. This means decreased profit margins for the typical political consultant experienced with direct mail or typical TV institutions.

They also see themselves apart from the communications staff in a politician's office. Chris Casey, author of *Hill on the Net,* about his experiences as adviser of the Senate Democratic Technology and Communications Committee, described the institutional resistance found in the Congress:

> The Senate by design is supposed to be slow to change. The House side moved quickly to get themselves some e-mail. The Senate, especially its Rules Committee, resisted. Someone told me, "There is no legislative purpose to e-mail, it will happen over my dead body." Another good example is that when the Senate set up internet access for offices, they only allowed three IP addresses per office: one for the exec, one for human resources, and one for all other staff. (Casey 2002)

Here, Chris reveals that the organizational resistance to technological innovation helps give consultants an excuse to bond. Frustrated with their candidates, parties, and PACs, IT political consultants sought each other out.

Deciding who is in the community often means deciding who is not part of it. The people most often excluded from the community's definition of itself are the traditional "old" media professionals and lobbyists. Television-era consultants are most certainly not part of the community, as Dove, an expert in issue-specific campaigns, points out:

> Old media perpetuate a myth that people don't have power. The traditional press keeps telling everyone that they don't have power. Old media have an interest in keeping people stupid and dependent on television. (Dove 2001)

Dove also sees the institutional divisions that keep new media and old media consultants apart:

> The established media didn't want to see it. People who know how to buy TV have been buying TV for a long time. They have historical data, and they know that if they want a certain demographic they will go to certain stations and certain timeslots. They make good money producing and placing the ads. (Dove 2001)

Some of the old media consultants fear that political hypermedia applications are not as scripted as television. More specifically, producers of content cannot always control how material is presented online because it is designed for users to explore. Vickey of Bush 2000 argues that older consultants fear the internet because "[having a Web site] is like having your own library, where someone can look up everything on a candidate. People will find something and use it against them" (Jagoda 2000, 88)."

Still, the e-politics community competes for the recognition of those within the larger community of electoral politics. Pollsters, journalists, and television commentators, when all is said and done, are still higher up on the political food chain. The older, more conservative cohort of consultants includes pollsters who are often wed to a world of partisan politics. However, when someone from the old political guard does "get it," the e-politics community praises them for vision. Several high-profile presidential advisers, such as Dick Morris and Mike McCurry, became the CEOs of e-politics firms, bringing in clients and financing.

The social distance that members place between themselves and other kinds of political consultants is also set between themselves and other kinds of new media dot-commers. Few of the firms have backing from Silicon Valley. They rarely contract out to large commercial Web site designers and do not, in general, participate in wider new media industry associations.

Thus, specialized conferences became an important way to reaffirm who was in the community. They bring the community together to fantasize about the possibilities of information technology, even when this is an exercise in absurd futurism. The conferences the community holds help to distribute knowledge about the technology and to provide opportunities for socializing and socialization. Conferences let them hear and tell stories about triumphant campaigns and dismal defeats. The conferences also help the community to find identity and access to the identity symbols. The conference network is a neutral social space among formal organizations that alone do not provide much in the way of social support. The conferences project and control discourse about what political hypermedia should and can be doing for the country. Conferences also recognize achievement, assign prestige, and provide access to limited foundation grant money. People compete for status through panel assignments, and both new and old members learn about the rules of engagement from more powerful politicians, consultants, and traditional media figures. It is at such conferences that propaganda and symbols are created or at least given value.

"Getting It" and "This Space"

For the consultants who specialize in political hypermedia, people who are "old media" strain to imagine how to communicate political information through anything other than the one-to-many paradigm of broadcast television. The language of "who gets it" describes, as Dan Solomon of Mindshare says, people who understand the ability of the technology to enable fine-tuning of messages. "People who go to Yahoo! financial [to buy e-mail lists] and buy the whole country are the folks who used to do TV buys," said Solomon. "They don't get the targeting thing."

Those who "got it" distinguished between both long- and short-term implications for the tools they were designing. As Casey said:

> At the beginning there were very few people who got the connect, who could think five or ten years down the road to the inevitability of how this was going to change politics, who could also think right now, to know how to incorporate this medium into a campaign. They could talk to you and tell whether you were doing something innovative.   (Casey 2002)

Thus, being part of the community meant distinguishing short-term goals in campaign victory and long-term goals in direct democracy.

E-politics business plans always have an idealistic paragraph or two that describes "this space" or this business field, as being empty but full of potential, a niche of opportunity for those who think innovatively. The rhetoric about this space most often appears in press releases and media interviews in which a set of corporate values and relations delimit the business's financial and moral obligations. These show this space to be distinct from the broader economic sphere of the new economy as well as the broader political sphere of campaign politics. It appears in common language when people have complaints of "crowding" in the e-politics space: "there's too many people in this space" or "there isn't that much revenue in this space." According to Bob Hanson, who started a business printing a directory of congressional phone numbers over a decade ago and now has a host of new media services, "We don't think there is room for a public company in this space. There isn't that much money to make." This space, the e-politics space, is situated within a larger social sphere of political interaction, but firms of different sizes and stages of growth populate it. Some argue that individual members of the e-politics community, cyber-active citizens, or the public at large can also reside in the e-politics space. Along with "getting it," occupying "this space" helps them to imagine both the physical and social characteristics within the community and to locate the community and its activities in some broader political topography. Just as a landscape or topography can hold many socially constructed attributes, this space includes a cluster of actors, organizations, settings, financial debts, contractual obligations, markets, clients and service providers, dinner meetings, social events, conferences, ideas, ideals, and dreams.

Shared Ideology

The language of community members, whether quips provided for the pundits and press or sales pitches to foundations and investors, is richest when they discuss the bigger social project to which they are contributing. Their shared ideology, as community members articulate it, has three components: revolution, direct democracy, and the marketplace. These components are particularly salient in the books, articles, and conference speeches of members of the e-politics community.

The language of revolution and the inevitability of technological change appears in company rhetoric because it helps to attract financial backing. A company's particular form of political hypermedia has to appear revolutionary in order to land investors. Companies feel they have to be more revolutionary than traditional media applications, and their fervor about the internet's role in politics has to be full of revolutionary zeal. Firms do this to distinguish themselves in the eyes of both venture capitalists and charitable foundations, both of whom provided financial and institutional support for e-politics firms. In either case, project proposals used the language of revolution in order to make the point of the effectiveness, a language similar to that used in Accenture's effort to capture the democratic imagination in an advertisement.

In their language, the process of the technological revolution not only will change campaigns, it will change who is willing to run for office. The e-politics community evokes the language of direct democracy whenever the role of technology in a political process is described. In his introduction to *The Net Effect*, Senator John D. Rockefeller wrote that "the internet makes political life more transparent" and that it has "already changed our political dialogue." This message of democratic renewal is particularly strong where community members have written in public forums (Berman and Weitzner 1995). While the most important aspect of the community's identity is its devotion to its e-politics project, the ideological platform of direct, Jeffersonian, democratic principles is the next most important aspect that binds them. "The community is four-fifths small 'd' democrat," a Republican presidential aide confessed. "Really ideologically conservative people are not very creative, and this is a very creative community."

This informational revolution extends to engaging ordinary people in politics, even as they themselves are "experts" in creating that capacity. According to Chris Casey, "We can use these technologies to return powers that for the last couple of centuries, the public delegated to experts." The most important aspect of their shared identity is their devotion to the e-politics project, a project that translates direct, Jeffersonian, small "d" democratic principles into software code and hardware design. Political hypermedia are often described as grassroots activation tools, or as mechanisms that at the push of a button can raise popular support or outraged opposition. The electoral mechanism metaphor is key to framing the importance of e-politics for the campaign that hopes to succeed.

The community also uses the language of the marketplace to describe how voters process information. Since the medium itself is thought to have revolutionized commerce, the new politics can easily be described as a kind of e-commerce, instead of in the realm of the public sphere. "Information is power, and improving access to information helps level the playing field between those who have money and those who don't," according to a pamphlet from Calvoter.org, a nonpartisan organization promoting technological ways of improving the democracy in California. "Direct access to data and intelligently filtered opinion from peers will turn American politics around." Like many in the e-politics community, the founders of Calvoter.org make the comparison of political information with other kinds of information: "This has been a clear consumer preference in many online markets, from financial services (with financial reports, regulatory filings, up-to-the-minute stock quotes) to healthcare (with medical journal studies, clinical trials, lab results)."

Voters are commonly referred to as "information consumers" who operate in an imperfect market. With the new political hypermedia, the e-politics community can help perfect the market for political information, so that candidates shop for votes, and voters shop for candidates and policies. The competition among competing views is good for democracy, and this competition is often framed in terms of the control that consumers can have when they shop for candidates and policy options. "Consumers should be in control of markets," advocated Phillips. "And the power of the internet is in transferring control." The development plan for a nonprofit citizen portal makes an interesting parallel with eBay: "We need a self-reinforcing, virtuous circle of trusting relationships between buyer and seller that have made the auction site famous. This circle is to be brought to politics." For the e-politics community, the competitive dispersion of political ideas and leaders can only lead to healthy deliberative discourse. Oron Strauss, a manager at Net.Capitol in Washington, D.C., believed that there were many ways to distribute political content.

> The internet changes the information flows, but doesn't change the transaction. The cognitive process of arriving at a decision is the same. Like aspects of commerce, data management, or customer relations, the internet doesn't change what you do, just how you do it, and hopefully it improves the process.

In this passage, the low level of education among citizen-consumers is described as a problem of inaccessible information. A politician is an eminently sellable product, and good market research helps immensely with product placement. This market-influenced language is particularly apparent in describing the aspects of business that sell voters' profiles (Vote.com, Voter.com, and Aristotle.com, as a part of their business models, all sell information about voters to campaigns). Often the language of the marketplace was also used by funders, whether venture capitalists, public institutions, or private foundations, who expected to see that some customer or client need was being met and who demanded deliverables through measures of customer satisfaction.

THE STRUCTURAL CODE OF POLITICAL COMMUNICATION

The e-politics community designs software to shape the flow of information in electoral politics. Software code embodies values when choices are made based on a designer's appeal to values such as freedom, privacy, democracy, justice, or transparency. A number of hardware and software systems have been shown to be normatively loaded manifestations of an inventor's solutions to technical problems (Norman 1989; Lessig 1999). In the case of hypermedia campaigns, it is not just that some new software and hardware systems are designed by people with a particular value set, but that their choices about an exostructure of media and information management shaped the way the rest of us experience and participate in political life.

One of the first attempts to define and compare political culture was Almond and Verba's classic *The Civic Culture* (1963), though their findings may not have stood the test of time (they argued that there was a participation explosion across their sample of young nations). However, their two-part definition is important because it laid the foundation for how contemporary social sciences analyze and compare political cultures. First, political culture is operationalized as an individual's knowledge about the formal organization of politics, his or her emotional commitment to the people in politics or political symbols, and his or her evaluation of how well the whole system works. Second, political culture consists of "objects": roles, structures, offices, politicians, policies, decisions, and enforcement mechanisms. The U.S. Constitution is a formal statement of many principles in political culture, but there are a wide range of other norms, rules, and patterns of behavior that governs political behavior, and the Constitution is one of the more formal parts of the democratic code. Outside the practice of politics governed by the Constitution, finance laws, or other formal dictates is the Realpolitik of behavior by candidates, constituents, parties, and PACs over which political science claims purview. All of these things are part of political culture in the United States. There is no correct or even consensus about the definition of political culture. But understanding a society's political culture must certainly begin with an understanding of its system of political communication. Such an understanding must certainly be informed by analysis of the norms, values, and patterns of behavior of the community that does the work of political communication.

The e-politics community felt united in their devotion to "upgrading democracy" in the United States with new communication technologies. Through their design of new technologies, the e-politics community shaped the material aspects of political culture. When its members spoke about organizing political campaigns, they used metaphors from the computer sciences in which they are expert. In designing the content and informational structure of hypermedia campaigns, managers often described four abstract elements of the political communication system:

1. political objects: actors, arguments, or icons
2. political processes: procedures through which actors find satisfaction or office; arguments find publicity or resolution; and icons find circulation
3. political events: the condition of an object at any particular point in process
4. political memory: the information supplies and filters that affect how we recall and interpret objects, processes, and events.

A country's particular system of political communication is defined by these distinct elements – objects, processes, events, and memory. These elements appeared in consultants' typologies of their own campaign projects, and shared understandings of these elements were the foundation for decisions about the information architecture of their campaign projects. Since the producer of political content occupies a privileged position similar to the producer of other "high" culture industries, it is worth exploring each of these four aspects in detail (Abercrombie 1991).

POLITICAL OBJECTS

An object campaign is organized to publicize a candidate or personality, an argumentative position on a public policy question, or an icon belonging to a political agenda. These kinds of projects are the least interesting and least challenging to many consultants because they require a standardized publicity strategy that "gets the word out." These kinds of campaigns include candidate campaigns where a political personality wants to figure more prominently in the news or an issue campaign where a lobbyist pays to have his or her public policy argument considered in the public sphere. In terms of political hypermedia, the object campaign is best exemplified by the Web sites for political personalities not running for office, Web sites for well-known public policy arguments such as those advanced by pro-life or pro-choice lobbyists, or Web sites for political identities with iconic status such as the Zapatistas. The object campaign takes few resources to maintain and rarely involves interactive hypermedia.

Actors, arguments, and icons populate a system of political communication. Actors are individuals or groups of people who organize to advance arguments or celebrate an icon. For example, a political party is an example of an actor who aggregates a set of citizens (other actors) based on their commitment to an ideology (a set of arguments) through a circulating icon (a donkey or elephant). Political parties are designed to take the energy, money, and votes of people with diverse interests into a large political organization formed around amorphous ideologies, general political platforms, or national-level issue positions.

Objects are socially arranged in a hierarchy that gives certain individuals, arguments, and icons greater currency or greater circulation in the public sphere. Frequently, objects are aggregates of other objects, resulting in a hierarchical system that gives overarching objects the most common features of their components. In this sense, political parties appear to be standardized versions of particular actors, arguments, and icons that make up party factions. Since objects are often standardized or aggregated versions of other objects, political communication is also a process of accommodating conflicting, competing, or idiosyncratic actors, arguments, and icons. Icons appear in the rhetorical repertoire of political leaders, the color and pageantry of political television commercials, and the papier-mâché of protest puppets. Icons have political attributes (the signified) and a range of descriptors (signifiers). Icons are representations or symbols of either an argument or an actor. The object campaign commodifies meaningful political images for widespread distribution and consumption and turns the descriptors into a kind of currency that can be spent by campaigns, businesses, foundations, and nonprofits. Arguments are the most basic statements around which objects and icons are allied. People have principles, but their commitment to an icon and their level of agreement with an argument defines their relationships with other political objects. Being "pro-choice" or "pro-life" means subscribing to a set of arguments about the status of women and the status of a fetus, knowing the iconic symbols of each argument, and being familiar with the political actors espousing such arguments.

POLITICAL PROCESSES

A process campaign occurs when consultants have been retained to advance a personality, argument, or icon through political scripted procedures. Consultants are instructed to achieve specific political goals, not just broadly promote a candidate or issue. Obviously, the most common process campaigns are for people who seek political office and issue groups who seek legislative relief for clients. In both examples, legislation dictates election rules and specifications. The procedure for getting a piece of legislation passed is knowable. There are, however, a significant number of informal rules about how priorities are negotiated by legislators and administrative officials, such that consultants are retained to help issue groups navigate formal and informal cultural schemata for passing laws. A process campaign often takes years of careful maintenance, a long period punctuated with important events that may require extra attention.

The battle between competing actors, arguments, and icons occurs through political processes – sets of socially defined instructional sequences for identifying the rights and responsibilities of citizens, the procedures by which citizens choose representatives, and the instructions for identifying the rights and responsibilities of representatives. Procedural rules in political communication systems are easy to exemplify. They include tax laws about who can contribute what amount to political candidates, franking rules for organizing discussion of party platforms or congressional bills, or FEC instructions that govern campaign advertising. In many democracies, the processes in political life seem automatic because they are clearly defined and widely known. In less democratic cultures, processes can still be well defined, but they may not be widely known (or transparent) or may involve only a small group of objects (such as actors, icons, or arguments). Ideally, processes enable objects to produce consensus and resolve differences efficiently.

Processes in political systems are the instructions for how actors engage, the response time or turn-around time for other actors, the communication channels among actors, and the system for verifying information, and they provide the institutional context in which objects interact. There are three kinds of processes in political communication. *Sequential* processes occur when an object moves through one process at a time. For example, a candidate must be elected President before he can sign a bill into law. *Concurrent* processes occur when an object moves through several processes simultaneously. For example, a political party must carry on internal debates about its platform and priorities on multiple topics, and party machinations over competing priorities eventually result in one or two prominent policy proposals. *Distributed* processes occur when several objects move through several processes. For example, the process of deciding how to clean up the environment requires that several different objects complete several processes.

POLITICAL EVENTS

An event campaign occurs when candidates or issue groups have a short-term, immediate goal that is an important part of a larger campaign process. Events such as nominating conventions, Supreme Court rulings, and human tragedies bring together multiple, competing candidates and issue groups. They compete for victory at the convention, vie for the sympathies of courts or the public, and jockey for leadership in the news headlines about a current event.

An event in political life is the immediate condition of an object at any stage in a process. The process state is the effect of instructions in a particular environment or moment in time. Similar objects – passing through similar processes at different points in time or under different circumstances – will look different when studied as events and the peculiar interaction of object properties and process instructions is brought to light. For example, two different Presidents can be impeached under the same constitutional guidelines, but each impeachment event is unique.

Often people point out that there is a big difference between what is inscribed in a country's constitution and what happens in the day-to-day negotiation of politics. The right to a private balloting may be guaranteed by constitution but not found in real balloting exercises. This is the difference between the formal process (execution stream) and an event (condition of an object at a point in the execution stream). No two events in politics appear the same because objects are caught in different stages of several processes. Although events themselves may not be scripted or studied in detail, they may seem highly structured because they are snapshots of process that are well specified. For example, we may understand the procedure for how political parties search for a vice-presidential candidate and the arguments for having certain kinds of candidates over others, but to understand the political system that produces a particular vice-presidential candidate we have to examine the event closely and the layers of processes and objects in context. In studying this event, we move beyond what appears to be a high-profile, open, and public quest but is actually a rigorous internal vetting for candidates from a party's elites.

In fact, several patterns of political behavior become clear when taken as "events." It is only the particular interaction of actors, ideas, and icons in the procedural context of an election that might result in negative advertising. The formal rules of voting procedures might guarantee citizen privacy as they vote, but specific events reveal how these rules are obeyed or broken in a particular election event. Actual voter turnout is a function of objects in multiple processes at a point in time.

POLITICAL MEMORY

A memory campaign often occurs when political personalities are no longer in the public eye, when political arguments have been won or lost by the turn of events, or when political icons no longer seem directly relevant to current events. They are efforts to manage how we remember, both in how much information is an active part of cultural memory and in how much is accessible for other campaigns that would have us remember personalities, processes, or events in a different way. Campaigns for presidential libraries and obituary campaigns are the best examples of projects where consultants are retained to shape how we think about our political system.

Memory is the fuel for political objects, motivating actors, grounding arguments, and perpetuating icons. Social memory is structured by a communications infrastructure that stores and delivers information about objects, and norms of institutional filtering that provide us with interpretive frames. It is through memory that objects are named and labeled, and the best example of political memory campaigns are campaigns about presidential libraries and presidential obituaries. In an effort to manage the immense amount of information that circulates in the public sphere during a political campaign, managers plan for three stages in the distribution of political content. The social *fetch pattern* of memory reveals when information is loaded into the open public sphere (when information can be accessed); the *placement pattern* reveals which objects get access to what information (who can access what; which markets get access to what information); and the *replacement pattern* reveals when information is removed from the open public sphere (when new information is introduced). Citizen access to memory is frequently random and haphazard, even for those with education and training, and often governed by those who manage the technology that stores and transmits memory. Political memory is easy to rewrite, and only technology allows versions of memories about objects, processes, and events to be stored for re-access and to preserve earlier versions.

Some objects, hierarchically ordered, have privileged access to the conditions under which memory is written and broadcast. The memory of a political system is in information about objects, processes, and events and how information about these three elements is identified, accessed, used, and protected. Objects often create processes for filtering memory such that information flow is restricted or distributed along with an interpretive frame. As a social frame, memory helps us to match actors, icons, and arguments with political processes and particular events. Our political memory assembles objects, processes, and events into a political system and is the collection of interpretive precepts that helps us to situate an event within a political process and to identify the important actors, icons, and arguments.

ANALYTICAL FRAMES FOR STUDYING POLITICS AND INFORMATION TECHNOLOGY

There are interesting discrepancies among the theories about technology, the findings of media effects scholarship, and patently observable change in systems of political communication. Conventional social science wisdom is that qualitative methods tend to be best for generating theories, while quantitative methods tend to be best for testing theories. In the rush to study new phenomena quickly, an enormous amount of the scholarship is reflective speculation that explores the democratic potential of technologies such as the internet. This is done either by imagining the best and worst-case scenarios about how political life might change as the technology diffuses or by performing large-scale survey research on how the public's media habits are changing. However, surveys of users often define the public sphere as the sum of commensurate voters who respond to a voter incentive structure that has been mediated by communication technology. To generate theories about the role of internet technology in the public sphere, we need an analytical frame for political communication that includes the organizational behavior of political campaigns. Analytical frames are systematic, detailed sketches of ideas – social theories – that researchers develop in order to aid the examination of specific phenomena. We should begin by exploring how a "media effects" analytical frame typically renders evidence about the role of communication technology in political life.

In the United States, academic interest in "media effects" began in earnest with Lazarsfeld, Katz, Merton, and other sociologists who constituted the Columbia School. They looked for a connection between television content, the organization of media interests, and popular culture in the middle of last century (Merton et al. 1946; Lazarsfeld and Merton 1948; Katz 1987). As media technologies diffused, these writers observed the growing reach of popular culture industries. They imagined a connection that was direct and causal, with technology causing a measurable change in the cultural, consumer, or political sophistication of the audience of individuals or households. This interest in the direct influence of communication technology on users, rather than the moderated relationship between designers and technology, or designers and users, was also a legacy of Lippmann and Dewey. They agreed that the machine age – symbolized by steam, cable, telephone, radio, railroads, inexpensive printing, and mass production – brought about new forms of political engagement. Their debates over the nature of deliberative democracy early in the last century shaped many of the current debates in political science (Lippmann 1947; Dewey 1954). Moreover, their optimism imbued technology with the power to change social relations. In 1937, Ogburn published a study that described the evolving inclination to look at the independent effects of technology on political institutions:

> Government in the United States will probably tend toward greater centralization because of the airplane, the bus, the truck, the Diesel engine, the radio, the telephone, and the various uses to which the wire and wireless may be placed. The same inventions operate to influence industries to spread across state lines.... The centralizing tendency of government seems to be world-wide, wherever modern transportation and communication exist.   (Ogburn 1937)

Here Ogburn relates transport and communication technology to government centralization, and many contemporary scholars try to make similarly direct, causal linkages from technological change to institutional change. After many decades, media effects research has shied away from models of causal relationships between communications technology and changing social institutions, and worked with more confined models of causal relationships between communications technology and public opinion or individual political sophistication. Even though the relationship between technological innovations and social institutions is interesting, media effects research has taught us more about individual voter behavior in experiential or narrow circumstances than about our democratic institutions.

The media effects frame assumes that if the internet has any influence on the shape and character of politics, it will be revealed in models of how internet use, controlling for other variables, influences voter sophistication or behavior (Wilhelm 2000; Rice and Katz 2003). This way of framing the role of communication technology in politics has inspired many attempts to model the effects of innovations, such as television, talk radio, or Motor-Voter legislation on civic engagement (Knack 1995, Knack and White 1998). Few quantitative studies about the effect of media use on civic behavior, however, have had enduring explanatory power. It is difficult to model how we actually learn or avoid political information because of the use of multiple media, multiple occasions of media use, and the intensity and time of media use. Much of the political science research uses statistical methods based on analytical frames of rational choice, economically driven actors, and political transaction costs and neglects more nuanced understandings of the cultural process of embedding norms in technological design, and the process by which people embed technology in their daily lives.

Indeed, the media effects frame has rendered contradictory findings on the effect of the internet on politics, as some researchers have found that the internet has beneficial effects on democratic institutions, while others hold that there are negative effects. Several senior scholars who have entered the debate over the societal effects of the internet have sought to polarize opinion between a "connection with the world" position (Etzioni 2000) and a "shrinking social universe" position (Nie and Erbring 2000). Of course, many of these studies and theories are based on media usage, so their contribution has more directly to do with how internet technologies affect our individual political sophistication than our system of political communication. Do new media information technologies have an effect on politics? The analytical frame of media effects has yielded positive, negative, and neutral answers.

POSITIVE POLITICAL EFFECTS

The argument that internet technologies are good for democracy is grounded in the claim that they can mitigate some of the more debilitating aspects of contemporary political communication. Anything that overcomes the effects of one-way, information-poor television and newsprint media helps democratic deliberation. These theories of the positive effects of the internet center on the ability of internet tools to foster civic engagement, to replace other forms of media that may have negative effects, and to provide information important to the voting process. In this frame, citizens have an inadequate supply of information from traditional news sources, limited interaction with public policy officials, and few opportunities to deliberate with each other. With this positive perspective, almost any problem in information supply can be overcome through interactive technologies such as the internet. Many networking technologies, not simply the internet, open up possibilities for new forms of governance and representation. Some argue that virtual communities can only add to the public sphere, especially when they grow around bulletin boards or chat rooms for exchanging ideas, mobilizing the public, and building social capital and empathy among the participants (Rheingold 1993, 2002; Schwartz 1996). It has been argued that African American families in particular can equalize their relationships with corporate and political elites with accessible communications media rich in information (Redd 1988).

Studies of local activism have revealed that internet tools facilitate social networking across traditional socioeconomic boundaries, engage people with group learning experiences, and draw new participants into public life (Brants et al. 1996; Wittig and Schmitz 1996; Tsagarousianou et al. 1998; Mele 1999). People who use new media avoid the harmful effects of traditional media, especially television, by experiencing politics more directly and interactively. The internet reduces the distance between government and the governed (Grossman 1996; Budge 1997). Television news seems to have more of an influence on public concern than the reverse (Behr and Iyengar 1985; Mutz 1995; Fallows 1996), so a multidirectional medium should create a news agenda that reflects public interests. Moreover, uninformed voters use media cues and informational shortcuts in place of becoming fully informed, usually benefiting incumbent Presidents more than challengers and Democratic more than Republican candidates (Ferejohn and Kuklinski 1990; Lupia 1994; Bartels 1996). Whereas traditional media create a political narrative that consists primarily of content from and about the primary political parties, internet technologies do not allow this reinforcing effect. Instead, they permits users to create new social contexts for themselves based outside neighborhood, family, or friendship ties, through which they may be converted to minority, partisan, or independent political positions (Burbank 1997). Using tools such as cell-phone networks to coordinate sudden, well-attended culture-jamming exercises, sometimes called "flash mobs," is an exciting new form of protest.

NEGATIVE POLITICAL EFFECTS

In contrast, others have argued that the internet is at best a global shopping mall and at worst a den of iniquity. Political content online is a base kind of political pornography in which important information is grossly simplified or, as Sunstein argued, is easily misrepresented, often altered, and increasingly tailored for individual interests (Sunstein 2001). Some have concluded that networked communication technologies can only exacerbate the worst features of democratic participation within industrial capitalism, because information exchange on the internet is driven by the commercial ethic of selling information. It would still, therefore, allow for tyrannous majorities, and would still facilitate negative campaigning (Klotz 1998b; Gutstein 1999; Barney 2000; Howard and Milstein 2003; Wicks and Souley 2003). Those communities that do form online are at best "pseudo-communities," intimate forms of communication that seem intensely interpersonal and at the same time a mass communication system that gives technology designers very effective tools for controlling the interactions and experiences of community members. Voters who are already committed to political parties are most likely to consume political information, so we could expect that providing such content over the internet would encourage groupings of the like-minded or clashes of the opinionated, not dialogues among the open-minded and inquisitive. Some researchers argue that the internet reduces social involvement and psychological well-being, which certainly would not be good for the future of deliberative democracy (Kraut et al. 1998).

Those who deplore the role of the internet in contemporary politics argue that specific tools – especially e-mail – can incapacitate political offices, distribute biased information to the electorate, and allow political interests to disguise their authorship of online content. In 2000, Capitol Hill received over 6.5 million messages a month, about 8,000 per representative and 55,000 per senator – a volume that doubled over the previous two years and doubled again two years later. The same technology that shows gun owners news stories about how guns are used to save lives also shows people who believe in restricting gun ownership stories about accidental shootings. While mud-slinging will always occur in any medium, many new media have the additional benefit of obscuring authorship and making content anonymous. For example, during the 2000 election campaign, Republicans were responsible for the Web sites Gorewillsayanything.com and Gorereinventionconvention.com, while

Democrats produced Iknowwhatyoudidintexas.com and Millionaires-forbush.com. In 2004, Republicans produced Senatorflipflop.com and Swiftvets.com, while Democrats produced Bushspeaks.com and Billion-airesforbush.com. As might be expected, these Web sites differed from both official campaign and party Web sites in both content and tone. Similarly, campaigns also used meta-tagging to make search engines return their own Web pages as a top search result when someone tried to search for information about political competitors, or Google bombing to associate unflattering words with particular political biographies. In other words, internet technologies may exacerbate and reinforce disconcerting political trends. Scholarship in the negative media effects frame argues that there is such a well-entrenched knowledge gap preventing lower-educated and information-poor groups from learning quickly during a campaign period that no amount of innovative technology can overcome their susceptibility to manipulation by campaign managers.

NEUTRAL POLITICAL EFFECTS

Still others have argued that there are few distinct media effects caused by increased internet usage. This line of argument holds that all that is good and bad about political life is replicated online. The pace of campaigning may be faster, and campaigns more efficient, but these changes do not make voters more sophisticated or more likely to participate in elections. Increased information alone cannot overcome the inequalities or biases among the electorate that are the real threats to sound electoral decision-making.

The internet's capacity to present an immense amount of information does not necessarily lead to more informed voters. This is similar to the C-SPAN "noneffect." Despite the broadcast of substantive legislative deliberations from coast to coast, few people watch the deliberations, and measures of political sophistication show no improvement since the cable channel was launched in 1979 (Entman 1989). There is a large population of "know nothings" who do not understand politics enough to value democratic deliberation or participate in it (Doppelt 1999). Regardless of the medium involved, there are substantial differences in information-processing skills and other barriers to civic engagement, regardless of how a particular medium covers political issues.

The media effects frame is well suited for studying general outcomes of mass media, but less useful for hypermedia, where user control permits so much more unique, mediated experiences. Close observation of designers – and the users who redesign for themselves – reveals how norms get embedded in technology and how technology provides users with both constraints and capacities. Media effects research may expose general tendencies and average experiences through broadcasting television content or standardized newspaper content. The positive, negative, or neutral effects of consuming content over mass media are important for technologies that people use mostly for content consumption. Since hypermedia technologies allow people to produce and consume content, the ideal analytical frame would be well suited for studying hypermedia use through both the production and consumption of cultural content.

The media effects frame lends itself to experimental research and studies with specific new media technologies. These studies are important for their controlled environments and for finding statistically comparable effects, but may not always teach us about larger trends in democratic practice. For example, experimental settings reveal that people with a sophisticated argument repertoire are more likely to participate in online debate and that a sophisticated argument repertoire is also one of the consequences of participating in online debate (Cappella, Price, and Nir 2002; Jennings and Zeitner 2003). Others have found cohort-specific connections between using the internet for political information and levels of civic engagement, interpersonal trust, and life contentment, though the models cover tiny amounts of explained variation (Shah, Kwak, and Holbert 2001). Studies of student media choices suggested that widespread internet use was unlikely to diminish the use of traditional news media, while internet users were less likely to recall the substance of the news they were reading online (Althaus and Tewksbury, 2000; Tewksbury and Althaus 2000; Tewksbury, Weaver, and Maddex 2001). Chatting online also seems to have a positive impact on political participation rates (Hardy and Scheufele 2005). However, since only one in ten internet users ever join political discussion groups or chat about politics online, it is important to move beyond the use of software-specific internet applications and controlled experimental environments to assess the multiple, varied forms of engaging political debate and interacting with political information online.

CULTURAL APPROACHES TO POLITICAL COMMUNICATION SYSTEMS

In recent years, the notion that culture matters has resurged in the social sciences, where culture is explicitly treated as a discrete unit of analysis (such as a nation-state, firm, or nongovernmental agency) or as a variable (emergent properties with historical consequences). Sometimes political culture is described as part of the error term to quantitative models explaining behavior and public opinion. Elsewhere, political culture is used to explain everything because it is described as the most fundamental, broad, antecedent cause of social behavior. Both Huntington's *Clash of Civilizations* (1996) and Putnam et al.'s *Making Democracy Work* (1993) are examples of arguments that ultimately retreat by deferring to the inevitable weight of political culture (Harrison and Huntington 2000).

There are, of course, richer ways of theorizing culture. In *Keywords* (1985), Raymond Williams maps out the development of culture as an independent noun, abstract process, or product of that abstract process. Culture has often been used as a synonym for civilization – for variation either within or among communities – but its greatest usefulness has been to distinguish between "human" and "material" development. In important ways, political culture is defined by both human relationships and the material means of transmitting information about those relationships, but we often leave the term undefined and avoid the components of material development – especially communication technologies – that are the most physical manifestations of cultural schema. Everyday cognition relies on cultural schemata, knowledge structures that represent objects or events and provide default assumptions about characteristics and relationships when information is incomplete (DiMaggio 1997). Although schema include both representations of knowledge and information-processing mechanisms, in the social sciences we rarely study those mechanisms that are in fact material.[1] Crediting mechanisms with structuration, a dark and uncontrollable grammar that writes society, is more the purview of Harold Innis, Marshall McLuhan, and Jean Baudrillard (McLuhan 1944; Innis and Innis 1972; Baudrillard 1978; Innis 1991).

In other words, research into political culture has largely excluded the material dimension of communication technology and treated political culture as ideological repertoires, not technological structures. For example, we know that political culture gives priority to some social problems and policy options over others (Hilgartner and Bosk 1988), that it is reified and resisted even in subsistence communities (Scott 1985), and

---

[1] A notable exception is emerging in the field of the social studies of science and technology, which takes as its foci the co-constitution of cultural forms, material objects, and political culture. See also Zarubavel's study (1992) of how information about the New World was diffused by early mapmakers.

that a formative characteristic of political culture in the United States is the dominance of independent political parties, which structure the vote but do not always offer meaningful and appealing policy options (Clemens 1997). However, the process of representing and manipulating public opinion heavily depends on consultants with skills in the use of communications media. A community of these consultants builds the tools that the rest of us use to compose, transmit, and consume political culture. Thus, a definition of political culture should include mental and material schemata, while acknowledging that people have different degrees of power over the organization of these schemata. Usually political culture is left undefined, but when it is used, it typically is used in two senses: either in a hard deterministic catalogue of the social constraints on individual action or in a liberating explanation of the community characteristics that provide the capacity of individual action.

The *hard cultural determinist* conception of political culture holds that political culture is rarely, if ever, composed afresh. Political culture emerges from social precedents. Studies of cultural path-dependence – including world-systems literature – often take this hard cultural determinist position. Hard cultural determinists tend to define culture as a set of collectively held values, which are in turn hierarchically structured so as to control different kinds of social relations (Parsons 1969). While individuals' attitudes to specific daily circumstances may change rapidly, their underlying value systems form slowly under the weight of history. Within this framework, there are no conscious agents of culture; cultural innovation can be rarely traced to individual action. Hard determinism is often used to explain behavior or attributes that one cannot (or does not want to) attribute to individual agency (i.e., a weak political culture, not bad presidential leadership; the culture of Nazi Germany, not Germans' personal morality; engineering culture at NASA, not individual responsibility for shuttle launch decisions). These explanations can, occasionally, feel like a catch-all for variation that quantitative models cannot explain: "Culture must contain the answers as we search for an explanation of the skill gap, the competence gap, the wage gap, as well as the pathological social sink into which several million African Americans have fallen" (Patterson 1997). In this view, culture is a set of obligations and burdens inherited from a previous generation. Culture plays a causal explanatory role because it is essential, largely immutable, and self-replicating.

In contrast with hard cultural determinism, the *free will* conception of political culture holds that people make choices all the time. We draw from a cultural tool kit as the need arises. With limited social or cultural capital, there may be some constraints on the range of tools available, but people are free to apply whichever resources they have at hand to engage with others and interpret social interaction. People use symbols, stories, rituals, and world-views selectively to compose strategies of action, and cultural sociology studies those strategies of action (Swidler 1986). Analyzing culture from the free will position uses what Bourdieu called the "subjective position," which foregrounds individual interactions because they are more easily visible to researchers than structural relations that are occupied and manipulated by other individuals, groups, or institutions (Bourdieu 1993). This approach to culture locates political struggle in personal reputations and personal acts of labeling, as Scott does when he writes about a "struggle of the appropriation of symbols, a struggle over how the past and present shall be understood and labeled, a struggle to identify causes and assess blame, a contentious effort to give partisan meaning to local history" (Scott 1985, xvii). In doing so, the free will position credits individuals with unique skills and creativity and often obfuscates structural context or socialization. Some communities have a culture that supports individual's hard work, educational achievement, and civic engagement; other communities have cultures that discourage their members from having these goals.

However, the hard determinist and free will perspectives may not be incompatible. The description of the political consulting industry at the beginning of this chapter reveals that individuals produce cultural schema that the rest of us live with. Our democratic culture is structured by a concrete system of political communication, which this community manages. Thus, an important part of political culture is the process by which someone with power makes choices about technology that affect the way the rest of us exercise power and make choices about technology. Closely observing the activities of a group of specialized political communication consultants yields their own understanding of the structure of political communication. Soft cultural determinism – defined below – relies on both human relations and material design to explain structural changes in the system of political communication, changes that provide both capacity and constraint for human action.

INFORMATION TECHNOLOGIES AS CULTURAL SCHEMA

Political culture is the set of ideological and material schema that constrain some forms of political action and expression while providing capacity for other forms of political action or expression. An analytical frame for political culture needs to integrate both the capacities of human agency and the constraints of material structuration. Moreover, the frame should capture power differentials because some people have more influence over the representation of knowledge and construction of information-processing mechanisms. Other people are confined by these schema, subject to ideological and material structures of communication and without the volition or skill set to participate in what Giddens would call the act of "restructuration" (Giddens 1990, 1991). But political culture has the qualities of a kind of exo-skeleton, a structure difficult to change deliberately and slow to evolve (Berger and Luckmann 1967; Bourdieu 1990; DiMaggio 1997). In the analyses in this book, communication technologies are the exostructure, the material embodiment of social choices in the writing of behavioral routines, scripts, and protocols. Although individuals have agency in immediate micro-level structuration (internal campaign strategy choices), participate with a small group in meso-level structuration (competition with other campaigns), and contribute in a small way to macro-level structuration (public policy outcomes), there is an exostructure of cultural schemata that only experts in campaign management have access to (political hypermedia).

In political life, this exostructure consists of filters that block or time the delivery of political information. Political information technologies influence our actions through the structured links they embody and imbue. Web sites, for example, reveal organizational affinities through links to other social groups and reveal ideological links through carefully presented premises and arguments. Overall, the model of culture as proposed by Bourdieu, Sewell, and Swidler seems to have been developed without awareness of the ways in which communication technologies, themselves a cultural product, provide a unified system of constraints and capacities for the exercise of social life (Swidler 1986; Bourdieu 1990; Sewell 1992). We should still strive for a theory of cultural change that explains the process by which schema are created and encoded into technology and constrain or enable civic action.

How then does political culture change? If we accept political culture as a kind of exostructure that supports the flow of information between citizens and leaders, how did those flows evolve, and what makes them change? To understand political culture, we need to analyze how political content is produced and how material technologies are built to communicate that content. Technological innovations and the institutional context of the development technology are both important for understanding changes in social organization (Orlikowski and Barley 2001). Social and material structures are both aspects of political culture. To understand truly the role of new media communication technologies in political culture, we need to analyze a narrative of how the material schemata – the supportive exostructure of political information technologies – has been constructed.

Political communication systems are perhaps best understood from a position of *soft cultural determinism*: that an important and often misclassified part of political life is the information communication technology itself. It forms a material schema, or cultural exostructure, that is not usually considered by social scientists. Political culture is an information filtering system that directs and restricts the flow of information between and among citizens and leaders. In democratic political culture, the information filters built in the service of a dominant political power are designed for calculated ambiguity, while the information filters built in the service of a radical or challenger power are designed to permit interpretive freedom. Political culture consists of objects (actors, icons, arguments), processes (rules and procedures), events (object condition at a point in process), and memory (analytical frames for recalling and interpreting objects, processes, and events). Digital democracy is a kind of political culture, a political variant that must be treated as a complexly coded system for organizing and acting on public and private preferences.

Political culture is a set of cognitive and material schemata for organizing the movement of socially significant objects through scripted political process in political events and for organizing the way we remember those objects, events, and processes. Political culture consists of cognitive representations, concrete social relations, and the information communication technologies that mediate these representations and relations. These schema, whether ideological or material, constrain some forms of political action and provide capacity for other forms of political action. In sum, political culture usually refers to ideological frames that help filter information. However, I argue that political culture is defined by material frames – information communication technologies – that also help filter political content. Political culture is usually treated as a hard deterministic force or as something permitting free will. I argue that political culture provides both capacity and constraint for action.

Establishing that the e-politics communities have power at this early stage is the key to the argument of this book; as agents, they have influence over these representations, relations, and technologies. It is important to establish how campaign consultants specializing in information technology have the power to dilute or concentrate control over our system of political communication. In keeping with soft cultural determinism, I argue that these campaign managers have access to both cognitive and material schemata.

In this chapter, I introduced the e-politics community. Not only does it have a common project – building a digital democracy – but it also has an overarching social organization with unique features. I discussed the shared norms, rules, and patterns of behavior among new media consultants, but I study their means of micro and macro organization in Chapter 4, where I develop a concept of epistemic heterarchy that distinguishes the knowledge-based, nonhierarchical complex system of organization. Because of the powerful position of this community's members, however, they inhabit a liminal space between large democratic institutions and the specific political choices of people, between abstract human relations and the material infrastructure of information communication technologies. Thus, I argue that one of the most important changes in democratic institutions is in the organizational behavior of the managers of our political culture: the way the political consultants, candidates, lobbyists, and activists manage information and communicate with each other and with citizens. They negotiate the transactions between individual political identities and shared political institutions we have all agreed to inhabit (Gerhards and Rucht 1992). I began this argument with evidence from conference transcripts, interviews, and observations from the Republican and Democratic national conventions in 2000. However, in subsequent chapters I discuss four representative political campaign management organizations: DataBank.com, Voting.com, Astroturf-Lobby.org, and GrassrootsActivist.org.[2] These projects have set out to digitize political culture, and I contrast them on two important axes of comparison: whether the political consultants are opportunistic or altruistic and whether their tools are designed to help in the production or consumption of political content.

[2] All four of these organizations are very careful to obey state laws that regulate which records can be sold to whom. They employ legal counsel that is committed to keeping the company's work well within the letter and spirit of the law.

TWO

Producing the Hypermedia Campaign

By 2050, a piece of software will be a candidate.
– Tracey Westin, DemocracyNet.org
(now Grassroots.com)

C ampaigns are complex exercises in the creation, transmission, and mutation of political symbols. The process of producing these political symbols changed in important ways over the last decade, largely through new tools for producing political campaigns. I illustrate my argument with findings from systematic ethnographies in two organizations devoted to digitizing the social contract. DataBank.com is the pseudonym for a private data-mining company that used to offer its services to wealthier campaigns, but through new media is now able to sell data to the smallest campaigns, nascent grassroots movements, and individuals. Astroturf-Lobby.org is the pseudonym for a political action committee that helps conservative affinity groups seek legislative relief for grievances by helping these groups find and mobilize their sympathetic publics.

There are several reasons to focus particular attention on the role of new media in political communication. Grossman's *The Electronic Republic* (1996) argues that we are moving into a third stage of democratic evolution. The early direct democracies evolved into representative democracies, and the new electronic media will bring us to a wired reincarnation of direct democracy. "Telecommunications can give every citizen the opportunity to place questions of their own on the public agenda and participate in discussions with experts, policy-makers and fellow citizens" (Grossman 1996, 48). He recognized, however, that it would take a deliberate effort to get technology to work in this way.

Whether or not we accept this enthusiasm for wired democracy, even the headiest theories of deliberative democracy argue that communications infrastructure can either be the great hope of or great bane to discourse. Dahl, in *Democracy and Its Critics* (1989), argued that communications technology could be harnessed to promote democratic values by making information available to the public in a timely and accessible manner. Putnam, in *Bowling Alone* (2000), also devotes a dozen pages to the question of whether new information technologies can be harnessed for their democratic potential. Even Sunstein's *Republic.com* acknowledges that these kinds of arguments about how information technology can be used are waiting for evidence about how it is being used. In this chapter and the next I analyze this evidence.

This type of empirical study of the social construction of new media is important for several reasons. First, the moment is ripe for studying the growth, diffusion, and institutionalization of a new communication medium, a process that involves both the social construction of technology and the technological construction of society. Second, not only are hypermedia interesting for their variety of communication modes (reciprocal interaction, broadcasting, individual reference-searching, group discussion, person/machine interaction) and kinds of content (text, video, images, audio). Because of this diversity, their reach and impact may be socially deeper than other media, such as radio and television. Third, many of the design choices made today will pattern the way the internet is used for decades to come. Understanding the normative structures and social assumptions of the designers will have both theoretical implications for our understanding of how culture is built and practical implications for those of us who use such hypermedia (DiMaggio et al. 2001).

As discussed in the Introduction, the punditry about politics online in the 1990s followed a tight script. Television communication systems, largely managed by political and media elites, constrained healthy political discourse. Candidates sent messages, and the viewing public sometimes paid attention. Political consultants and academics collaborated on a science of political marketing (Mauser 1983; Selnow 1994). Information had a relatively short life, television messages were fleeting, and their independent effects were difficult to verify. In conventional wisdom, the age of cyber-politics is inherently democratic and aterritorial. Candidates and citizens send and seek data about each other's preferences and voting histories. Cyber-politics turn at a much faster pace, and political elites have less control of spin and impact because hypermedia rely on citizenry for message turnover. Massive volumes of information can be stored and easily accessed, making it possible to verify campaign messages and, presumably, catch lies and mistakes. Negative effects, if there were any, would come through devious political hacks but would not be a result of the way the hypermedia system itself was designed. But beyond the punditry, what role does the hypermedia campaign have in the public sphere?

I argue that the very way political culture is produced has radically changed through the growing use of political hypermedia, such as relational databases and the internet. Contemporary communication technology has radically altered the organization of political power, and I present several examples of how this has happened. More important, those who have traditionally held control of political knowledge have lost much of this control to those with the ability to design and operate political hypermedia. *The production of political campaigns is increasingly the purview of either technocrats, whose choices about technology design affect the distribution of political power, or nontraditional actors who, equipped with political hypermedia, exercise the same marketing capacity as traditional political actors.* The new system of producing political campaigns has immense implications for the meaning of citizenship and the basis of representation.

THE DIGITAL LEVIATHAN

Rousseau's notion of a social contract, into which we enter when we participate in any kind of organization, is often set in contrast to Hobbes's notion of the Leviathan state hegemon that protects us and shepherds us through a life that would otherwise be nasty, brutish, and short. Hobbes's state of nature, dominated by passions, woe, and madness, was in sharp contrast to Rousseau's stable political order, in which people contracted with one another to defer political authority to leaders who acted in good faith. Both the French and American revolutions were political events in which citizens radically redrafted the terms of their social contract, codifying the roles and responsibilities of both citizens and leaders in foundational documents such as the Declaration of the Rights of Man or the Declaration of Independence. Of course, only a small group of rich men drafted the terms of these new social contracts, but they worked under the assumption that citizens at large were parties entering into an agreement that would be monitored and enforced by responsive, transparent, and accountable institutions.

Understanding how a couple of specific organizations work will help build some theory about how new media campaigns manage citizens today. In my fieldwork, I studied a number of PACs, lobbyists, political party planning committees, and other kinds of political technology consultants and found that they were defined by the motivations of their founders and by the clients they hoped to serve. I have selected four organizations, representing each of the four possible combinations of motivations and clients. In the next chapter, I introduce two organizations that consider "constituents" to be their primary clients. In this chapter, however, I introduce two organizations that consider "campaigns" to be their primary clients. These two organizations differ in that one is run by a group of altruists who hope to improve the democratic process with their political technologies, and the other by a group of entrepreneurs who hope to make a profit with their political technologies. The staff of each of these two organizations can teach us about the daily work of political communication, but also something about the trajectory of political culture in the United States.

The Opportunists at DataBank.com

DataBank.com recently adopted its new name. For several decades the firm was one of the top direct-mail companies, having helped put several Presidents and hundreds of senators, representatives, and governors into their offices. From the start, the founder, whom I will call "Larry," had used computing equipment to store political and demographic information. As stand-alone computing power improved and networked, Larry was able to expand his databases and make them relational, linking multiple sources of data through multiple cases. Data mining is research into the implicit and emergent information that resides in a data set compiled from multiple sources originally collected for other explicit purposes. Different organizations have collected an immense amount of personal data for many years, and increasingly, the data are digital. In 1999, the firm went online, offering access to its data services for the modern campaigns that need to feed on data twenty-four hours a day.

I had to work to convince Larry and the other staff that my research objective was not necessarily to expose or embarrass them. Many newspaper articles had profiled their operations, and some members of the professional community thought that their work violated even the lowest privacy expectations. That their seed capital came from credit card companies is often held against them. But one of the reasons I chose DataBank.com to observe is that its customers are successful, which is the best form of advertisement in this industry. Its offices are unusually secured, even for D.C., with shaded windows and expensive computer security. Larry told me he had several motives when he finally granted me access:

> I actually try to publish our research. Collaborating with academics gives us credibility, though we have been screwed by journalists looking for a sensational story. What we are doing here is innovative, and once in a while I see that even traditional pollsters are experimenting with new media survey instruments.

Larry is clearly aware that his work violates common privacy norms, and he thinks academic collaboration will help to legitimize his business. As an example, he gave me an article by the head of the Harris Poll, one of the world's oldest and largest public policy polling firms, on using the internet for marketing research (Taylor 2000). The sensational coverage DataBank.com sometimes concerns its skilled data mining. Larry and his staff made a business of compiling and analyzing data about voters and public opinion.

DATABASE MANAGER The Database Manager is a software tool for archiving data. It relates data points about demographics and policy preferences at different levels of aggregation, so as to extrapolate individual demographics and policy preferences from group data. It generalizes from individual demographics and policy preferences to group attributes. Larry's first employee, Dave, described three stages in the evolution of their Database Manager tool. Early on they had very basic material: names, phone numbers, addresses, political leanings, and some demographics. Eventually, they merged several large private databases, mostly about consumer activity and public health records, producing more layers on political and market behavior. More recently, they have been able to collect highly nuanced data on political preferences from the internet by inviting voters to complete detailed political profiles in exchange for goods and services. They started out in the early 1970s with an addressing service for direct mail. The most devout Republicans and Democrats in a district would provide their mailing addresses and phone numbers, and Larry and Dave would maintain records and sell them to candidates and campaigns as necessary. In the mid-1980s, they met a prominent political scientist who wanted to conduct a survey with the nation-wide samples they had collected. The condition of making their database available was that they would get to see the results. The response rate was not great, but Larry and Dave mapped responses back to respondents, turning their list of mailing addresses into a political database. The next campaign that approached them for help was offered access to opinion data from several key districts. With this data the campaign won handily, so Larry and Dave hired several people to start looking for other sources of voter data.

> Dave: Obviously, we knew who were registered voters. On top of addresses and political affiliation we started layering whatever else we could find. The most difficult thing was figuring out how to maintain sensible "cases" in the database. We wanted each case to be an individual. But often census data, social science data, newspaper polls comes in aggregated forms so that people can't do precisely what we were doing – reverse engineer survey responses. We maintained individuals as cases, but often individuals were given attributes that were averaged variables for the community around them – family, block, neighborhood, zip code, electoral district, municipality, county, state, region.

As an ethical practice, survey researchers are supposed to remove any information in a data set that could be used to link responses to specific respondents. But even without names and phone numbers, it is possible to reverse engineer some databases so that good guesses can be made about who revealed what to the social scientists. Using this technique, DataBank.com has been assembling information on the electorate for more than twenty-five years.

Larry and Dave consider themselves successful executives, but get a lot of personal satisfaction from thinking that they help "lubricate" deliberative democracy. "We help lobbyists identify sympathetic communities, and we help politicians understand what the people want," says Dave. With only fourteen employees – all computer scientists – DataBank.com occupies a small, two-story Georgian house within sight of the Library of Congress. The company has two important tools for clients: its detailed voter database and its Message Tester software. "Privately, I believe there is great wisdom in the collective, more than in any elite circle," confesses Larry. "I think leaders should be shackled to public opinion." The firm has one female employee, Sally, who was hired about ten years ago.

> Sally: I was one of the first data-scouts they hired. They hired four of us and our only job was to look for data. Newspapers, think tank reports, social science surveys, marketing research, anything that was politically or demographically relevant we coded and entered.

We had a code for data quality. After two years of merging databases, the company had an incredible resource.

These statements reveal that the relational database was designed to be scalable, so that clients with strategic needs in specific electoral districts would have the most relevant aggregated or disaggregated data. Moreover, Dave and Sally reveal that the multiple sources of data on seemingly unrelated topics can be preserved and related on the basis of complex categories of social identity: economic surveys, business surveys, and city, county or state surveys of land use, industrial growth, health care, educational needs, labor needs, transportation patterns, and migration.

By the late 1980s, Larry and Dave had impressed a number of large firms and important candidates with their alacrity in helping campaigns to win. But operations were expensive and the database was getting unwieldy. Larry reveals that many of the layers were from questionable sources and that there were other desirable privately held data sources available: credit card data and other forms of commercial data.

> Larry: We had grown as much as we could. We had a great system of inputting data as we ran across it. Pollsters would occasionally share their stuff, but the next level was to merge with something deep, something long-term and comprehensive. As a business we suffered between campaign seasons. I was sick of hiring student interns.

Privately held firms with large customer bases were often most aggressive about collecting data on customers and about actively lobbying government to protect market share. These firms collected data on their customers, partly to improve customer services and partly to equip their lobbyists with information. Ostensibly, their customers were someone else's constituents, so it made business sense to use the political clout of their customers to advance their business interests.

> Dave: We had helped an alliance of credit card firms stifle a congressional privacy initiative several years back. They had produced information about constituents in key districts for the specific campaign but wouldn't let us look at the raw data. Both of us knew that with records on purchasing habits going back decades, they had one of the most potent private databases in the world. We needed them next.

They convinced one of the firms to invest in DataBank.com. In exchange for access to purchasing histories, Larry offered up a significant interest in the firm. Sally reveals that she and her bosses were trying to find consulting opportunities for their firm by inferring political opinions from private shopping habits.

> Sally: Most income data are self-reported and I don't think much of that. But that company's data were amazing! Sensibly calculated estimates of income, classifications of luxury purchases, health-related purchases we could analyze for the health lobby, gun purchases we could analyze for the gun lobby, gas purchases we could analyze for the oil lobby, and so on.

Luxury goods and food purchases would reveal something about an individual's class or disposable income, and magazine subscriptions might reveal something about that person's political leanings. As the technology has improved, DataBank.com has been able to merge more detailed and varied forms of information. More important, the quality of data has gone from being broadly demographic (such as class, race, gender, and general political attitudes) and attitudinal (such as political norms, policy preferences, and religious affiliations) to *psychographic* (such as thinking patterns, discursive habits with friends and family, and parenting styles).

Today, DataBank.com has basic information on 150 million registered voters and more detailed profiles on four of every ten adults in the United States. The market price of political data has fallen dramatically. In 1995 the firm's rate was about ten dollars for two variables on a thousand names. By 2004, just 50 cents bought two descriptive variables on a thousand people, and that descriptive variable could include information about credit card purchases, income, race, voter registration, and any other information that might inform a political lobbying strategy. However, the data that Larry and Dave prepare for political campaigns have come (1) from sources where citizens gave explicit informed consent for its immediate use, but not for extended and relational use, and (2) from sources where citizens did not give informed consent but have nonetheless left a data trail, primarily from credit card purchases and Web site visits. Recently, DataBank.com has made its service available over the World Wide Web, so that clients can directly access and pay for the data they want. Larry and Dave say they are especially proud of their online services because now everyone has access to data that were once available only to presidential candidates and big budget campaigns.

In other words, anyone can be a customer, and by making this data so accessible, they feel they have made political culture more democratic.

MESSAGETESTER Recently, Larry and Dave began experimenting with ways of using new media to test political messages. The more traditional consulting firms run focus groups for certain clients, but this is an expensive procedure not guaranteeing representative results. Rather than present ten people with a campaign ad and get their feedback face to face, why not run the ad to a thousand people and measure their feedback? The MessageTester software is an application that distributes a range of possible campaign ads to a representative sample of voters and canvases those voters to see how they pick up on subtle variations in political messages.

> Larry: Campaigns go to a lot of difficulty to test a message. They have always "practiced" delivery. Candidates rehearse their speeches in front of test audiences, and political parties throw position scenarios by focus groups. The latter is especially necessary for bigger groups that have to be careful with positioning that satisfies both financial supporters and electoral supporters. Those are different groups with different interests.

Here, Larry reveals how political hypermedia play an important role in contemporary campaign strategy: negative ads, potential running mates, and policy positions are empirically tested on subpopulations through a range of text, audio, and video material. Using the information they already had on the electorate, DataBank.com strategically distributed free WebTV boxes to key households across the United States. In exchange for free access to the internet, members of the household might be subject to a survey once a week.

> Dave: The WebTV boxes arrive at the door and are easy to install. The first survey they do, as part of the setup, establishes the demographics within the household and the environment in which the WebTV box is set up. This helps us know what kind of people we could ask after and helps control the survey environment. The box sits on top of the TV, and once a week a little red light on top of the box flashes on, indicating that someone in the household is needed for a survey.

Here, Dave reveals how much thought he and his designers have put into controlling the test-taking environment of their subjects. In the first few months of the program, they experimented with instrument effects by varying colors, pictures, music, and video stimuli. For a long time they could not build a random sample but could build purposive samples and had other techniques for getting close to the most important goal: a representative sample (Witte and Howard 2002).

I met someone from a major lobby group in the DataBank.com offices late one Friday in May. He was in to pick up a test report that several DataBank.com staffers had spent all night on. The lobbyist told me, "I'd much rather work with recent private information and reactions to my ads than models based on old publicly available data." On Monday, the lobby group decided they needed to run some issue ads as soon as possible. They scripted four possible ads, each with different levels of message strength. On Tuesday, they produced the thirty-second radio spots at a studio in New York. On Wednesday, the spots were beamed to DataBank.com's offices and put to a purposive sample of 200 households in Chicago, where the lobby wanted to be heard. Two of the ads attacked a local politician, and two ads just expressed the opinion of the lobby group; one of each type was narrated by a woman, one by a man. Each person in the sample listened to two of the radio spots and was then asked whether he or she felt the ads were fair and whether he or she felt outraged enough to contact elected officials. The test group found the attack ad with the male narrator too negative and discredited the lobby group, but the attack ad narrated by the female narrator was tough yet acceptable to the sample. By Thursday night, results were coming in: The DataBank.com analysts picked out the ad that listeners in the right demographic would respond to well. The lobbyist gratefully picked up his report and would have the winning spot on the air in Chicago by Monday. "For bigger accounts," Larry told me, "we can move even faster."

There are four aspects to DataBank.com's strategy for narrowcasting political content. The first is humanizing the candidate or issue, which involves making candidates seem like you or making issues relevant to you by repeating known information about your own life in the portrait of the candidate or description of the issue. The second is simplifying the message through four or five key themes chosen for you, themes they know will distract you from contrarian information. The third is emotionalization, whereby key words that sensitize you and trigger visceral reactions are deliberately chosen from what is known to trigger visceral reactions from people with your demographics and attitudes. The fourth aspect of narrowcasting is actually the appeal to celebrity, whereby you are promised special status in an exciting group effort.

THE ALTRUISTS AT ASTROTURF-LOBBY.ORG

Whereas DataBank.com is a privately held firm, the nonprofit group Astroturf-Lobby.org was set up by Mark and Charles to help political action committees with internet communication strategies. The firm has two full stories of a building on Connecticut, Avenue in Washington, D.C., along what Charles likes to call the "towers of power" – the corridor of important political consultancies that stretches between the White House and Dupont circle. Mark works especially long shifts. Like doctors, he is always on call and will respond quickly if one of the pagers or cell phones on his belt rings. Also like doctors, he is on twenty-four-hour rotation periods with his colleagues so someone at the nonprofit is always awake to maintain spin control for clients. Although Astroturf-Lobby.org helps PACs from different parts of the political spectrum, Mark usually finds personal affinity with Republican groups. "I have the same goal as the activists," Mark said. "I'd like to get a million people. I want the Speaker of the House to be able to send e-mail to a million people about how the latest tax package benefits them. I want to be able to circumvent Peter Jennings." Mark has worked for a number of Republican issues and is particularly angry about how what he calls "the liberal media" spins his campaigns. "Constituents always complain about feeling disconnected from Congress because the media don't transmit a GOP politician's message clearly," Mark said. He has met the staff at DataBank.com but disagrees with their theory that the internet should be used to draw people into political dialogues.

> Mark: These people are assuming that the obstacle to participation is the labor; I think the obstacle is personal interest. Why is it better to have more people participating if their level of interest is so low that they can't even get off their butts to get a stamp and write Washington? Are their opinions really valuable if they can't afford 33 cents for that opinion? If they will blubber in front of the local TV cameras but not be bothered to actually vote? Or worse, like in Florida, they try to vote but don't take care to learn how the ballot works?

Here, Mark reveals a core Republican sentiment: that the most valuable political opinions come from people who are willing to spend time, effort, and money to form and express an opinion.

Mark used to work as one of "Nader's Raiders." He was the key logistical person for the New York City Earth Day of 1990, one of the proudest moments for contemporary environmental activists. Although he now works for Astroturf-Lobby.org, he says he does not think of himself as a cynical person – the Earth Day 1990 poster is proudly displayed in his office – but he does seem to have grown in a different direction since taking work as a political consultant.

> Mark: There are these idealists who go out and build a Web site or business around creating democratic reform. There's no business in democratic reform. You gotta represent one side or the other and you gotta help your client win.

Even though most of Mark's clients are conservative, one of the clients paying for his advice is Amnesty International. The organization called one day in early 2001 to make sure the latest details of a torture case were up on its Web site. Mark stopped in mid-conversation at the instant one of his pagers went off. It had been triggered by a call from Turkey and was a signal that a fax was coming in with details about an urgent appeal for attention to a case of torture. Amnesty's agents in Turkey were not equipped with e-mail but could call and fax, so the case history poured out of a fax machine down the hall. Mark ran down, grabbed the fax, and walked it one flight up to one of the IT staff who maintain Amnesty International's "wide-area" communications. The facts of the case were entered into a database, which generated an action alert to everyone on Amnesty's volunteer roll who had said they were particularly interested in doing something about torture cases in Turkey. These people, mostly in the United States, Canada, the United Kingdom, and Australia, were sent a form e-mail, a dossier about the case, and a list of contact names, numbers, and addresses of people to target for a letter-writing campaign. Journalists around the United States received a special briefing packet. The arrest and torture had begun that night in Turkey; it was 4 P.M. in Washington when Mark's pager went off, and the action alert was formatted and sent out by 5 P.M. On the East Coast some members of Amnesty International would get home after work to check their e-mails and find an invitation to send either an automatically generated protest letter or one customized by as much activist fervor as they were willing to muster. The fact sheet might have made a few newspaper deadlines on the West Coast.

Astroturf-Lobby.org had activated a small public interested in this specific issue. Within forty-eight hours the letter-writing campaign had exposed and embarrassed the Turkish government into releasing the torture victim. This process of bringing digital sunlight to a political problem is championed on the Amnesty International Web Site.[1] But activating people with bland old text files is not what excites Mark, and here he reveals that one of his goals is to build as much surveillance and tracking technology into political hypermedia:

> Mark: I want to send out Flash files full of information – mini political commercials. Now if you forward the e-mail to your friend, this Flash file will connect with our server, let us collect the information on the transaction, and update the flash file with the latest information.

With commercially available software, Mark can watch how his members are reacting to political events: what they feel deeply angered by, how quickly they are willing to act, how widely they are willing to draw on their social network, and with whom specifically they correspond. In other words, he can track the affinity network.

Charles, the company's co-founder, is proud of the collection of photos he has on his ego wall: Reagan, Bush Sr., Clinton, and Bush Jr. They pose with him at different events; other political personalities are pictured, even ones who did not win the offices they chased. Charles pioneered the art of satellite-coordinated political actualities and electronic press kits. In 1996, with Clinton and Gore approaching the Chicago Democratic National Convention on different trains, he set up the first moving-train interview feeds with a network of helicopter and satellite relay stations. One of his favorite stories is of his time as an aide to a senior senator, who in a quiet moment in the month before retiring thanked Charles for helping him remember everybody's names. The senator candidly pointed out that he would not remember Charles's name by the end of the month. "With all this new technology, we improve the political memory," Charles tells me. He described the process that political parties have to go through to adapt political hypermedia.

---

[1] Accessed http://www.amnesty.org/ on 06/2001: "Amnesty International has launched a new online network – FAST (Fast Action Stops Torture) – as part of its worldwide campaign to stop torture. As soon as Amnesty International hears about an imminent threat of torture, FAST instantly sends out an alarm to its network of activists around the globe. Cell phones ring, pagers buzz and computers chime, instructing activists by the thousands to sign electronic letters of protest. Within hours, the threat of torture is exposed. Once exposed, it is nearly impossible to carry out. . . . When you sign up with FAST, you transform your computer, cell phone, handheld or pager into an instant action tool – a tool with the power to save thousands of people from the horrors of torture. You also become a part of a worldwide community of activists determined to prove that human rights violations can – and will – be stopped."

Charles: Political positions are always full of contradictions, and we have to manage the paradoxes that become apparent when the party muckity-mucks decide to build a Web site. It comes down to me to juggle the party planks so that the paradoxes aren't as apparent or only appear to someone who does really deep surfing into the site. Before the internet the important political campaign managers had a kind of speechwriter's role, mediating between the different schools of thought that exist within a campaign. Now we don't have to mediate so much, we just organize the paradoxes so that they don't appear to clash.

Here Charles reveals that political parties actually pay him to help cloak contradictions in their political platforms. For Astroturf-Lobby.org, this subterfuge is possible by gathering intelligence on a Web site's visitors and showing them the content from which they are most likely to take satisfaction.

ASTROTURF COMPILER SOFTWARE To help manage these contradictions, Charles and Mark developed the Astroturf Compiler, a software package that allows lobbyists to build a sympathetic community of supporters through informational bulletins. The software also allows people who are sympathetic with a lobbyist's campaign to pass political information along their own networks of friends and family. Whereas a social movement grows when people with grievances meet, agree on a common agenda, and organize for political action, the Astroturf Compiler is for lobbyists who already have an agenda but need to find and organize members of the voting public likely to subscribe to the agenda. Mark has an unusual definition of a democratic "representative." He also says "every issue has a lobbyist," and lobbyists are usually the ones who hire him to find them their supporters.

Mark: The chlorine lobby needs to be able to say, "We represent X thousand chlorine lovers in America." I find out how many people in the U.S. love chlorine. We don't always need to contact those people, just need to label them as chlorine lovers, and figure out what districts they are in. To be strong in politics is to have the best quality information about what your constituents want. Being strong in politics makes all other political values possible.

According to Mark, his clients are grateful when he finds sympathetic voters for them but are just as grateful when he can estimate the number of people they can legitimately claim to represent and when he can covertly gather information on these unaware constituents. Given that the firm has grown up through several technologies, I found the organization an ideal site for studying the transition to internet politics. "One of the important changes I have seen," Mark tells me, "is that these days the thing we are researching and promoting tends to be an issue, not a candidate. They're special interest groups, or special interest groups acting behind a candidate; the object of our promotions is an issue position, rarely a person." He and his staff said they feel that political charisma is rarely important even in the most high-profile debates or electoral contests; what appeals to people are a candidate's policy positions.

The firm has developed good techniques of mass customization or narrowcasting. The chief information officer spent most of his time coming up with ways to "slice and dice" data that would reveal new things to customers. Hunched over his computer terminal, he describes how his conclusions about popular opinion can help to identify and define groups of people who might be "susceptible to push or pull," and those who were susceptible would be sent some political propaganda designed to push or pull that particular person's opinion a specific way. "We don't actually generate the content; that's up to the campaigns. But I can tell a campaign what Citizen Q would like to hear, and what his address is. I can also hand over his phone number and sometimes an e-mail address," said Mark. This set of software applications, however, is not just a benign system of giving voice to people whose opinions have not been counted. Lobbyists who use the Astroturf package can actively change the political landscape and influence representatives. They not only get more accurate information, they actively agitate on issues and then forward the results of that agitation, still relying on money and technology to influence legislators.

VOTEMOVER The VoteMover software is based on a set of algorithms that relate campaign expenditures, constituent correspondence with elected officials, and legislative outcomes. These relationships vary by policy topic, so good poll data help the staff at Astroturf-Lobby.org keep algorithms up to date. They can trigger and direct phone calls, e-mails, and telegrams from the right constituents at the right time to the right elected officials. "A good poll is a plebiscite" was the first declarative statement Charles made for my notation as he put his feet on the desk on my first day with the organization. The offices always seemed dark, and in his large front office I realized why. He explained that they had double-paned and shaded the windows to prevent too much sound or light within the building from escaping to snooping instruments outside.

"Polls and plebiscites used to be expensive, but now we can run them over the internet. More important, we can start to anticipate public opinion as long as the datasets are kept fresh." Almost every person I spoke to in the firm, including a couple of its clients, were convinced that the top political leaders desended on polling numbers. Some thought it was an unfortunate dependency. Others argued that we would all be better off with more "positive and negative feedback loops" between leaders and citizens, "clear signals of approval and disapproval," and the building of "direct connections between leadership and the led." Still, one of the major locations of blockage in the political system, according to Mark, is the legislature itself. "Take hand gun control," he offers. "Seventy percent of Americans want tighter gun controls, but the political system has been incapable of meeting that public demand." This problem can be resolved, he thinks, by giving activists and lobbyists the tools to channel public opinion at strategic places and important times. But here is where Charles and Mark disagree. Whereas Charles thinks a seasoned political consultant will know how to best strategize campaign communications, Mark wants to model political life with as many statistics as possible.[2]

If a campaign comes to them with clear legislative goals, Mark applies a range of analytical tools to figure out which members of Congress will be most sensitive to constituent correspondence, and the degree of the sensitivity. The company has done enough campaigns that it can roughly predict the rise and fall of public, journalistic, and congressional attention. But if the campaign can tell them how many votes they need to move in Congress, Mark can make more precise calculations about how many letters, phone calls, e-mails, and telegrams need to be thrown at each member of Congress. Mark spent last summer going through all of the company's records to catalogue all of the "campaign inputs," such as campaign dollars, financial contributions, television advertising minutes, Web site banner ads, and phone calls. Then he compared all

[2] For example, the National Education Association, nervous that Congress would slash funding for education in the fiscal 1999 budget, took on the Juno Advocacy Network and Pam Fielding of e-Advocates to help turn around the campaign. Of Juno's 6 million subscribers nationwide, 225,000 met both the geographic and demographic criteria of the new effort: parents in key districts who might be concerned about education. These parents wrote 20,000 e-mails, and education won a 12 percent budget increase. Certainly, there was a larger context to the turnaround, but campaign insiders credit the targeted e-mail campaign. Citizens who take advantage of the basic, free e-mail service of Juno Online must fill out an extensive demographic and psychographic questionnaire, which is then used to target advertisements they see as they read and write e-mail, for example, "Send Your Child to a 21st Century School," "Tell Congress to Support Education," and "Act Now" in rotating banners.

of the "citizen outputs," such as telegrams, letters, phone calls, petition signatures, e-mails, and office visits. He even put in data on the particular members of Congress involved, such as size of mandate, length of experience, party, and region of the country.

Since Mark can then purchase data from DataBank.com on the profile of particular districts, he can estimate what resources the campaign will need to leverage specific members of Congress. Mapped onto a list of the campaigns he and his clients considered successful, Mark presents potential clients with a set of formulas for political "wins." He knows the company would never take on big tobacco or military contracts, but he also knows that he has a broader definition of what counts as a "progressive cause" than he did when he was working for Nader. Charles is also a "hacktivist" who spends time at night, he admits, undoing some of the damage he does during the day by helping people and issues he considers to be marginal and ill-equipped to battle with the big guns of political hypermedia.

> Mark: I think politics has always been driven by data; it's just that the data on the electorate [were] never very accurate. The reason traditional politics has been about class or race politics is because individual policy preferences could only be meaningfully categorized by class or race. Now I can differentiate between nine gradations of nose-pickers, and political culture produced over new media is going to have the same nuances . . . or is it fragments?

> Charles: I've been with this consulting house for almost twenty years. When we produce a political campaign today, it tends to be about consumption and lifestyle issues, not about class politics. More important, we use the new media to produce issues, not leaders. Leadership roles shift from issue to issue and the political faces we use on one issue are different from the ones we use on other issues. We create issue-specific leaders, and they rarely have purchase outside their issue. Not like the old days of party umbrella politics.

Frequently, Mark is seconded to campaigns for significant chunks of time. He is valued for his skills in modernizing campaign communications and organizational structures. The real political change is happening not on the internet but *because* of the internet, Mark says. "It allows us to communicate and collaborate with others remotely. We're aware of what is going on around the HQ and the broader campaign without leaving the room." The folks who really make a difference in their campaigns look at the internet as a tool that should be integrated within the entire campaign communication and organizational structure.

When he meets new clients, Mark tells them about a recent example of how his political science works. Astroturf-Lobby.org has done enough campaigns over the years that it has developed records of each campaign case and some rough formula for campaign success. Of course, certain issues have more traction with different segments of the population, but the general relationship between campaign dollars and legislative or electoral success can be mapped out. In one example, the client wanted to move four congressional votes from "nay" to "aye" on a complex pharmaceutical regulations bill. These were "soft votes," meaning that the four key representatives did not have vested interests in the legislative out-come and were voting on the basis of strategies negotiated with colleagues on other pieces of legislation. Mark knew from previous experience that congressional offices are more sensitive to telegrams or couriered letters from constituents than e-mails or posted mail. But the authors of these telegrams had to be constituents from these four specific congressional districts. So Mark worked out the likely formula for political success.

At the time, $350,000 would buy a communications strategy including three million Web site banner ads, targeted in these four congressional districts in one week. Banner ads on political topics generally had a 1 percent click-through rate, meaning that one person in a hundred who saw the ads would follow through to read more about the topic. In Mark's experience, 9 percent of the people who read about a campaign will join it as members, regardless of the topic, issue position, or author. Moreover, about one in ten people who join a campaign are actually passionate enough to write a letter to their member of Congress on the topic. (See Fig. 2.1.)

Working backward with this formula, Mark and his team decided that they would need about 270 telegrams per week, channeled at the four congressional representatives they needed to impress. To get 270 tele-grams, they needed 2,700 people to join what they termed an "astroturf" movement, which meant that 30,000 people in these four key congres-sional districts would have to learn abut the campaign message, which meant that three million banner ads had to be purchased. At the time, three million banner ads cost about $350,000, so with additional con-sulting fees, Mark could give this pharmaceutical lobby group a fairly good estimate of how much it would cost to win their campaign. In the end, three of the four "soft votes" changed their votes within the first

Millions of Internet Users in Four Key Congressional Districts

Specific Campaign Strategy	General Campaign Model
$350K buys 3 million banner ads	(Predicts 1% click-through rate)
30,00 people learn of campaign	(Predicts 9% accept message)
2,700 people join campaign	(Predicts 10% will write telegrams)
270 telegrams to Congress	(Predicts 60-70 telegrams / week from constituents will change Congressional opinion)
Telegrams distributed among Congressional offices until they make concessions	(Predicts 4 Congressional votes moved)

Figure 2.1: Astroturf-Lobby.org algorithm for producing a political campaign.

two weeks. The remaining congressman received about fifty telegrams per day from constituents – until he too changed his mind. Few of the members of this astroturf movement would have known that the infrastructure and staff of their organization was provided by a publicity firm. As one of the firm's commissioned reports advises its clients, "There are some campaigns where it would be undesirable or even disastrous to let the audience know that your organization is directly involved . . . it simply is not an intelligent PR move. In cases such as this, it is important to first 'listen' to what is being said online. . . . Once you are plugged into this world, it is possible to make postings to these outlets that present your position as an uninvolved third party. . . . Perhaps the greatest advantage of viral marketing is that your message is placed into a context where it is more likely to be considered seriously" (Bivings Report 2002).

HYPERMEDIA AND THE PRODUCTION OF PUBLIC OPINION

Over the years, the cost of organizing a political campaign has grown, along with the power of advertising managers and publicity experts within campaign hierarchies and their dependence on public policy polling. Producing a political campaign strategy involves defining a problem and then delineating the issue public that is a client group to be represented or an audience to be activated (Walker 1991; Schier 2000). This consensus group has boundaries, but whereas traditional media could communicate only within large boundaries – either territorial or demographic – the internet is used to target issue publics on the basis of shared political preferences. Lobbyists use the political hypermedia to help the community grow and discover itself and to activate the issue public as necessary. Like the firms that discover the value of turning their "customers" into "community members" to promote long-term loyalty around product identity, political parties and lobbyists use political hypermedia as a means of seeding and maintaining political subcultures. These communities are both a risk and a benefit for the interest groups who seed them. On the one hand, hypermedia communities operate without the information gaps that encumber traditional political parties. On the other hand, DataBank.com and Astroturf-Lobby.org can activate these issue publics for a fairly specific policy option.

Until companies such as DataBank.com and Astroturf-Lobby.org developed political hypermedia, campaigns were bloated, ad-hoc organizations that relied on big financial contributions to target voters with blunt survey instruments. The hypermedia campaign is a lean, mean, fighting machine that uses new media for surgical strikes with accurate information and complex models that anticipate voter preferences. But this system of political hypermedia brings more campaign producers to the field. By designing these tools the e-politics community broke the oligopolistic control of several important media industries: traditional pollsters and consultants who designed, distributed, and assessed mass media political campaigns. Today, candidates' campaign teams, lobbyists, and individuals with a political agenda have access to many of the same data sources that the mass media campaign managers once sequestered as the basis of their expertise.

Political hypermedia are designed to foreground simplified issues and background candidates. Mass customization or narrowcasting helps draw out information about individual preferences in such a way as to tailor political communication. But in many ways, political hypermedia equip constituents with the same communication tools available to leaders. The media allow people to form their own political groups, and these groups have been shown to exercise their own patterns of control over political content, group maintenance, and recruitment even though they are conducted entirely online (Hill and Hughes 1997).

Even though the public internet is used in interesting ways for both campaign logistics and the production of messages, other kinds of private, digital, and networked technologies are used in the hypermedia campaign. Both Astroturf-Lobby.org and DataBank.com could have built systems to allow their human rights activists or concerned senior citizens to send e-mail to their elected officials. But both organizations know that congressmen do not check their e-mail and that policy advisers in congressional offices are most sensitive to telegrams, phone calls, and faxes. So their political hypermedia tool took constituents' letters, as typed into a Web site form, and printed them along with properly formatted delivery orders for the courier, and campaign staff sent the printed letters directly through a courier service.

THE SCIENCE OF PRIVATE OPINION MEASUREMENT

Political hypermedia have been designed to enact the principles of direct democracy through constant canvassing. As an invention, the microscope radically altered the way scientists understood the world. Old theories could be tested anew, and our knowledge of the microbiological worlds increased significantly. In the same way, political hypermedia have altered the way political consultants, politicians, and academics understand voter behavior and the relationship between candidates and constituencies. Leaders' comments, committee votes, and fund-raising efforts get recorded and catalogued, while the subtle eddies of public opinion get regularly monitored. There is still some mystery about the causal patterns, but the ability to predict outcomes has improved dramatically by refining the formula for legislative success, testing political messages, and studying personality psychographics on top of demographics. As Larry from DataBank.com described, "This truly is a new kind of political science." DataBank.com and Astroturf-Lobby.org teach us that political hypermedia are deliberately designed as surveillance media. Governance requires counting (Foucault 1991).

The political communication produced over hypermedia is based on the unique relational databases that campaign managers have been able to build. First, information about voters is standardized and comparable across geography, time zones, electoral districts, and media saturation. This means reducing and individuating data about larger social groups into attributes of individuals or it means generalizing from data about individuals to larger social groupings. Second, the consultants do their best to sell not just the raw data but the flow of data, addicting political candidates and issue groups to the feedback loops that both vilify political positions and warn of opposition. Thus, the political information appears in multiple forms, both as cues about what lines to say in a speech or what colors a candidate should wear and as cues and color suggestions for other clients with different perspectives.

Many of the professional new media communications consultants believe that the more data they can collect on citizens and candidates, the more transparent and responsive this dyadic relationship will become. Citizens will read candidates properly, and candidates will read citizens properly. There always have been pollsters and focus groups, but their work is now much more scientific, much less of an artistic practice among hard-nosed, seasoned political insiders whose "gut checks" drive campaign strategy. These tools can empower people and groups outside the Beltway, but they also make the work of political insiders easier. Citizen attributes were once the quietly held property of citizens. Now these attributes are quantified, bought, sold, and analyzed on a massive, yet personalized scale.

> Morris: On the one hand, you want politicians to make their public policy decisions informed by public opinion, but the data [are] usually used for persuasion, activation, you know, "what rhetoric will scare voters because they hate my opponent," which is not truly civic. That's the rub.

Even though banner ads are no longer a major source of revenue for internet advertisers, they do help interested parties collect information about the people who use political hypermedia. They allow organizations to track users and their habits and create relational profiles for use as political marketing tools. The profiles help campaigns search for the ideal customers for their cultural products.

The technology also allows political parties to gather information on where Web surfers are going, to analyze that data to figure out what their ideological leanings are, and target ads to the Web pages they visit. Campaigns learn about how their members learn.

> Republican consultant: What's fundamentally different from TV, radio and the newspaper, is that we are able to measure who got content, how often they got it. You could never do a *real* reception study. Now we can tell who saw what and how long they took to read it. The internet has an ability to measure, even with protecting

individual privacy. Nielsen ratings are grossly imprecise in comparison. I think the world in which you are able to understand what the public is thinking is a better political world.

Democrat consultant: Bumper stickers don't get people to vote. Name recognition, excitement over issues, controversy, and leadership do get people to vote. The new tools may help generate excitement. We may be able to excite people more easily if you target the right people. It's cool to do that – to reach the right people at the right time about the right issues. No question about it, the targeting science is getting much better. To get this response, you need to start off with raw numbers. We make the parallel with telephone sales: If you make fifty phone calls, you'll have ten short conversations, and two will be a serious discussion, and 1 will buy. Just like direct mail. This stuff isn't being reinvented. It's being perfected!

For the most part, this true political science is being perfected through private experiments conducted under contract for larger polling houses, lobby groups, and political candidates. Of course, what makes the experimentation possible is the large sample size possible with e-mail and Web-based survey instruments. Statisticians refuse to say that a particular sample size is needed to justify the claim that a survey is "scientific," but the more cases in a random sample survey, the tighter the confidence interval is. Some survey firms maintain panels of hundreds of thousands of people, allowing for both tight confidence intervals and experimentation. "It's the difference between buying 100 lottery tickets and 100,000 lottery tickets," Larry told me. Some have likened the evolution of political hypermedia out of polling to the progression of scientific method out of alchemy. Political consultants always looked for the mysterious relationship between television audience reaction and voter approval, but that was unmethodical alchemy compared with researching strategy options over political hypermedia:

Dave: There is a big hole in our industry's ability to credibly describe that branding or messaging capability. But the television world has had a lot longer to develop it, and there is a language that is used between the people who make the commercials and the people who measure their effectiveness to the point now where you know that if you place a thousand gross rating points (GRPs) in this market with this message, you are going to move public opinion. And so, one thousand GRPs actually means something to public opinion. But we are already starting to develop the metric for predicting the effect of one million impressions.

Several political hypermedia projects found that it was easier to test hypotheses and float ideas over political hypermedia. According to Tim Vickey, Webmaster for Bush Jr.'s successful 2000 campaign, "Campaigns have a direct link to the public and they won't have to dump everything out there and hope everyone sees it. Not only will they be able to drill down [their message] on the people they want to talk to, but they'll be doing it a lot cheaper, too" (Jagoda 2000, 88).

Although the VoteMover tools could be used to enhance any campaign's strategy, they are often used in conjunction with the Astroturf program that is designed to create the image of public consensus where there is none. Inside the planning group, they call this "creating a public in urgent need of representation," and once they have defined this group of voters the client PAC steps up to represent the unique, transboundary constituency. For example, during the summer conventions, Astroturf-Lobby.org agreed to help a number of HMOs and pharmaceutical companies to lobby the government to prevent Medicare from expanding its coverage of prescription drugs. This PAC wanted government subsidies, but only through private insurance providers. Mark and his strategists calculated which votes they needed to move in Congress and how many voters in each constituency would have to be mobilized, and then worked out how much it would cost to "activate" that number of constituents. Then, in conjunction with one of the country's leading publicity firms, they created a PAC that claimed to represent senior citizens concerned about having the right to choose their own HMO. They advertised the existence of this social movement and its concerns in key markets, inviting other seniors to join by giving donations, providing e-mail addresses, and volunteering time. In a few months of television and online advertising, this social movement went from 0 to 310,000 members. (The people at Astroturf-Lobby.org love working with older demographics because seniors are most likely to donate money and write letters.) Mark did not have to organize across the country; he accurately predicted how much the social movement would cost and then used a range of hypermedia tools to complete the task. "The technology doesn't just activate voices, it amplifies voices."

Mark and the Astroturf-Lobby.org team believe that their political communication tools help the public gain access to government through

founded and organized by professional lobbyists who consider the appearance of an aggravated public to be a useful tool in the service of a
paying client. Members may be profiled but not actually contacted or in
contact with one another, and are not always aware that they are being
represented. Moreover, they may have similar grievances but not have
a shared identity based in a collectively defined set of grievances and
shared commitment to a collectively defined set of political solutions.
Instead, the lobbyist defines the grievances and enunciates the solutions. Members are invited to participate at the grace of the campaign
managers, and these managers provide hypermedia tools that give members the capacity to reach politicians and policymakers within the constraints of software designed to parrot the voice of the lobbyist's client.
For example, one of DataBank.com's clients set up a service by which
senior citizens who wanted drug benefits added to the federal Medicare
program could write to legislators. Essentially, it was a service by which
senior citizens could add their name and party preferences to a letter
already crafted to advocate that such a drug benefit be administered
by private service providers instead of an official government agency. In
other words, the lobbyist's clients were seeking to preserve some business
opportunities by creating the appearance of a sympathetic public.

Nonpolitical actors – citizens outside the dominant political circles
who feel they need to organize to get the attention of elected leaders –
usually begin grassroots movements. However, the members of Astroturf
movements are genuine people with sincere grievances and legitimate
demands (as are the sponsoring clients). They are not self-organizing;
lobbyists construct the Astroturf movement when they decide to make
tactical alliances with public opinion. Members may not be aware that an
industry lobby group sponsors their social movement, that a professional
IT staff manages their movement, and that the movement might be
suddenly shut down if managers decide that the tactical advantage of
organized public opinion has passed.

Consultancies such as DataBank.com and PACs such as Astroturf-
Lobby.org have an important power: the ability to produce political
content. An effective political campaign is about defining and acknowledging the stakeholders, framing arguments, and creating icons, and all
three of these kinds of political objects are much easier to manage using
the new communications tools that have been developed over the last
decade. Information is still power, but having raw data does not a king
make. Instead, the power of the hypermedia campaign is in manipulating data, revealing the sensitivity thresholds of opponents and potential

supporters. These data are used to produce opportunities for exercises in thin citizenship and to render data shadows for occasions where citizens are not engaged but need representation on specific issue.

Political hypermedia tools help campaigns produce content, improve their organizational efficiency, and track public opinion better. In describing an application to a political client, Mark described the ability to "virtually walk the precinct." The customization technologies allow a campaign to produce content from guesses, calculations, or genuine foreknowledge of likely public interests. But as we see in the next chapter, citizens also use these tools to read public opinion and track the behavior of their elected representatives. Tracking the behavior of the unelected representatives – lobbyists who have become the primary basis of representation – remains difficult.

Having defined and problematized the notion of political culture by looking at the work of people who produce hypermedia campaigns, the next step is to analyze the work and words of those who build tools for consuming political content. In the following chapter, I argue that political interests outside the Beltway, even individual citizens, now exercise the power of many of these elite political consulting firms. The consumers of political content are invested with the ability to produce their own content. In other words, political elites build ever more confining schema for individual consumers of political culture, but such consumers also have the power to design their own schemata. It appears with these examples that the producers of political content have designed political hypermedia to provide one key service: to relieve citizens of the deliberative task with technologies that entrench cultural schema. By design, mass media systems in the United States restricted the range of options available for the consumers of political information to respond. This machinery consists of filtering technologies that enable some citizens to make sense of contemporary political information. In the next chapter, I introduce two firms who are building this machinery.

THREE

Learning Politics from the Hypermedia Campaign

> Politics is what happens when one person tries to repre-
> sent another person's interests. E-politics is what hap-
> pens when one person uses a good technology to project
> their own interests into the right places.
> — Morris, chief operations officer,
> GrassrootsActivist.org

> What happens to the public sphere if nobody goes out
> in public?
> — Dania, marketing director, Voting.com

Technological innovations can radically alter the organization of power in politics, and it is almost impossible to distinguish political systems from their communication technologies. Whereas the previous chapter concerned how hypermedia are used in producing political campaigns, this chapter deals with how political communication is consumed through hypermedia. I describe the work of Voting.com and Grassroots-Activist.org, pseudonyms for two organizations that specialize in helping citizens consume political information. Building on ethnographic evidence, I argue that political hypermedia have been designed to open up the market for political information about both citizens and campaigns. This open market, however, has immense implications for the way we consume political content. I conclude by describing the process of *political redlining*, which occurs when citizens use hypermedia deliberately to construct their informational networks or when campaigns use hypermedia to contextualize the information they provide to a purposefully structured public.

In 1922, Lippmann published *Public Opinion,* a foundational text for political science. Lippmann attempted to reconcile the Jeffersonian gospel of devout citizen engagement with the practical challenges of having voters sophisticated enough to actually contribute to complex decision-making processes on a wide variety of issues. "The democratic ideal as Jefferson moulded it," Lippmann wrote, "became the political gospel, and supplied the stereotypes through which Americans of all parties have looked at politics." (Lippmann 1960, 270). Lippmann found the Jeffersonian standard of democratic participation to be impractical because few citizens could be sufficiently omnicompetent, omnipresent, and omniscient, and most actually seemed to conduct political debate with a staple of fictions, symbols, fragments, and stereotypes. For Lippmann, this was an almost insurmountable problem with deliberative democracy. Since the news media could never take on "the role of translating the whole public life of mankind, so that every adult can arrive at an opinion on every moot topic," political processes must necessarily be dominated by minority opinion (Lippmann 1960, 362). The people who organize to speak loudly in the public sphere are more likely to get their way. This conclusion has been reiterated by countless studies of political communication.

In the last decade, political science has mapped out many of the shortcuts we use as citizens, shortcuts that allow us to form our policy preferences quickly, as needed, minimizing the work of learning new information (Ferejohn and Kuklinski 1990; Lupia 1994). To keep up with the tides of political opinion, pollsters had to begin rewording their survey questions. Questions about public policy preferences had to include clues and prompts to guide respondents on the range of plausible answer options (Stimson 2004). Plato first observed a gulf between voter sophistication and practicable discourse when he distinguished between people with different substantive "metals" and argued that some people made better citizens than others. Even the contemporary theories of Barber, Dahl, and Mansbridge imagine an ideal polity, one optimized to handle complex public policy problems by balancing the size and sophistication of membership with the quality and quantity of information. Often, the most intractable problems of deliberative democracy are framed as problems of information quality or quantity (false, incomplete, imprecise, too complex, too reductive), and no established communication tool has been able to serve a large polity made up of people with different levels of political sophistication by providing access to a large supply of information on very complex policy problems.

Communication systems for distributing political information are often proposed and designed, but the social institutions to support these imagined possibilities rarely form at the same pace.[1] The republican and parliamentary democracies that emerged out of eighteenth-century revolutions were designed so most people would, through the election process, need only occasionally to process such vast amounts of information. For citizens, the immediate challenge of voting is in choosing someone to solve social problems. In a direct democracy, the most valuable information helps citizens to assess their alignment with candidates' opinions on social problems and policy options. In a republic, the most valuable information helps citizens to assess candidates' ability to solve problems once put in office. But there are several kinds of social institutions for coordinating complex decision processes. One of the most important social institutions, built for coordinating the supply of goods and information for large numbers of people with complex demands, is the market. Political hypermedia are the technological manifestation of a deliberate institutional design project: the construction of political life *as* information markets.

For many citizens, the process of consuming political content during the 2000 and 2004 campaign season differed from that of previous elections. Digital tools allowed text, audio, and video data to be manipulated by citizens and sent to or received by as many people as desired with geographic destination limited only by the quality of network services. Since 2000, political hypermedia have increased the range of filtering options for consumers, allowing them to decide who communicates with them and what kind of content is communicated. Increasingly, consumers can vet the information they receive and then share it over personal communication networks of family and friends. This process of choice and distribution makes them less dependent on vertical, hierarchical, communication networks of campaign organizations and media outlets. More important, by participating in a socially constructed market for political information, citizens became consumers of political information.

---

[1] There are a number of examples of the role of new technologies in restructuring social relations, but these examples tend to be about tools introduced in the workplace, not media systems in the public sphere. See Barley 1986.

SOFTWARE AND SURVEILLANCE

Voting.com and GrassrootsActivist.org are good examples of the kinds of contemporary organizations that work within the marketplace for political information (Howard and Milstein 2003). Both collect and sell detailed profiles of citizens using traditional survey and data-mining methods, and both developed three kinds of powerful new media tools to complement these traditional methods. Their "spider" programs crawl through the Web, automatically collecting Web site content, such as a person's e-mail or physical address or an organization's press releases. The organizations often employ spam, or unsolicited commercial e-mail, to gather or spread information for political marketing campaigns. Spyware, a kind of software that Voting.com and GrassrootsActivist.org covertly install on users' computers during internet use, reports a user's Web activities back to the sponsoring organization. In addition to covert installations, spyware is sometimes installed with the under-informed agreement of the user, who often later forgets about its presence. Many companies have developed variations of these tools for their particular business needs, but Voting.com and GrassrootsActivist.org apply these tools to gathering political information. They differ from the organizations discussed in chapter 2 in important ways. Whereas DataBank.com and AstroturfLobbby.org are organizations that help campaigns to produce political content and sell arguments to the public, Voting.com and GrassrootsActivist.org provide the public with tools for *consuming* political content.

THE OPPORTUNISTS AT VOTING.COM

The founder of Voting.com, Chris, graduated from Yale in 1996 with a B.A. in political science. He loved politics and wanted to participate in the dot-com boom that his friends had joined in. Voting.com's peak publicity period coincided with both the dot-com industry bubble and the hot summer of conventions in 2000. On election day, the Voting.com Web site broke all previous records for page views. However, only a few weeks later, with the business model in question and the outlook for all Web-based businesses dimming, the company was forced to close.

Voting.com was designed to be the first "voter portal," a Web site offering multiple new media services to the discerning voter in search of quality political news and debate. Chris wanted to identify the set of essential citizen services that could be provided online (such as vehicle and voter registration forms, tax forms, and municipal, state, and national government documents), so that Voting.com could also provide these for a modest charge. However, a wide range of governmental agencies and news media already provided these services, and Voting.com failed to find a workable revenue model. Over the three-year life of the company, Chris could find only three real sources of revenue. Initially, they sold political paraphernalia online, such as buttons, bumper stickers, and T-shirts. Later, when the company was at its largest, they sold data about their users. Finally, when the company was almost bankrupt, they sold off the designer chairs he had bought for his staff.

At first, he had some angel funding from his grandmother. His business plan proposed several sensible ways to make money from the public need for political information, and with all the enthusiasm for dot-com investment opportunities, he found venture capital in short order. Actually getting the money to transfer into his company's accounts was tedious, but when it came, it came big: $3 million in the first six months, $25 million at the end of the first year, and another $70 million at the height of the summer campaign season. Once into the work of building a voter portal, Chris and his team found that their business model articulated noble goals but did not prioritize their goals clearly. Voting.com tried to have its own active news team compete with the other major new sources. They did some original reporting during the election, unlike most other voter portals, but burned through their money during the campaign year. The day after the election he fired forty-five people – half of his staff – and the firm was on the fuckedcompany.com index within a month.

The management team for Voting.com consisted of Chris and two other core members. Jeff was an academic who had started a policy project on e-government at a prominent West Coast university, and when funding ran short, the project was "sold" to Voting.com. The terms of the deal are closely guarded, but Jeff stood to make more money as the chief operating officer for Voting.com, and Voting.com benefited from the prestige of academic affiliation. Dania graduated from the same Ivy League college as Chris. They met through a family friend during Chris's quest for funding. Dania had a background in statistics and had worked as a customer relations manager at a large investment bank after graduation. Although she started in a lower paying marketing position in the banks, she had worked her way up the ranks quickly.

Voting.com was like many other start-up dot-coms in that the executive team meet either virtually or in informal settings – in this case, on the basketball half-court Chris built at the back of their loft. During the summer months of 1999, Voting.com acquired office space in Providence, Rhode Island, so Chris could be near his girlfriend who was in her last year at Brown. The loft space was big, airy, and remained under construction for three years, not unlike the firm's software applications. Voting.com's design staff occupied the bulk of the space, though several times during the year his "territory" within the firm was redrawn as the marketing and client services divisions were assigned to his management, then reassigned, then returned to him. Around 6 o'clock every day, after being on the phones trying to drum up business and placate investors, Chris would make a latté in the kitchen and then shoot hoops. He would bellow that he was "holding court" and thus accessible to staff. Any employee could approach him with problems and questions as needed (though they might have to play basketball with him during the conversation), and court would remain "in session" until late in the night.

The original business plan was based on software applications that let citizens find compatible politicians, but the plan was made at a time when banner ads alone were thought to generate sufficient revenue. By 1998, promising an investor a large number of "eyeballs" was insufficient. Chris decided that to build the best voter portal in time for the presidential election, he would need to use this portal to generate public opinion and polling data, the types of data needed by the most informationally voracious presidential, congressional, and issue campaigns (Table 3.1). They expected to be able to make money by running a one-stop information shopping source for both citizens and campaigns: a voter portal that would provide condensed political information for inquisitive citizens and concise voter profiles to campaigns hungering for measures of public opinion. Under Chris's leadership, the company developed two main suites of applications, the OpinionBot and the CandidateShopper, which are now copied in various forms by other political consulting firms around the country.

Table 3.1 summarizes the demographic and attitudinal information commonly collected for mass media political campaigns. These variables allow pollsters to make direct inferences about public opinion, and the data usually come from telephone surveys.

OPINIONBOT Like many e-politics projects, the OpinionBot applications evolved significantly over the life of the firm: investor demands, customer demands, perceived opportunities, and input from staff constantly reshaped the firm's goals and technologies. Rarely did software ideas and innovations supplant one another in sequence. More often

Table 3.1: *Public Opinion Research in Mass Media Campaigns*

Direct-inference demographic and attitudinal variables

Variables

Age

Education: highest grade

Employment: full or part-time, retired, not working for pay, disabled, student

Gender: male, female, sexual preference

Family status: married, living as married, divorced, separated, widowed, never been married; same-sex partnership, number of children

Hispanic or Latino: Mexican, Puerto Rican, Cuban, or some other Latin American background

Income: average yearly household

Media use: television: network, local, cable; radio; newspaper; magazine; internet; frequency, average hours

Participation and sophistication: party membership, registered to vote, voted last election, likely to vote next election, signed a petition, attended a rally, wrote a letter to a politician, gave time or money to a campaign, knowledge of basic current events

Party membership and ideology: Democrat, Republican, Independent, no preference, other party; very conservative, conservative, moderate, liberal, very liberal

Policy preferences: specific policy questions, push polling

Race: white, African American, Asian or Pacific Islander, mixed, Native American/American Indian, other

Data sources

Telephone random-digit-dial surveys, face-to-face interviews, computer-assisted telephone interview systems, focus groups

---

they were conflated so that at the peak of its earning power the OpinionBot was a package of applications designed both to summarize and to generate fresh multimedia content.

For the first few months, the Voting.com design team thought OpinionBot would be a straightforward survey instrument. People would visit the site and respond to a daily question about news headlines. They would have only simple yes/no answer options, and a tally of the day's responses would be sent to the newsmakers themselves. This involved a little preparation work for Jeff, who was the news editor. He phrased questions in a neutral way, wrote basic arguments to summarize the positions, found the e-mail addresses of whomever he thought might be interested in the results, and sent everything to the operations staff by midnight each night. Eventually, he decided to ask politicians the same question of the day, but found that most would not give a straightforward responses.

> Jeff: The questions were not designed very carefully. For some of the questions, there was no variation among respondents, and less variation among candidates. For example, one of the variables asked about favoring the legalization of marijuana. None of the candidates were saying yes, until we added a libertarian, of course. I also discovered little variation in user responses, so they weren't getting much purchase in distinctions between candidates with this question.
>
> . . .
>
> Another example was the question "Do you favor or oppose a $1 increase in the minimum wage?" With that kind of precision, if you agreed with Bill Bradley, you would say no because he advocated a larger increase. This is where the profit motive interfered – we didn't spend money on developing our methodological smarts.

Other than Jeff, Voting.com did not have trained social scientists working to develop the sophistication of their instrument. They knew their questions were simplified and the answer options limited. In surveys, variation in responses is important because it confirms that the investigator sufficiently understands both the topic at hand and something about the range of likely opinions in a population. If there is no variation in response options, the dominant response option probably hides variations of which the surveyor is unaware, meaning the respondents were not offered the chance to express important variations in their opinions. One of Jeff's interns came up with most of the questions. The results themselves occasionally generated news headlines, but it became clear pretty early on that most of the respondents they were sampling were Republican. Still, Jeff maintained that they were doing valuable work:

> Jeff: This is still beautiful because it's about transferring vast amounts of information and knowledge. A lot of people don't have information. However, it is costly to collect this information well. People are already starting to ignore the information that comes to them.

Voting.com rarely got reactions from the elected leaders, government officials, and other policy experts who were being deluged by the public opinion e-mails generated through their OpinionBot software.

Even though Jeff had hoped to post news stories about how the OpinionBot had influenced prominent elected officials, when he made a couple of calls to friends on the Hill, he learned that most e-mails went unanswered because there were simply too many of them. Occasionally, a congressperson would ask, "How's the mail?" on a particular issue, and if staffers had been reading the office's e-mail (senators and representatives almost never read their own e-mail), then OpinionBot results might have been noticed.

The solution to this dilemma was an obvious opportunity for Jeff: OpinionBot should be not just about collating people's opinions and pitching public opinion at elected officials, it should be about catching opinion at the other end. Voting.com had built an application for throwing large amounts of data about public opinion at government offices and agencies. Why not build an application to help congressional offices process all of this information? The application to generate e-mails about voter opinions would become the public service for citizens; the application to collate this flood of e-mails would be for sale to congressional offices. Chris gave me a tour of this new version of OpinionBot.

> Chris: So we have this flake from Oregon who logged in and put
> their name and address on this form letter that says, "I think
> you should endorse the Kyoto Protocol." From his postal code
> we know that these three officials are the most important politi-
> cians who could possibly have any influence on this endorsement
> [Oregonian senator, President, EPA administrator]. All three will
> get this form e-mail. At the other end, this senator's office receives
> the e-mail, confirms that it is from someone in his district, con-
> firms that the topic is probably "environment," and responds with
> this form "Thanks for writing, the environment is important to the
> senator, too," letter. If the person is not from the senator's district
> they get a note pointing out that the senator's first priority are his
> people [constituents in his district].

Of course, people often write their own long e-mails, and others will write in and say that the senator should not endorse the Kyoto Protocol. So the operations staff designed a software system that would not only count e-mails, but also do automated content analysis so that the senator's office could identify constituents, what they are writing about, and how passionate they are, without having to read the thousands of messages that arrive each week.

On Christmas Day in 1999, Dania joined the basketball court discussions. She revealed that while 45,000 users had provided profiles of their voting habits and political preferences, no one had analyzed the data, integrated the findings into software design, or packaged the data for resale to Chris's pollster contacts. Dania was immediately given the title of "research director," reporting directly to Chris and Jeff. Her salary went up 25 percent to $85,000 a year, and she was made responsible for extracting and analyzing data from the firm's existing operations. Even though she did not have any staff under her, other sections of the firm were instructed to make her requests for cooperation a priority. She worked with Jeff's team to extract data from the server logs, advised the marketing people on their strategy, counseled the election news editor on what stories to run, and packaged data files for the sales people to offer to the pollsters.

By the primary season, Dania had a rhythm: Every few days she could extract data from the servers, build basic models to control for the overwhelmingly white, male, Republican sample, and sell a short analysis paper to one of Chris's pollster friends. The papers sold for $2,000 each and become the firm's showcase product. She usually remembered to wipe out the personally identifying information of respondents before sending the raw data files on to the pollsters, but recalled one occasion when she accidentally forwarded all the personally identifying information. She had drawn up plans to design another software application that would automate the whole process, but given the crush of priorities, Chris decided that Dania would continue to clean the data by hand until things stabilized. Her work generated intelligence for their own marketing department, survey results for the news department, and voter profiles for pollster and lobbyist clients.[2]

It took Dania a couple of months to set up a comfortable rapport with the operations guys. Most of the women in the firm worked for the marketing or customer relations department, and she felt that the operations staff did not respect the priority of her work because she was female. They considered their work too fundamental to be bothered with analyzing server logs and data files. Sometimes it would take her a week to clean up the garbage files they sent over, and another week to

[2] Dania radically rewrote the privacy policy on Voting.com's Web site when she began mining this data, and only a few of Voting.com's regular customers ever complained about the changes. Those who did complain received an apologetic e-mail and were told they could leave the service if they disagreed with how their profiles were being used.

produce something the company could sell, because they were perpetually redesigning the way the basic portal collected information. Since
she was earning money for the firm, she eventually convinced Chris to
reassign a couple of operations guys to do the drudgery of data mining,
and Jeff unhappily surrendered two staffers in what he insisted had to be
a temporary arrangement.

The newsroom broke a couple of big news stories during the 2000
primaries; within a week a major investor bought into the Voting.com
project. This made the staff – and investors – think that Voting.com
could compete with the major TV networks as the one-stop voter portal
for political news. Even with most of a $70 million commitment from
investors already reserved for salaries and invoices long past due, Chris
had some money to spend. Jeff and Dania remember executive meetings
where Chris spoke about a small company, founded in D.C. by some business school faculty who had developed content analysis software similar
to OpinionBot. Chris made a good case for the purchase, saying it would
allow them to leap ahead with an aggressive new offering: an application that would move beyond demographics into psychographics. He
passed out a package on the new subsidiary, Mensa, as he introduced
the five new employees to the Voting.com team. Chris stated that they
would report directly to Jeff and Dania "as necessary," but he told the
new employees that they could come straight to him with good ideas or
management issues.

The Mensa team, as they continued to be described even after they
were acculturated, would develop psychographic variables on the Vot-
ing.com users. Their company literature described important differences
between demographic variables such as race, gender, and income, which
pollsters usually used to model political opinion, and the psychographic
variables that can help anticipate a person's reaction to an idea or their
likelihood of following opinion leaders.[3] Jeff described the project late
one night when he and Chris had pulled beers from the company refrig-
erator and were debating whether voters would ever lose trust in the
portal.

Jeff: If you watch someone's movements on the internet, you aren't
just finding out what topics people are interested in, you can also
learn a lot about how somebody thinks by following how they jump
from one site to another, and follow links. It's very invasive. If more

---

[3] An example of a similar service, provided to corporate marketers, is the WebFountain
technology of IBM's Almaden Research Center in California.

people were aware of how cookies and spyware worked, they might start to pull back.

Mensa had developed software for sifting through correspondence to extract detailed psychographic information about individuals. The application had originally been designed to work over the instant messaging systems used by investment bankers. This kind of program was called a spider because it crawled around the internet looking for text content to catalogue. Originally, Mensa had hoped it could identify which investment bankers seemed to be the opinion leaders who could anticipate changes in share prices or move the market with their commentary. In theory, Chris thought the same could be used to study voters. For example, the Mensa software compiled a range of statistics and summary data from chat rooms, listservs, and e-mails, and Chris sold data on neighborhood opinion leaders – the "supervoters."

The new employees from Mensa redesigned the OpinionBot software to bring opinion leaders of a discussion board or listserv into sharp relief against opinion followers. The software could comparatively measure how sophisticated users were, along with identifying the issue on which they were writing. All the Voting.com crew had to do was figure out how to get their users to generate content. They experimented with content from public web-boards, IRC, Web chats, and other conversation forms. Since Voting.com had subscribed to wire services for news stories, they could tell what users were reading when they created their "MyNews" personal news pages. They could also track users as they deviated from their news page, as some people would use the links provided by Voting.com to dig deeper into background stories, source documents, and news analysis or opinion pieces. Some would also use the interactive opportunities to respond to news through the online polls, message boards, chats, and live event interaction.

After the summer conventions in 2000, Voting.com predicted a Republican sweep of congressional races. I thought it was risky for a voting portal to make such predictions, so I asked Jeff to speculate about why this prediction was made. "Possibly because the Republican consultants on their advisory board won an argument with Chris," he speculated. "We took a lot of heat, and then he had to do serious backpedaling with his Democrat and progressive board members to keep them involved." By this time Voting.com had more than 100,000 subscribers, and with the push of a button Chris told all of them that Republicans would sweep Congress. Chris brushed off criticism that his act cost the company credibility. He felt that Voting.com's users would avail themselves of the CandidateShopper tools and make up their own minds.

CANDIDATESHOPPER One of the important services that drew voters to Voting.com was the special matching service that told voters which politicians in their districts would most closely approach their ideological position. After completing a range of questions about voter norms and attitudes on key issues, Voting.com would reveal the ideal candidate for every elected position, from dogcatcher up to President. It was one of Voting.com's core applications from the very beginning, and only in the darkest hours did Chris consider selling the privilege of recommendations, a practice widely criticized but common among search engines (Introna and Nissenbum 2000). In a heated executive meeting in a financially tight month he made the case:

> Chris: It's no worse than the way soap companies pay to have their detergent products situated prominently on the shelf. The companies don't pay to have their rivals removed from the shelves, just for a prominent position. Couldn't politicians pay us for the same kind of prominent reference?

Chris was very cautious in making this argument, and Jeff immediately pointed out that the most of the Voting.com users were relatively sophisticated and trusted the portal to provide them with unbiased information. But the executive debate often bogged down when people interchanged the words "client" and "customer," "citizen" and "user." These terms were used to refer to either the political-information–seeking clients/consumers they had set out to serve (voters), or the campaign staff and pollster clients/consumers who were paying for data (candidates). Users were anyone who used the Web site, clients and customers were either the pollsters who paid for data or the people who opted to Voting.com's services, and citizens were people who should benefit if they used the Web site. There was confusion because the management team was hoping to serve citizens and meet commercial obligations with the same strategic choices. Thus obligations to users, clients, customers, and citizens were conflated as Voting.com's business models evolved.

The CandidateShopper application became the primary source of text for the new Mensa group's psychographic software. Voting.com users were offered the opportunity to engage in chat rooms set up on the Web site. Voting.com did not need to steer debate or choose topics. It let users set up and monitor their own groups on their own topics. Voting.com's in-house legal counsel felt that the terms of the privacy agreement, which already stipulated that user information would be shared only in an aggregate form with third parties of Voting.com's choice, covered Mensa's systematic analysis of chat text. Two of the Mensa team members were specifically assigned to filling out the database of information on particular users of the Voting.com software. It was their job to surf the net and acquire other data sources on users, just to help fill out the picture of who was saying what. Their working list of items to identify included the many pieces of personal information commonly found online. Table 3.2 summarizes the degree of sophistication that the software had for assessing a writer's commentary. Political information includes details about personal identity and opinion that allow researchers to make relational and explanatory inferences. This information about individuals is collected from a variety of sources, including credit card purchases, internet activities, and academic surveys, and it might be used to infer, for example, a person's political preferences.

During the campaign period, OpinionBot was able to gather and correlate a significant amount of data on the interests, habits, buying practices, and political preferences of the Vote.com users. Although only the text-based system was put into use, Jeff structured the system to be ready for images, audio files, and video clips.

> Chris: Essentially, we have managed to place information about almost every aspect of our lives on one Web site or another. Almost every organization is found online, and their information, if not properly protected, will be available for search as well.

> Dania: Demographic variables are not a sensible means of assessing or predicting political opinion except through the blunt instrument of old media surveys. Why would we try to associate political opinion with skin color or genitalia, now we can estimate a person's particular policy preferences with their preferences on related issues?

Even people with little internet experience leave some kind of electronic data legacy in the course of their day, and Chris's research team could still make inferences about these people through electronic records such as social science data, neighborhood data, or credit card purchases. Once the text-based system was working, the priorities changed and Chris had Jeff move the operations team on to other tasks. One of Chris's best customers, a polling consultancy that buys demographic data, was

Table 3.2: *Public Opinion Research in Hypermedia Campaigns*

OpinionBot indirect and direct-inference content analysis variables used on the Agora	Mensa indirect-inference psychographic variables collected on CandidateShopper and MyNews
Variables	*Variables*
Capitalization	Same demographic variables identified in Table 3.1
Commonly quoted text strings	Purchases: guns, birth control, gas, medical
Emotional symbols: emoticons	Magazine subscriptions
Missed and extra letters: syntax errors, spelling errors	Group characteristics disaggregated to individuals: region, state, city, electoral
Random, unique or repeated text errors: improper spelling, typographical errors, Dvorak-specific errors, Palm- or Newton-specific errors, Qwerty-specific errors	district, zip code, census block, city block, family
	News topics of interest: MyNews use records, pattern and number of followed links, time on page views, issue choice
Tabulations	Opinion leadership
Vocabulary statistics: common words, technical jargon, medical words, slang or youth words, drug-related words	*Data sources*
Vocabulary itself	Electronic records: server logs, credit card companies, membership lists, social
Writing analysis: word frequency – single words, word roots or multiple word combinations for entire text or subsections; cross-references and concordance between two texts, average number of sentences, average words per sentence, average number of syllables in file, average number of syllables per word, average number of syllables per sentence, ratio of different word forms to total number of words	science surveys, spiders, spam, spyware, user names, e-mail and IP addresses, chat room names, ISP choice, instant message profiles, social security numbers, phone numbers, resumes, customer loyalty cards, bank records, message-board posts, schooling history, court appearances, identification on corporate Web sites, online lifestyle content (alt.com), other political or hobby Web sites, school alumni listings, employment information, professional
Data sources	associations, sporting organizations, social or psychological support groups,
Spiders, spam, spyware run on hypermedia content such as message boards and the Agora	religious organizations, newsgroup membership, magazine subscriptions, public advocacy groups, dating services, library membership, peer-to-peer download groups, direct digital TV ordering services

particularly intrigued by political hypermedia and "getting more of this psychographic stuff." Twenty years ago, this consultancy had pioneered the art of "push-polling": deliberately manipulating a survey instrument either to plant misinformation or to test a respondent's tolerance of hypothetical situations. Planting misinformation worked only in small races where they could carefully select a neighborhood and could trace the effect on an electoral outcome. Testing hypothetical situations worked only on more sophisticated respondents because hypothetical scenarios can be difficult for many people in a random-digit-dial sample to understand. This pollster thought that if you could push public opinion with a phone-based poll, you could certainly push public opinion with political hypermedia.

The pollsters commissioned Voting.com to develop another addition to the combined software system of the OpinionBot and CandidateShopper: an avatar that would crawl the web. Voting.com already had a catalogue of public chat rooms they had set up for their users, and another collection of chat rooms they had set up for the city newspaper of a large East Coast urban area. Voting.com extended the functionality of their spider software not only to catalogue content, but also to contribute content back to the online conversation. The avatar could sign up for newsgroups, chat rooms, and instant message networks, dropping gossip or drawing attention to a particular Web site. The avatar could then note who reacted to the gossip on the chat and who clicked through to visit a Web site. In one of their reports to investors, Voting.com claimed that since they had so many politically sophisticated users, they could use the avatar to influence and track the country's opinion leaders, thereby affecting electoral outcomes.

Campaign managers hired Voting.com to help customize their messages for a significant proportion of the voting public:

> Chris: There's no such thing as mass culture, especially mass political culture. It's a false assumption that old media, especially the television, feeds. It's actually very difficult to produce one television show that everybody likes. It's nigh impossible to produce one political candidate that everybody likes. Many people will like the candidate, and the rest will hold their nose and consider offering their support to the lesser of several evils. There is no homogenous public opinion with undiscriminating preferences. Finally we have an information medium that can supply a heterogeneous polity with diverse candidates and issue positions.

Here Chris makes good use of the language of the market. There are diverse informational needs in the electorate, and many of these consumers of political information can be pleased with a choice from a diverse range of informational services. Yet while Voting.com built some innovative political hypermedia tools, the company had its critics within the e-politics community, such as Morris, who worked for a nonprofit rival organization, GrassrootsActivist.org:

> Morris: They got to the position of first mover because their interest is not in promoting civic values. The way they word the questions are intentionally inflammatory, intentionally disabling any meaningful political action. It's not a deliberative democracy site. It's an entertainment purpose site. The only damage it really does is that it draws people away from real deliberative tools and other public spaces and lowers the standard for what the public expects, so that's been an opportunity lost. But it's not as insidious as some of the more aggressive models.

In sum, the founders and developers at Voting.com saw business opportunities in developing hypermedia. While the OpinionBot and CandidateShopper applications help people research candidate and issue positions and help campaigns learn about constituent grievances, they collect an immense amount of information that many would consider private. They do this without the informed consent of users, and rarely is there a way of opting out. Voting.com delivered customized information to users, but this information, while privately prepared for delivery to a specific Web site, was also packaged as data on user's online research and sold to political campaigns. Thus, mass internet use was turned into data about particular behaviors and preferences (Webster and Lin 2002).

In the last desperate weeks of the firm's life, the founders began negotiations with a major software provider and ISP (internet service provider) to merge databases and combine resources, but they could not make it work. As the Florida 2000 election debacle was being resolved, Voting.com spent the last of its credit. Jeff and Dania came to work one day to find the elevators to their loft barred. Each was escorted to their desks by security guards to collect their things. Most of these things were toys they had collected and displayed to delineate their space in the open concept loft and to associate youth and play with work and risk. Ironically, they were most upset about not being allowed to remove their personal information – private e-mails, browser settings, and other documents – from the computers they had used while working at Voting.com. While they had worked to gather private information, in the end they lost access to their own private information that had collected on the company's servers. The company's crash was nasty, with many true and untrue stories being catalogued on Web boards. In the end, the company had two assets sold off as part of their credit management strategy: One hundred expensive Herman-Miller chairs, some never used, were sold to NYsit4less.com, and the detailed profiles of 170,000 voters were auctioned off to a prominent journalist.

The Altruists at GrassrootsActivist.org

Voting.com was one of several privately held firms that tried to create a business by providing information services to citizens. But these firms had nonprofit rivals who thought political hypermedia should be developed as a public service. A crew of Silicon Valley Web designers who wanted to provide logistical support to fledgling social movements founded GrassrootsActivist.org. They had met while working for various dot-com projects around the Bay Area, and in mid-1998 several of them happened to be unemployed at the time. Although the internet bubble was still going strong, this still meant cycles of quitting or being laid off and quickly making new plans. Rather than visit their headhunters, they got together and decided to live off savings for a bit and start up GrassrootsActivist.org:

> Morris: I wanted to build this archive so that anyone interested could look up a candidate's voting record and donor list. For democracy to really work, you need an accessible archive of political heritage. Sure, there have always been archives and records in D.C., and the rich lobbyists could pay to send in researchers. Now the information is truly accessible.

The operation had the tax status of a nonprofit but had an organizational culture like the dot-com firms from which almost all employees had come. They had the top floor of an old building completely remodeled to their liking. The elevators always opened onto a hive of activity on the loft floor. A doghouse had been built into the wall of the reception area for Morris's golden retriever, Poochie. To the right of the elevators sat most of the staff in an area with the atmosphere of an open newsroom, with many young faces sharing messy desks. Most had headphones and listened to music downloaded with the latest file-sharing software. To the left of the elevators lay a series of subdivided section's, not quite finished, where people worked on different projects. At the back of the building was the kitchen, deliberately tiled with a strong material that could resist scratching when they moved the large speakers and foosball table around for parties and dances. Morris and Sam shared an office, desk facing desk, between which hung a framed antique pillow made from a tattered antebellum American flag. While Morris and Sam were the nominal heads of the organization, there was a working committee of six to ten people and an ad hoc group of a dozen other consultants, friends, and family who were retained to help the organization. This structure had parallels in the dot-com world, though, unlike Chris at Voting.com, Morris and Sam almost never acted unilaterally.

GrassrootsActivist.org was managed by a "working committee" who thought of themselves as quiet activists. I met several people who had previously been sole proprietors or self-employed but were now happily bought out and employed at GrassrootsActivist.org. For a couple of years they had done dirty work in the dot-com world, and since they shared a vision of what was wrong with democracy, this was their opportunity to do noble work. One Friday night I caught a bunch of staffers in the lounge articulating these critiques:

- Representative democracy is supposed to be one person, one vote. Now it's one dollar, one vote. Less in some states!
- This is a revolutionary tool for political communication. Can you imagine being able to ask millions of internet users to boycott a product or bombard an elected official with protests?
- Lobbying is more of a democratic process now because technology has made activating more people less expensive.
- The danger is that we'll have a fragmented public sphere – knowledge niches in which people won't know what's going on in spheres they aren't interested in; political action will support narrow interest groups, not broad-based interest groups.
- American politics is already fragmented. The internet will add fluidity and ad hocness. I like "accelerated pluralism."[4] The lesson of vote-swapping this round [in 2000] was that you could use the internet to cut across fragmented communities to build coalitions.

---

[4] This is reference to a paper by University of California at Santa Barbara political science professor Bruce Bimber, "The Internet and Political Transformation: Populism, Community, and Accelerated Pluralism." *Polity* 31(1): 133–160.

- But the point of all this work is to reduce the number of nodes, or degrees of separation between a citizen and the President. In this sense democracy should be more direct.

Here the staff revealed an important point of consensus: Whether or not they shared political ideologies, they concurred that democracy in the United States faces some serious *operational* challenges, and that political hypermedia have a role in overcoming those challenges.

Identifying social ills was an important exercise for many members of the project, and their discussion revealed both sophistication about the problems of deliberative democracy and intention about how those challenges could be overcome with technology. Of course, not everyone had exactly the same solutions to the problems they identified. Some thought they should design tools to push information that a campaign deemed important into the view of citizens, while others thought they should design tools to enable users to manage political information themselves. The macro solution was that technology could help democratic discourse, but the specifics varied slightly for each person. For Sam, one of the founders of GrassrootsActivist.org, the solution was a collaboratively filtered discussion board that would allow peer and end-user control of information filters. From very early on in its conceptualization, this tool was aptly named the Agora.

AGORA GrassrootsActivist.org's most user-driven tool was designed as a digital incarnation of the public sphere. The Agora is a peer-review system for sharing political commentary. It is a messaging system designed to create a direct relationship between thoughtful commentators and audience size. "We wanted to create a real public sphere, getting as close as possible to the one imagined by philosophers." There is collective control over the issues that are open for debate, and a peer review system for promoting the quality of debate. New members log in and are invited to comment on any issue. New members are limited to 200 words of commentary, and their ideas are randomly shared with ten other respondents. The people in this micro-public sphere rate the thoughtfulness of the contribution, and as a quantifiably good reputation builds for new members, they are granted more time on the digital soapbox. The system will also allow comments to circulate more widely, facilitating the rise of public intellectuals and opinion leaders who shape debate with high-profile comments. Smart, succinct writers do well in the Agora. A commentator can earn the privilege of having their 500-word thinkpiece shared with 100 people, their 1,000-word editorial shared with

1,000 members, and so on. Contributors can also lose their good reputation in this peer-review system.

GrassrootsActivist.org has a detailed digital library of information available for citizens who want to read up on public policy debates. The library is on the World Wide Web and has several components, including a collection of streaming audio and video of candidate position statements and advertisements, a searchable database of campaign finance information that reveals who contributes what to particular candidates, and a tool that lets voters compare candidate and issue positions. They also link to THOMAS, the searchable database of congressional legislation. All of these applications are designed in the hope that motivated voters can become more politically sophisticated and start their own grassroots campaigns with good information.

Sam and Morris, designers of the Agora, think that political scientists and pundits are too cynical about the political sophistication of the public. On the contrary, they think that citizens are disengaged but sophisticated in ways not measurable with the standard survey instruments and burdened by the wide range of reasons we have for avoiding politics (Eliasoph 1998; Doppelt 1999). They are immensely proud of the Agora, and hold it up as a prime example of how political hypermedia restructure the public sphere. They do realize that not everyone wants to participate in a public sphere by writing commentaries for public debate, so they eventually added a reference guide to political "blogs."

Web logs are becoming increasingly popular online. "Blogging" is a public act in which the author knows others may visit and read the content. The blogger will link to other blogs and form a topical ring, and the author may react to the content posted in other parts of the ring. Sam was a regular blogger himself and thought that political blogs were an important new media manifestation of the public sphere.

> Sam: I built one of the first Bradley fan sites. I had maybe 150–200 visitors a day before I registered with Yahoo!, then 600–700 afterwards. Did some spamming at Harvard – an e-mail that listed the ten reasons to vote for Bill Bradley [in the 2000 Democratic primaries]. Some people would forward the link, and some would write in and say they liked the site.

But even he realized that blogs were a peculiar kind of public space. "They are little publics with their own facts and no unbiased media to corroborate what is put down. Exit is really easy. People who live next to each other engage or ignore each other. Online, if you disagree with the direction of the topic at hand, you can easily leave, so discussions become conversations of the like-minded. Most bloggers link to like-minded bloggers." Morris was more proud of his online cataloguing tool for political ideas, made accessible to all over the internet.

SMARTVOTER.ORG The SmartVoter.org application actually began as a collaborative project with a group of libertarian internet users in Northern California. In the early 1990s, Morris was getting tired of all of the complex ballot initiatives within the state.

> Morris: I have twenty-two different people I personally elect to represent me at the federal, state, and local level. California may have more representatives than other states, but most citizens have between ten and twenty-five people who represent them. In 1994 I had an idea for a personalized voter guide. It took the work of having to figure out what political districts they were in – the Web site told them.

Morris turned his ranch near Sacramento into a summer camp for undergraduate students. He provided a small stipend, and students came and maintained the ranch during the day and catalogued political campaigns at night. The students worked on a master database of voting records, financial contributions, ballot initiative positions, PAC activities, and more for all the states in the union. "Just putting the information up for all to see promotes accountability," one of his interns told me. Recently, they received a big grant from a foundation and to catalogue a greater variety of media artifacts for public access:

> Morris: People want a curious mix of primary and secondary sources. At first we provided access to raw data: unprocessed video footage, actualities, whole press releases, and draft legislation. Increasingly, we provided access to tools that make virtual citizens. They don't have to be quite as engaged because we collect secondary sources, build comparative charts and interpret events. I've heard that described as virtual democratic discourse, but I think it's just as good because more people can make up their minds more quickly.

The most recent applications added to the Web site are similar to those available on commercial Web sites, but repackaged as being particularly useful for grassroots organizing. Users can set their preferences on how GrassrootsActivist.org will filter political information, so only the most topically relevant and textually reduced content is brought to the user's attention.

Members of the GrassrootsActivist.org team have their favorite stories on small campaigns that made it big. Jean's favorite story is about a woman in upstate New York who successfully fought to maintain federal support for a network of shelters for battered women. Although the program had been in operation for some time, the bill to reauthorize the expenditure was up for debate and it had been stalled between the White House administration and congressional leaders. This activist wanted to start a cyber-campaign because the major lobby groups were not working online to coordinate and rally the real victims and those who benefited from the program. Grassroots Activist.org gave her the lowest consulting rates possible, and had one week to build the site since the legislation was set to expire. After her day job she went home and worked on the net looking for supporters.

> Jean: The campaign took fire. We generated 160,000 e-mails to Congress, got 36,000 members on her list, and collected $6,000, which is chump change to a large organization but it helped her pay bills. She had to take out a home equity loan to raise $30,000. Established organizations could tap their funders and networks – she started from scratch.

Senators get "one minute" to speak before bills are voted on, and these opportunities to have the floor tend to be used for self-aggrandizing or relating constituent stories. When this activist asked her listserv to help collect stories for a senator's minute, she collected more than 2,000 detailed, personal stories about domestic violence in four hours. After the legislation was passed, the campaign did not stop. When Nike ran a television ad about an ax murderer chasing a hapless woman in her nighties and Nikes, she activated her grassroots network to express outrage through phone calls and e-mail to Nike and the broadcasters.

Sarah, another team member, helped to organize a campaign called "Stop Dr. Laura." On her talk show, Dr. Laura repeatedly derided the gay lifestyle – referring to homosexuals as "biological errors." This enraged gay communities in many cities, and Sarah's campaign coordinated the protest. First, she used the internet to spread news of Dr. Laura's comments to cities where the show did not air. Second, she relayed the direct phone numbers, fax numbers, and e-mail addresses of the television network executives, political leaders, and advertising executives to her network of volunteers. These volunteers deluged the show's producers and advertisers with complaints and threats of boycott. Over several weeks the show, was relegated to late-night time slots before being dumped altogether.

> Sarah: Some closeted lesbian cop in the South wrote me to thank me for producing the only source for this news. A gay journalist at a straight paper in Maine wrote to say that the Stop Dr. Laura campaign inspired her to stand up for professional benefits at work. A high school kid in Georgia organized his class to contribute to Stop Dr. Laura. That is the change. To me that's a cultural change. It's how people view themselves. It has made more people political actors. It ignites old idealism. Many people care about these issues, but don't take the next step to actually get involved. The net provides that extra piece of outrageous information that triggers activism.

Here Sarah reveals that she used political hypermedia to locate the opportunity for a citizen's action at the moment of outrage and to reduce greatly the transaction cost of political participation.

> Sarah: As a private individual, I now have 18,600 people on my e-mail action list. I am not an organization. Proctor and Gamble is one of the largest advertisers in the U.S., spending millions of dollars on advertising annually, and in two weeks we got them to dump Dr. Laura. It was a Web campaign, exclusively Web-based. A few degrees of separation took my news and e-mail alerts to senior editors for Fox News and the *L.A. Times.*

Sarah not only has consumed information from political campaigns but has produced her own political campaigns as well. In another example, she was also instrumental in making a public display of Timothy R. McVeigh's dismissal from the Navy after McVeigh admitted on an AOL homepage that he was gay. "It took from Tuesday night when I started until Monday morning when [Clinton's Press Secretary] Mike McCurry was asked about McVeigh at the White House press briefing." For between $50 and $1,500 dollars a month, "after-work activists" organize many of these campaigns with tools from GrassrootsActivist.org. "For $50 you can start your own social movement," reads a project pamphlet. Unfortunately, cataloguing all of these movements to weigh successes against failures, comparing hypermedia activism with traditional activism, would be an impossible project. But for GrassrootsActivist.org, the point is actually to keep track of elected politicians, and they have a

Web site that tracks the daily activities, spending priorities, and legislative voting records of prominent politicians.

The projects led by GrassrootsActivist.org staff include inspiring examples of small campaigns that bring injustice to the attention of the public. Some tools that provide basic documentation to the voter are not unlike Voting.com's CandidateShopper, but GrassrootsActivist.org does not sell user data. (Interestingly, neither Morris nor Sam was aware that Voting.com's OpinionBot spider tool was picking up content from the opinion pieces written for their Agora system.) GrassrootsActivist.org's online forum comes close to the ideal public sphere, a space for discussion where succinct, smart commentary is rewarded with clear signals of trust and confidence: the invitation to contribute more. Such tools also allow self-channeling, however, so that people can choose to remain part of social rings that discuss a narrow range of issues from specific perspectives. Even though it would be impossible to keep a balance sheet of how much time is spent in public places such as the Agora and private networks such as Web rings, we can still draw conclusions about changing patterns in the way political information is consumed.

The staff of Voting.com and GrassrootsActivist.org have several shared goals. First, they worked to increase the volume of information that can be exchanged among citizens and leaders. Currently, much of this information is simple and highly aggregated. Most of the information about public opinion is collected, simplified, and spun by pollsters and the media. Second, they make it possible for this exchange to occur without real temporal or spatial constraints. Third, they decentralize control over mass communications. This process has two components: increasing the control that information consumers have over what messages they receive and when, and increasing the control that producers have over which audiences receive which messages and when. In this rubric, citizens are consumers of political information who should have the right to select which messages to receive. With these two cases in mind, we now need to assess the democratic costs and benefits of building an open market for political information.

POLITICAL COMMUNICATION AND THE OPEN INFORMATION MARKET

Television used to be the single most important mass media conduit of political content in the United States. By the 2000 elections, the technology of television systems was supplanted and subsumed by a range of technologies that both amplify its importance while denying its future as a unidirectional broadcast tool. Candidates still had to look good on television, and their consultants still bought expensive TV campaign ads that reached many prospective voters. Television was the primary target for information produced by political campaigns. However, it was not the primary source of data about public opinion, nor a high-quality source of political information about campaigns, nor the medium of choice for the most politically engaged people. Those who built hypermedia tools for consuming political content designed two-way communication tools, provided access to vast supplies of information heretofore restricted by geographic and institutional barriers, and created online communities of continuous learning, often based on users' pre-existing ideological alignments.

As in other cultural industries and other markets, the political culture industry fully exploits the available technical resources in producing campaigns. Among the new media political consultants, a language of "clients" and "customers" and "political information consumers" is used over just "citizens" or "voters" to refer to the occupants of the public sphere. Much of the rhetoric from those who produce campaigns is not about diverse political opinions and alternative policy options but about rationalizing the system by which information flows between electorate and elected. The public sphere was once a chaotic system but is now organized in a system of information markets, information consumers, and profit sources for consultants who can work that system.

The technologies of mass communication created markets for political information because media such as radio, television, and newspaper required data about listener, viewer, and reader demographics to be effective. However, these more traditional media structured a homogeneous mass of citizens differentiated by only the most basic demographic or geographic features. The technologies of political hypermedia deepen this market enormously by differentiating among citizens, differences indirectly inferred from what we write and the psychographic assumptions that can be made from their purchases and other secondary sources.

The common analytical frame for theorists of deliberative democracy has situated citizens in a public sphere, whereas those who actually produce campaign content have an analytical frame that situates users in a market for political information, where identities and opinions are bought and sold. Thus, one of the most important roles for hypermedia in politics is in opening up the market for political information. Voting.com and GrassrootsActivist.org reveal important changes in the

structure of the market in which individuals' and groups' political identities are manufactured and sold, and important changes in the qualities
of the product itself.

The Market for Political Information

For the most part, Voting.com's business comes from clients who
wanted to survey the public about commercial products and services and
target them with political messages. In contrast, GrassrootsActivist.org,
a much smaller organization, is a specialized consultancy for aspiring
activists. However, both models increasingly play an important role in
the marketplace for political information with three kinds of services.
First, when industries form political lobby groups, both Voting.com
and GrassrootsActivist.org help these lobby groups legitimize a political cause by identifying the needs of group members. A lobby group
will often claim to represent both the firms in an industry and the consumers of that industry's goods or services. Thus, information about the
importance of the industry to the economy becomes a source of political legitimacy. For example, the Chlorine Lobby Group (as discussed
in chapter 2) is sponsored by chlorine manufacturers who claim to represent chlorine consumers. Second, both Voting.com and Grassroots-
Activist.org do *direct-inference* public policy polling for clients. In other
words, they survey users about political topics and use basic demographic
features to explain variation in responses. For example, a direct-inference
question might ask, "Do you support the President?" or "Should the
government offer universal health care?" Third, both Voting.com and
Grassroots Activist.org increasingly do *indirect-inference* public policy
polling, collecting data from survey questions, demographic data, credit
card purchases, internet activity, or voter registration files and making
inferences about opinion. They might infer, without actually fielding
survey questions, that a woman over fifty-five years old, living in New
York, registered as a Democrat, and spending a significant amount of
her income on pharmaceuticals, is very likely to think the government
should offer universal health care. Moreover, purchases of guns, birth
control, or other items can help researchers make indirect inferences
about a person's political attitudes.

With new media tools, the research staff at Voting.com and Grass-
rootsActivist.org amassed so much data from so many sources that complex relational databases were used to extrapolate political information
without ever directly contacting a respondent. In important ways these
data are cleaner than that collected from traditional survey methods

because the contact, cooperation, and completion rates are higher when someone volunteers for a survey online. Moreover, much of these data came from observed behavior, not reported attitudes. The public does not need to volunteer its opinion because its responses can be inferred. Depending on how the organizations use new media for their research, they are more likely to construct better, more targeted samples, to contact more people who are likely to participate, and field surveys with higher completion rates. Raw data may be cheaply purchased by anyone through the Web sites that Voting.com and GrassrootsActivist.org maintain, although more advanced analysis and premium data are available at greater costs. In sum, today's commercially available political information is multisourced, nuanced, and clean and can be transposed among different units of political analysis, from named individuals and households to residential blocks, zip codes, and electoral districts.

Democratic Representation through the Market?

The contemporary market for political information now includes a diverse array of actors, including advertising and public relations agencies, media and entertainment companies, university research institutes, pollsters, nonprofits and private foundations, political parties, internet service providers, and PACs. Both Voting.com and GrassrootsActivist.org, however, made deliberate efforts to associate with academic research institutions to increase their legitimacy. They host conferences, sharing their commercially valuable data with academic researchers, and use university names liberally throughout their corporate identity literature. They buy, sell, and trade political information that in its raw form can be cheaply sold to any citizen with internet access. In other forms, aggregated and relational, the information is more expensive and priced at a point that only the more high-end lobby groups can afford. The cost of polling has dropped substantially, such that political information is not just available to Presidents and political parties. Competition between organizations in this market has driven the prices of political information down, distributed the product among more political actors, and made a rich variety of productions – the market for political information is more open than ever before. Ironically, the market for political information has been democratized and liberalized, making political information available to both elite campaign managers and average citizens and ignoring the common privacy norms that might have become a regulatory constraint on the kinds of information available in the marketplace. The managers of issue publics reach directly into the private lives of individuals to sift for supporters.

The market provides political data in real time, allowing campaigns to adjust the tone or content of their messages according the audience. The market provides relational databases not just for demographic information and historical analysis but for psychographic information and predictive analysis. The market provides software applications for merging many different forms of electronic data and for dynamically integrating this data with hypermedia that push content and shape the experience of citizens looking for information online.

Even though individuals' identities and opinions are bought and sold digitally, the technologies that allow indirect inference about opinions make it less necessary for political organizations to attend to freely voiced views. Customizing political messages is an old marketing trick, but the tailoring that is possible with new media is so much more powerful that political information today is a significantly different product. Customizing political messages to the degree possible with new media does violence to the public sphere, restricting our future supplies of political information based on assumptions of the opinions and identities of our past. Increasingly, an important part of our political participation occurs somewhat beyond our control, co-opted into a highly privatized and often covert market sphere where our political information is traded, channeled, and filtered, denying a forum for its direct, free, and deliberate exchange.

Whereas information about public policy opinion used to be expensive to collect, highly reductive, and shared among a limited number of powerful political actors, it is now much less expensive, highly nuanced, and widely available. More important, pollsters used to rely on direct questions about political opinion, but now they can also extrapolate political information from observing our commercial and noncommercial activities.

Many political hypermedia projects, from both firms and nonprofits, are designed to equip either political elites or average citizens with the same tools that commercial enterprises have for marketing their goods and services (Howard and Milstein 2003). "Competition and efficiency works in the market," Chris of Voting.com told me. "It should work in the marketplace of ideas and the marketplace of politicians." With the political application of new media, the market grew to have a more diverse group of actors buying and selling political information, as well as a wider and deeper range of that information. While I have been writing in the abstract about consumers, citizens, and users, it is important to note that these abstracted individuals are real people. All too often, the literature that searches for positive, negative, or neutral political implications of new media tools also speaks of abstracted, isolated technology users and misses interesting changes in the qualities of political information and the structure of the market in political information. Companies such as Voting.com and GrassrootsActivist.org will have created profiles of the majority of readers of this book. At least four of every ten readers will have been profiled in detail, with their names linked to a set of political, economic, cultural and psychographic variables. These detailed profiles are used to draw direct and indirect inferences in both the commercial and political spheres. Political actors use this information to design the targeted messages that we receive. In the end, this means that a growing amount of the political and consumer content we see has been tailor-made for us alone, while others are getting messages uniquely tailored for them.

Although Voting.com and GrassrootsActivist.org are pseudonyms, they reflect real companies with managers who envision "a world in which politicians become so well informed about public opinion that there is no need for direct democracy" (Lewis 2001). On one occasion I prodded Morris by saying that "the political magic of the internet is in being able to compare what a candidate tells loggers in the north of the state with what they tell environmentalists in the south of the state."

> Morris: How can you do that if every page you look at is customized per user? When I go to a really good e-commerce site, they are showing me things to buy, based on what I've bought before. Politicians are doing the exact same thing, and so will issue groups. This is the inevitable danger of the technology, and there is little we can do to stop it.

Although concerned about the "inevitable danger," Morris is one of the campaign consultants building the dangerous tools. Since many who work in e-politics have come from the world of e-commerce, it is not so surprising to see the language and norms of the market used to recast political life as a form of e-commerce.

Such detailed knowledge about individuals is used to exercise panoptical and discursive power (Foucault 1977, 1999; Poster 1990, 1995) but is also a key component of the surveillance duty of governance (Giddens 1987; Webster 1995; Scott 1998). Contemporary political theorists may agree that the state is defined as the social organization that has legitimate control of both the machinery of violence and the machinery of surveillance, but an open market for political information allows other entities to have purview over political information. With hypermedia, both political and commercial organizations can conduct political surveillance of the citizenry.

POLITICAL REDLINING AND ISSUE PUBLICS

When Lippmann wrote that the news media could never effectively manage the exchange of information between political leaders and citizens, he probably did not imagine that campaign managers would use another institution – an open, digital market for political data – to structure this exchange. We have placed our personal lives into the open market as data points for political dossiers and profiles. Voting.com, for example, charged about $70 for two variables on 1,000 people, but the quality of its psychographic data was well above that of other data firms charging lower rates. As a public service, they collected information about political donations and built a publicly searchable donation database, allowing users to see how much their neighbors had donated and to which political candidates or issues. Since political inferences are increasingly made from shopping habits, we continue to generate data for campaigns' statistical models as long as we conduct electronic transactions. Political culture used to be generated by elites or small groups of people operating through widely institutionalized media or party organizations. Now lobbyists and issue publics generate political information for their own consumption. As citizens, we increasingly live in a political subculture that has been conceived with us in mind.

Even the GrassrootsActivist.org project, which sought to build tools for political learning and had relatively altruistic motives, helped to develop some problematic communication strategies. On several occasions, I met clients in the waiting room of GrassrootsActivist.org. "Their tools have let me identify certain people and give them extra political attention and services," one told me. "The data let you target. Who wants to target nonvoters, for example? Big waste of time." Another told me that she was a big hit with her parent company because she could segment audiences to specific groups. "If you have an issue like pro-tobacco, where you need that small microcosm of society that supports you, you only let your audience see your message." In other words, even the hypermedia tools created by altruists are used for political redlining.

"Redlining" is an old term used to refer to the organizational practice of identifying the parts of a community that are difficult or problematic to serve. Most often the term refers to how organizations decide that some people, by virtue of neighborhood attributes and perceptions, should be offered low standards of service and indenturing obligations. These neighborhoods would be circled in red ink as places where insurance companies would give uncompetitive rates, banks would have more demanding repayment plans, government agencies would make fewer investments, or real estate developers would refuse to build new ventures. Most often neighborhoods made up of racial minorities or low-income households would be denied the opportunity of competitive insurance rates, loan packages, municipal infrastructure, and real estate development (Massey and Denton 1993).

Political redlining is the process of restricting our future supply of political information with assumptions about our demographics and present or past opinions. As I use the term, political redlining occurs in three ways over hypermedia. First, political redlining can involve delimiting which population is less likely to vote and designing informational services only with likely voters in mind. Second, political redlining can occur when someone decides to filter political information for Web site users who have signed up for content. Third, redlining can occur when an individual chooses to privilege some information sources over others by relying on Web rings for content or by setting topical preferences with news portals. Informational segregation occurs when political lobbyists take excessive amounts of information on some potential voters while ignoring others, pursue informed consent from some voters but not others, or offer opt-in or opt-out privacy policies to some voters but not others. Some pollsters will take data snapshots of a neighborhood or issue public and then neglect to revisit the site for changes in public opinion, decline to dig deeper for subtle variations in opinion, or change privacy policies midstream just to collect and sell more data. It is more common to use aggressive and deceptive marketing strategies online, strategies that take advantage of the technological inexperience of new users, users with poor search skills, or users with different levels of education or linguistic comprehension. This means, as with other forms of social inequality, that the elderly, poor, and racial minorities are most likely to be victims of imposed political redlining.

From the point of view of campaign managers, political redlining is reasonable because politicians have specific constituencies. As with the case of AstroturfLobby.org, campaigns will exclude voters who cannot be activated against the particular politician being targeted. Redlining traditionally refers to the organizational practice of refusing to serve communities based on race and income. In the political sense, redlining also refers to the campaign practice of declining to serve a community if it is not part of a sensitive electoral district or declining to serve individuals if they are perceived to be less sensitive to the political issue. In other words, if a community is not in a politician's service area, it is not targeted by a hypermedia campaign. If a person is not an engaged citizen likely to feel sympathetic – a suspected nonvoter – he or she is not targeted by a hypermedia campaign.

Political redlining is discriminatory; campaign managers build hypermedia not just to segment, but also to factionalize the public. The designers perceive a set of sensible social segments, primarily defined by political grievance and opinion, and set about building technologies that help these communities to coalesce. Often these segments also align with gender, race, and class boundaries, but issue publics are primarily distinguished by ideational, not demographic factors. Demography and public opinion are not always related, and it can be very difficult to predict one's ideas based on demographic characteristics. For most pollsters and political campaigns, however, demographic profiling has served as the best means of aggregating the personal politics of millions of people into identity profiles. From the start, political hypermedia have been designed to get around this problem of focus and scale. Informational segregation creates environments for narrowly focused political dialogues or closely edited political updates.

A number of theorists have feared that new media might fragment social perception, experience, and ideology. Political hypermedia are designed not only to serve politically sophisticated citizens with the information they desire, creating what Kling called "boutique politics," but also to equip any consumer of political content as a producer of political content (Kling 1996). The cultural industries that Horkheimer and Adorno critiqued are similar to the political culture industry of campaign managers:

> The ruthless unity in the culture industry is evidence of what will happen in politics. Marked differentiations such as those of A and B films, or of satires in magazines in different price ranges, depend not so much on subject matter as on classifying, organizing, and labeling consumers. Something is provided for all so that none may escape; the distinctions are emphasized and extended. The public

is catered for with a hierarchical range of mass-produced products of varying quality, thus advancing the rule of complete quantification. Everybody must behave in accordance with his previously determined and indexed level, and choose the category of mass product turned out for his type. Consumers appear as statistics on research organization charts, and are divided by income groups into red, green and blue areas; the technique is that used for any type of propaganda.   (Horkheimer and Adorno 1972), (p. 123)

What Horkheimer and Adorno observed in the construction of a popular culture was supported by my observations of how Voting.com and GrassrootsActivist.org design hypermedia tools for political redlining. Horkheimer and Adorno were criticizing the tools and industry of traditional media. As the next chapter illustrates, hypermedia are not hierarchical nor is their content mass-produced. Hypermedia do depend on classifying, organizing, and labeling consumers. With hypermedia, though, many of these schema – and the tools themselves – are actually constructed by individuals, with or without their informed consent. But even if we have grievances against mass media industries, such as the pollsters and consultants who produce political campaigns, there are at least two ways that modern hypermedia campaigns can disenfranchise. Mass media, such as broadcast television, seemed to constrain the supply of political information available to the public and provided little capacity for user-driven political learning. Unlike the mass media critiqued by Horkheimer and Adorno, hypermedia are both a structure of constraints and a system of capacities.

When the producers of political content make choices about what information a consumer will see, they structurally impose limits on how the consumer will navigate and what the consumer can learn. For example, if I rely on my labor union's Web site as a news portal, that union's editors will be making important choices about what information is presented to me. In this sense, producers structurally impose a political context on the hypermedia world I inhabit. Companies such as Voting.com and nonprofit charities such as GrassrootsActivist.org provide these structures of facts and link. However, because I, too, am equipped with political hypermedia, I can choose to visit other portals, create my own portals, or rely on friends and family to pass on political content to me. When the consumers of political content make choices about whom they trust for information and what form that information should take, they construct a network of information suppliers by validating some and disapproving others, in effect imposing limits on themselves by privileging some sources of political content over others. For example, I can choose to have The *New York Times* send me updates about environmental news but can avoid news about developing countries and can visit the blogs of my friends to keep up to date on Canadian politics. Consumers individually construct a trusted political network from which they draw information. Whereas campaign managers can use political hypermedia to bond voters to a campaign so the campaign becomes the primary source of political information, citizens can use political hypermedia to bridge campaigns so they have multiple information sources.

POLITICAL NETWORKS, INDIVIDUALLY CONSTRUCTED

Lippmann's solution to the logistical challenge of deliberative democracy was for citizens to disengage from the hyperbole of Jeffersonian democracy and "tie their expectations, and reasons for political participation, to specific criteria of improvements in health, housing, education, freedom, pleasure, and other material necessities." In this sense, Lippmann's solution to the direct democracy paradox was for multiple, private interests to bear on how government should behave. I call these issue publics, or small groups of people who are activated on the single issue about which they feel passionate but who remain uncommitted to broader policy agendas or consistent party ideologies. My notion of the issue public is similar to Lazarsfeld's idea of the political crusade, where a citizenry may be lethargic on a number of complex political issues but is likely to be aroused by a few dramatically simplified issues (Lazarsfeld and Merton 1948). In other words, political hypermedia allow us to construct our own conduits for political information, linking our subsequent supplies of information through networks of trusted sources, the friends, family, and news sources that we are biased toward. Political hypermedia allow self-regulation by way of redlining – people assemble their own networks for conveying political information.

> Jeff: We are going to have candidate or issue campaigns where every person sees a different message from the same group, even if they contradict each other, because they can send different messages to different people and they'll tell you whatever you want to hear. Why else would you tailor? Political parties and candidates are always afraid that a singular issue like a labor or women's stance will turn off people. The reason this is so attractive for political

people is that they can put walls around it so that only the target audience sees the message. That is really powerful and that is really dangerous.

Private citizens can program their own informational filters, approve a social network of peers to review and filter news, or accept the filtering choices of a campaign with which they feel affinity.

> Morris: We're all excited for different reasons. Sure, we all think the junction between the internet and politics is really neat. Our clients have more political power. The pragmatists who like to win, whatever side they are on, and the idealists who think the political world is getting better because more people are interacting. But people aren't interacting. They are segmenting themselves. They are self-segmenting themselves into little boxes of self-identified communities on the internet. It's causing more interaction between like-minded people. I'm not working for a revolution; I'm working to get my clients to win. There are certain issues I really care about, and fortunately we've got clients who work on those issues.

These comments reveal the difference between campaign managers' abstract desire to be good for democracy and the practical desire of winning their campaign. Of course, political hypermedia itself does not segment citizens, but it does allow campaign managers to segment the public and enables people to segment themselves.

Social movements arise as people find community around shared political projects. It is much easier to create some kinds of communities online, and much easier to have like-minded people join groups based on shared ideology.

> Morris: Issues that would never have been explained by politicians or made public by news media can now be made more salient by advocates for whom those issues are important.

> Sam: The internet facilitates aggregation of large groups of like-minded peoples that can help create political interest groups and weaken the influence of nonrepresentative special interest groups. I think it is actually a more balanced form of direct democracy.

The shopping and marketing tools developed for commercial applications online are applied to political ends. Viral campaigns, spam, and mass customization applications pioneered by dot-com firms to market goods and services have been adapted by political campaigns peddling candidates and ideas. Tools for conducting market research are applied to help garner public approval. For the political consumer, other tools facilitate comparison, such that the voting and financial contribution history of several candidates can be compared the way one might compare airline tickets or cell phones. Consumers use political hypermedia to bridge information sources.

Until recently, the supply of information was haphazard and almost exclusively mediated by consultants, spin masters, and the news media. Choice lay in the medium or vehicles for content, less in selecting the content itself. Newspapers and television present information in a linear form, and the consumer of political content had little control of information's form, presentation, or meaning. Because it is incumbent on users to identify the actors, objects, and icons they wish to follow, these hypermedia technologies deliver only what is asked for and reduce the probability of being presented with political content that the user did not ask for. Many users still choose to rely on traditional media to make the judgment calls about what they see, but it is increasingly easy to bypass the filters of traditional mediating institutions. With political hypermedia, either editors have been trusted to filter information or users have pre-configured their own filtering preferences.

POLITICAL CONTEXTS, STRUCTURALLY IMPOSED

Political portals, online bulletins, e-mail updates, and membership news are different forms of highly structured information sources. They provide a political context for the news, often framing events as outrageous while simultaneously providing a means for expressing discontent to a carefully chosen political leader. Clients of organizations such as Voting.com and GrassrootsActivist.org, from the AARP to the ACLU to Democrats and Republicans, to the NRA and to the NAACP, have an interest in framing the news for their members. For members who provide these organizations with data and sign up for news updates, these organizations can spin news and provide context.

Political constituencies were geographically based, but now they are grounded in both issue and media. The ideology of content online is unbundled from a unified party ideology, even when hosted on a party Web site. Although staff from Voting.com and GrassrootsActivist.org admit as much, the most public campaign managers confirm that they package different parts of a campaign ideology for different people. Ben Green, who worked for the campaigns to elect Gore-Lieberman in 2000 and Kerry-Edwards in 2004, said:

> Campaigns could slice and dice their database and e-mail lists to reach whichever segment of supporters they considered most important at that moment. We had a Pittsburgh page and a whole Pittsburgh email distribution list and many such lists looked to be very, very geographically specific, demographically specific. We had close to 40,000 people build their own web pages on the Gore site, effectively producing campaign literature and emailing it out to other people. (Jagoda 2000, 80)

Democrats crafted messages with data from Voting.com and application services from GrassrootsActivist.org so they could build the "multiple faces of Al Gore." Instead of "one size fits all" politics, the campaign increasingly targeted its messages:

> Green: We had a lot of different outreach efforts, Gore.net, Students for Gore. They all worked together and they had a net effect. Campaigns will be able to target their messages – they can send individual emails to a female who is thirty, thirty-one, thirty-three, or thirty-five. Through email, voters are a click away from getting involved, whereas with television, they are not.

Targeted e-mail built community by creating the impression that there may actually be an issue public to be sympathetic with, if that person feels unwelcome under the large umbrella of party politics. Political organizations use the hypermedia tools to extend their community. For example, the AFL-CIO uses www.workingfamilies.com to offer internet access to union members for less than twenty dollars a month. The AFL-CIO plans to finance the purchase of a computer for as low as $600 and to bring its families online for less than thirty dollars a month.

Issue publics may also be thought of as brand communities. In fact, contemporary political life has many such brand communities, and political hypermedia are designed to help monitor and control these groups and to make sure members stay in the fold. This is why major lobby groups allow users to personalize their Web site in ways that permit users to choose from within carefully designed informational structures. When users treat the NRA Web site as a news portal or create MyNRA, they subscribe to a political brand community. According to one of the founders of GrassrootsActivist.org:

> Sam: It takes a lot of creativity to build a communal ethos, but political candidates or issue positions are a natural source of affinity and a bulletin board or chat room is a good way of keeping volunteers and fans involved. We want people to meet one another online, to talk and trade stories, and to feel loyalty to the campaign. Of course, we want people to find community, as long as they stay focused on the candidate or issue position I am promoting.

Of course, the campaign manager's understanding of voter demographics, loyalties, and positioning of the major players defines this notion of "community." Simmel describes this kind of group as one in which interaction, solidarity, and the pursuit of common purposes do not depend on every member's intimate knowledge of every other member but on a generalized sense of community (Simmel 1950). More accurately, issue publics differ by how much knowledge members have of each other and by their understanding of membership. The issue publics that grassroots activists created with tools from GrassrootsActivist.org tended to allow members to learn a lot about each other's grievances. Members built empathy and participated in forming campaign strategy. In contrast, the issue publics that lobbyists created from Voting.com data tended to prevent members from learning much about each other, or even learning of their membership. These members did not design campaign strategy but were activated and channeled as needed.

Voting.com and GrassrootsActivist.org constructed tools for political clients who want to provide an informational context for their members. Presidential candidates, congressional offices, and government agencies hired them to help with political targeting. Citizens generate a significant amount of political information online, and this information is sold, often without the users' knowledge. Content generated by members of issue publics or redlined communities was particularly valuable as it helped to sell psychographic data to pollsters and campaigns. First, the appearance of voluntary membership in an issue public attracts other members, whether or not a potential member is aware of how volunteerism is being activated. Second, the act of contributing to the issue public by filling out a poll or submitting an opinion often reinforces loyalty to an issue public, such that a member who is drawn into a debate is less likely to switch out to a competing one. Third, the content collected by both groups allowed them to make both subtle and complex adaptations to their software, which blurred the distinction between the production and consumption of political culture, the form and content of the media, and activated or mobilized political communities. Fourth, it allowed managers to design sophisticated customization tools, so that members of an issue public consumed content that was most likely to satisfy their interests. Finally, it gave them voter profiles – detailed and inexpensive demographic and psychographic information. Political parties and issue campaigns, therefore, use hypermedia to bind consumers ideologically.

Whereas political contexts are structurally imposed, political networks are individually constructed. Traditionally, the political information created by the Democratic and Republican parties was structurally imposed through party bosses, local elites, and noninteractive communications media. *Consistent with the theory of soft cultural determinism advanced in chapter 1, political hypermedia have been designed to allow individuals to assemble their own political networks while allowing managers to better control the political context of news and information. As a result, political culture consists of both chosen networks and imposed schemata.* Although both forms of ideological redlining are worrisome, they have different implications. First, the political content delivered through traditional media systems tended to allow the first kind of political redlining, the structural imposition of political contexts, an imposition we as consumers had little control over. Citizens have always been able to use their own networks of friends and family for political information – word of mouth – but it has been very difficult for citizens individually to construct their own television stations, radio stations, and newspapers. That political hypermedia allow us to construct our own informational networks, working around the structurally imposed political contexts as we see fit, is the real freedom in contemporary political culture.

Whether political redlining occurs when people self-select their own networks or are channeled by campaign managers, issue publics are the result. Political culture is no longer a mass culture; it is particularized and segmented through the new political science. Even the most progressive members of the e-politics community adopt marketing strategies, transforming the idealized public sphere with consumerism in the realm of political activities. The internet makes it easy to comparison shop for computers, books, or politicians. More accurately, it lets users mix and match a political platform of their own, constructing their own activist agenda and receiving targeted messages from the large candidate and issue campaigns. Someone who wants a political program that is progressive on environmental issues, conservative on domestic fiscal policy, and hawkish on foreign policy can comparably measure how close candidates come to meeting those expectations. For those likely voters who need an extra reminder to show up on election day, GrassrootsActivist.org now offers a computer-assisted telephone service for calling likely supporters at home the night before an election. Potential supporters are telephoned and played a pre-recorded message reminding the voter of their affinity with a particular political agenda and collective identity.

In his study of the Paris Commune, Gould found that protest networks did not create new collective identities, but instead activated identities that members already possessed (Gould 1995). Similarly, Schier made a useful distinction between mobilizing protest and activating protest (Schier 2000). In these conceptions of politics, multiple, overlapping issue publics constitute a political culture. Hypermedia consultants at Voting.com and GrassrootsActivist.org described activating a protest in similar terms. Political hypermedia have been designed to permit political actors to activate issue publics by aggregating citizens. With such accurate data on individual grievances and policy preferences, it becomes possible to aggregate citizens in ways they may neither suspect nor approve. Small groups of people form endogenously, redlining through self-selection, or exogenously, redlining through lobbyist channeling. These discursive communities are irreducible because the only basis of group loyalty is either agreement on a single political issue disassociated from other issues or because members do not realize they have been so grouped. Unlike Gould's activist networks, joining a protest community does not parallel the time or resource commitment on a par with supporting the Paris Commune in 1871, or even participating in civil disobedience as anti-globalization activists do. Instead, political hypermedia activate people for five-minute protests, in which opinion is quickly registered and sent for quick processing by elected leaders with relevant responsibilities and jurisdictions.

Issue publics are specialized consumption communities for political communication. Their power has been theorized by Dahl, who argued that government legitimacy depends on a careful balance between acting on the weak preferences of majorities and the strong preferences of minorities (Dahl 1956). Their power has also been located in studies, for example, of public attitudes toward Israel (Krosnick and Telhami 1995). They are an intensely politicized minority whose individual members are closely focused, whose information stream is closely managed, and whose energies are strategically directed. But how are the hypermedia campaigns of these issue publics, lobbyists, political parties, and candidates actually organized? Do they operate differently from mass media campaigns, or have they had an impact on how mass media political campaigns are constituted? Four political consultancies, DataBank.com, Astroturf-Lobby.org, Voting.com, and GrassrootsActivist.org, illustrate some of the different goals and strategies used in contemporary political campaigns. The next step, taken in chapter 4, is to understand the organizational behavior and form of hypermedia campaigns.

FOUR

Organizational Communication in the Hypermedia Campaign

P olitical campaigns, whether advancing a candidate or an issue position, have always had to be flexible and adaptable organizations.
How has the process and organization of political campaigning changed
with the proliferation of hypermedia technology? Even though the role
of technology in the organizational behavior of firms, hospitals, stock
traders, and academic networks has been well researched, relatively little has been written about the impact of new information technologies
on political organizations (Barley 1986; Orlikowski 1995; Barley 1996;
Barrett and Walsham 1999). Networks have become a prominent analytical frame for organizational research (Emirbayer and Goodwin 1994;
Podolny and Page 1998; Contractor and Monge 2004). As a consequence,
scholars of political communication have begun to study how political
information flows among citizens, with limited attention to the role of
new media in organizational units of analysis: party and campaign organization. Moreover, archival work has revealed the myriad ways organizations control people and resources through information management
tools (Yates 1993), and both New York's Silicon Alley and California's
Silicon Valley have become important contemporary field sites for studies of organizational innovation with new media technologies (Saxenian
1994; Pratt 2002; Neff 2005).

Political campaigns are important sites of technological and organizational innovation. Recent studies of campaign organization have posited
the growing role of professional pollsters and professional fund-raisers.
Even though pollsters supply campaigns with important information
about the electorate, and fund-raising professionals generate revenue,
information technology experts have become dominant, often managing both the pollsters and fund-raising staff. Because it is rare to treat
large political campaigns ethnographically, little is known about their

information flows within the campaign and how these flows pattern relations within the organization and between constituents and the campaign. Nonetheless, these campaign organizations are important actors on the national political stage. Whether a candidate is campaigning for office or a lobby group is campaigning for legislative relief to its grievances, big-budget campaigns often captivate the attention of elected officials, news media, and the public.

In the previous two chapters I analyzed a number of examples of contemporary political campaign strategy. In this chapter I make some generalizations across political hypermedia campaigns and make two arguments about change in the organization of contemporary campaigns. First, the flow of information through hypermedia campaigns is significantly different from the flow of information through mass media campaigns. Second, the structure of campaign organization has evolved as a consequence of these information flows, and I develop a theory of epistemic heterarchy to explain these features. Information technology experts built their political values into the tools and technologies as they campaigned, with direct implications for the organization and process of campaigning. The transformed campaign – a hypermedia campaign – is the organizational instantiation of the capacities and constraints of information technologies.

One of the challenges in treating a campaign ethnographically is coming to terms with the organizational boundaries of different kinds of social movements. These are treated loosely in the literature, and the distinction between a social movement and a campaign is often just that a campaign has some formal organization. In my fieldwork, I found four types of campaign organizations, with important nuances in the kinds of organizations that campaign in contemporary political battles, and these nuances vary by the source of their normative order, the source of membership, the kind of affinity network they have with other groups, and the internal staff structure.

What we call a *grassroots or social movement* is a group of people who consensually and consciously generate a normative order that becomes a source of personal identity for members, some of whom may serve organizations which promote the normative order. A *lobby group* is an organization with wealthy corporate or private donors that exogenously set a normative order that may or may not be an important source of personal identity for an organization's staff, but usually is the basis for the organization's strategic affiliations with other like-minded organizations. A *candidate campaign* is defined by a leader who endogenously generates a normative order that becomes a source of identity for staff and members, which is the basis for strategic affiliations with other like-minded political leaders and which can sometimes be reworked by the members who are attracted to support the leader. In contrast, an *implanted or astroturf campaign* is an organization with a wealthy corporate or private donor who exogenously sets a normative order that may or may not be a source of personal identity for the organization's staff, that can be the basis for strategic affiliations with other groups, that may be a source of personal identity for a larger membership, but that cannot be reworked by that wider membership.

THE DEVELOPMENT OF CAMPAIGN ORGANIZATION

Most scholars of political campaigning make distinctions among the pre-modern campaign, the modern campaign, and the postmodern campaign. Between the mid-nineteenth century and 1950, local party volunteers took the pulse of member opinion with party meetings and local canvassing efforts. There was little centralized control of campaign logistics. The news media consisted of a partisan press, radio, and local posters or pamphleteers, who brought relatively low-budget local public meetings and whistle-stop leadership tours to the attention of a stable, partisan electorate.

Mass media campaigns, run between the 1960s and late 1980s, were long, nationally coordinated campaigns run by professional consultants and specialist advisers from a central party headquarters. Occasional opinion polls helped the campaign to keep on top of public sentiments, and the nightly television news broadcasts were the most important medium for publicizing closely managed campaign events. The costs of these campaigns grew immensely for televisable media events and political commercials, which had to be targeted at increasingly fickle cross-sections of the electorate. The postmodern campaigns that developed in the 1990s remained nationally coordinated but operationally decentralized. Presidential campaigns in particular now have a permanent quality, applying impression-management strategies from the beginning of primary contests through the election cycle, through the term of office, to legacy campaigns or preparation for the subsequent electoral contest. Ever more professional consultants use regular opinion polls and focus groups to produce ever more costly, targeted campaign television ads and events, trying to manage news production for segments of the electorate no longer in stable party alignments (Dinkin 1989; Norris 2000a).

145

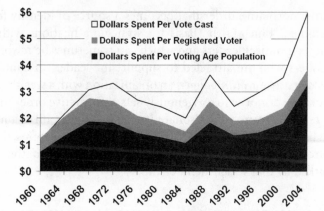

Figure 4.1: Presidential campaign budgets per voter, registered voter, and voting age population, 1960–2004. *Source and Notes:* Calculated by the author, using voting age population, registered voters, and total votes cast from the Federal Election Commission. Population of registered voters for 2004 is estimated. Total spending is adjusted to 2004 U.S. dollars, with data for 1976–2004 from the Center for Responsive Politics and data for 1960–1974 from M. L. Goldstein, *Guide to the 2004 Presidential Election* (Washington, D.C.: CQ Press, 2003).

Many campaigns seem permanent, organizations that smoothly transition from manipulating public opinion for the purpose of winning electoral office to managing public opinion for the purpose of legitimating governance from issue to issue (Blumenthal 1982; Ornstein and Mann 2000).

Figure 4.1 reveals several important trends in the cost of political communication for presidential candidates in the United States since 1960. The amount of money spent per voting age population, per registered voter, and per vote cast has been adjusted to 2004 dollars. There are many factors that affect campaign spending in a particular year, including the rules governing contributions, the health of the economy, and the skills of campaign fund-raisers. But from the point of view of campaign consultants, this figure reveals several of their industry's imperatives. First, the population of registered voters used to be about the same population who voted. A good list of registered voters was safely assumed to be a list of people who would vote on Election Day, but there was an incentive to spend some time and money trying to draw in new voters. Second, the total amount of money spent on campaigning has increased about tenfold, from almost $80 million in the 1960 campaign year to over $700 million in 2004. Much of this is due to the cost of television advertising, though the purchasing pattern has changed in a crucial way. Instead of buying national time for standardized political messages, campaigns have been spending more to air multiple ads targeted for specific markets. Hypermedia tools collect intelligence on the cultural cues needed to help customize a message and distribute content either for obvious political commercials or subtle news actualities.

Third, the pressure to spend campaign resources only on known voters has grown over time, especially since 1992. Here, the declining voter turnout is part of the denominator effect that has created such a gap in the ratios of campaign dollars spent per voting age population and campaign dollars spent per actual voter. Given the same budget in 2004, a political communication strategy targeting the voting age population spends about three dollars per person, while a strategy targeting reliable voters can spend six dollars per person. The imperative in contemporary political communication strategy is distinguishing between someone who is eligible to vote and someone who actually votes.

Indeed, hypermedia campaigns may be more fleeting than permanent: They quickly appear in specific parts of the country and dissipate when no longer useful; their objectives narrow and particular; their legacy and impact difficult to trace; and their true political goals obscure. The most important permanent attribute of the hypermedia campaign is really its data, especially data that helps political communication strategies distinguish politically inert nonvoters from people who can be activated for a cause and vote. Profiles on voters, donors, volunteers, and candidates and other strategic information used to disappear between campaign seasons. It might have been kept by consultants as part of the expert resources they could offer future clients. Now such data are passed among affinity networks of consultants and campaigns. It is merged and held independently of any particular campaign project, available in the marketplace.

I have been using the term "hypermedia campaign" to describe the particular campaigns developed with new media such as the internet. The dominant feature of the new campaign may not be, as Norris describes, costly targeted campaign television ads but cheap, targeted campaign ads designed and distributed through hypermedia. Such costly television ads were an exaggerated feature of the bloated campaign structure before hypermedia. Today's campaign is reflexive, less expensive, and operates in a political sphere with fewer (media-based) barriers to entry. More important, the people who consume political content can turn around and produce it over hypermedia. The exercise of producing and consuming political information is increasingly conflated. The mass media campaigns broadcast content produced by the elite management consultancies to large numbers of people. In contrast, the hypermedia campaigns narrowcast content to purposefully selected people, and the content itself is significantly shaped by data from the small, targeted audience. In astroturf campaigns, elite managers significantly control the informational schema through which political action occurs, while more endogenously formed social movements can purchase similar data sets and software tools on the open market. As revealed in chapters 2 and 3, people do not always know they are contributing data to a campaign. They may agree with the campaign agenda while knowing little of its true motives, or can begin a campaign that competes well against those of larger, well-financed lobby groups.

Surprisingly little has been written about campaign structure and organization, even though a political campaign can represent a social movement in concrete form, propel candidates or issues into the national spotlight, raise millions of dollars, and unite millions of members. Even though qualitative methods are used in studying many other kinds of social organization, ethnography is rarely used in the study of political campaigns. We do know that political campaigns have become increasingly professionalized, a process that began when campaigns started to take on professional pollsters and fund-raisers to maximize the amount of information collected on the electorate and the amount of money collected from supporters (Herrnson 1992). Most common are studies of campaign finance and fund-raising. But less is known about how campaigns manage personnel resources and structure their work.

IDEOLOGUE ELITES, CAPO MANAGERS, AND CODING GENERALS

There are three observable ranks of status among political campaign IT consultants. I label the older, articulate owners of e-politics consultancies *ideologues*; those who manage the complex personnel, financial, and informational resources and commitments *capos*; and those who do coding and provide day-to-day technology support *generals*. The people in these categories are technology staff and volunteers, paid professionals and academics who give hypermedia specific political applications by putting content online and doing opposition research. They build tools for campaign logistics that help to collect donations, organize volunteers, and gather intelligence on voters. They tend to be less wedded to political party or large ideological packages.

> The online politics community is bipartisan at this point. Repub-licans and Democrats have more in common than they have sepa-rating them. The community defines itself against political profes-sionals who rely on television and direct mail and offline methods, and what unites them across partisan lines is their commitment to develop politics online. (Cornfield 2000)

Hierarchical organizations are, by definition, groups in which subgroups or individuals have specific roles, reporting relationships, and degrees of power. I found three distinct roles, differentiated by the kinds of organizational power each had and the amount of technology work in their daily routines.

The *ideologue elites* do most of the conceptual work in imagining how technology can be applied in democratic deliberation. These are the heads of firms, who may be minimally involved with day-to-day opera-tions but are frequently occupied with political alliances and returning media phone calls, generating good quotable quotes, networking with other firms, chasing clients, writing thought-provoking monographs, and keeping up with the foundations and academics. The technology elites tend not to work on raw data. They spend their day reflecting on the successes and failures of important campaigns. They dialogue with clients and link successful projects from the academic, nonprofit, and for-profit world into new tools for clients – whether those clients are academic, nonprofit, or for-profit. They carry epistemological authority because their statements about the future of democracy are what inspire the imagination of investers, clients, and employees alike. They specu-late and interpret out loud, sometimes saying the ridiculous just to hear the sound of their own voices. In the end, they generate many ideas, leave them to be implemented by others, and then appropriate the work as if the real labor was in dreaming the dream, not actually slaving over code for weeks on end. They see themselves as altruists, working for a campaign but ultimately responsible for the quality of the democratic process.

Ideologues read the well-respected deliberative democracy theorists, from Dahl to Mansbridge and Barber to Popkin. Part of their work as ideologues is in turning theories of deliberative democracy into critiques of contemporary political discourse in general and political opponents in particular. They harness this vibrant intellectual tradition to inspire a discourse about the tools necessary for a new responsive, transparent public sphere. They connect the daily drudgery of coding and organization to the myth and ceremony of direct democracy. At Astroturf-Lobby.org, Mark keeps a training manual called *The Human Side of Intranets*:

> In your job as intranet project manager, you will assume the role of cheerleader for this new communication medium. This is not like creating a new brochure; this is a whole new thing. The ultimate success of your project will depend on how well you handle this "evangelist" role. Evangelists are usually technology pioneers. They are advocates of new systems and processes. They spend a great deal of their time educating people about a new concept. They provide a continual stream of information about the technology and its advantages. They do this to build support among management and to create a demand among potential users. (Koehler 1998, 47)

The e-politics community is a small technocracy, a social elite who has a vested interest in technological development and helps to generate the rhetoric that new media are unquestionably good for society (Postman 1993). They participate in the marketplace of ideas, trying to build a social capital with elite candidates and lobbyists.

The capo managers do the hard work of organizing resources for specific campaign projects, a skill set similar to that needed to manage favors, territories, and personalities in a Mafia-like *famiglia*. "We have to manage all the peculiar personalities who generate code, translate the fantasies of the company spokespeople into meaningful deliverables, and barter for time and talent resources with other managers in the project," reported Jeff, who worked as chief operations officer for several projects at Voting.com. "All of it has to be kept in the head because it's kind of like participating in some kind of underground economy – a black market for time and talent." They are not part of the economy of discourse about technology and politics that occurs outside the project; they participate in the internal economy of personal and technical resources within the project. They do the more mundane work of signing clients, hiring employees, and making sure that projects actually get off the ground and meet deadlines. Some are pendants, eager to train to become ideologues. To be a *capo* is actually to assemble and repackage information and handle the bulk of the architectural work involved in turning a big democratic dream into a working application. They do not really have the status of the ideologues, but they are responsible for carrying out the design aspects of the project.

> Mark: I don't have the same decision-making role I used to have. Now I simply pass on information about decisions that the tech guys under me have made to other parts of the project. Not all of my team can sit in on board meetings – though they sometimes try to – so I feel like I spend more time reflecting their opinions upwards than being a conduit for decisions made above me that get handed down. Besides in any given day client priorities change, new possibilities emerge, forcing us to constantly reexamine where we are going. This is why experiential knowledge makes the junior people so important – our planning committees can't meet every day so a lot of the power and authority rests in the small groups who make time-sensitive decisions on their own.

The junior people with experiential knowledge about technology and politics are the third grouping of e-politics professionals. Even though they are junior staff in age and training, they can aptly be labeled an army of generals.

The *coding generals* do the raw coding, graphic design, and data collection. "The strange thing is that we're all generals," said Sally, who did much of the data compilation for DataBank.com. "You know that saying that 'an army fails when it has too many generals.' We are sort of low in rank in that there is a mass and for the most part we take assignments, but they treat us better than any army grunts, and if we want a foosball table or a beer party, by God it better happen." These technical engineers are a lower caste only in salary and engagement with the public; they have the daily responsibility of design decisions and coding for the projects to which they were assigned. "I'm told I have a lot of power but I do not seem to command anyone," Dania said of her marketing job at Voting.com. "I'm like a general in an army of generals." They carry out the client service aspects of the work. Some of them are not as invested in the big democratic project as the managers or elites, but they do participate in the e-politics conferences.

> Charles: We have a suite of tools that we customize depending on the needs of our clients, such as database management, grass-roots activation tools, ad tracking capabilities, and credit card distribution – a very sophisticated back-end technology suite. Each client has different needs and contexts and the architecture of your

Web site is a fundamental embodiment of your strategy. So we don't believe that just off-the-shelf tools work in most cases.

The coding generals implement the digital democracy, and modern campaigns themselves are dependent on their specialized IT staff.

Larry: If they disappeared, the institution would fall on its face. Sometimes this does happen because organizations have trouble redistributing these skill sets. These people work extra hours, take on more responsibility, and put up with little internal recognition.

To examine loyalty, campaign managers create interesting tests for prospective staff. Prospective campaign staff must at least tolerate the normative goals of the campaign and its particular objectives. During an interview, the senior managers will test for loyalty to the campaign by querying job candidates on their attitudes toward policy options that actually belong to an opponent. To test for loyalty to the project of digital democracy, potential employees are asked to describe the risks of benefits of a digital democracy in their own words. How job candidates respond to this question often determines whether they are hired by the campaign and their status within the organization once hired. Senior technology managers reveal the norms of the campaign but also their higher project. This higher project – wiring up democracy in the United States – requires innovation in both information technologies and organizational form (Beniger 1990).

In the introductory chapter, the hypermedia campaign was defined by the processes of organizational adaptation that go along with technology adoption, rather than by the specific technologies used in a communication strategy. The hypermedia campaign was defined as an agile political organization defined by its capacity for innovatively adopting digital technologies for express political purposes, and by its capacity for innovatively adapting its organizational structure to conform to new communicative practices. Chapters 2 and 3 revealed how campaign goals and relationships among political leaders, campaign staff, and client groups have adapted, but here we must take a more in-depth look at the information and organizational process of the hypermedia campaign.

INFORMATION PROCESSES AND ORGANIZATIONAL BEHAVIOR IN POLITICAL CAMPAIGNS

Much has been written about the lasting impact of forms of organization in the dot-com corporate world, where innovative organizations are needed to help manage risk, resources, and responsibility. From the point of view of campaign managers, the most worrying trend is that their candidates need to be conversant on many more issues. "At least the traditional way of doing politics forced candidates to pick three particular messages and stay on them throughout a campaign, across the country," one Democrat manager told me. "Now a candidate has to be multimessage." To overcome this challenge, campaign managers began to use the hypermedia technology itself as a logistical tool in their own operations. "It allows us to communicate and collaborate with others remotely," reported Charles from Astroturf-Lobby.org. "We're aware of what is going on around the HQ and the broader campaign without leaving the room." Within the e-politics industry, it is common to refer to the old campaign style as a mass media campaign because of its notably different information flows and ways of organizing.

Political campaigns adapted their own internal structures and their own media habits to take advantage of the capacities of political hypermedia. In a banal but fundamental way, the new tools had an effect on campaign logistics in 2000. For example, Ben Green from the campaign to elect Gore-Lieberman built a hypermedia "publishing system that allowed those communications staffers who worked at three or four in the morning to push stuff out onto the web – without having to talk to a tech person" (Jagoda 2000, 81). A decade before, the Republican National Committee was spending $8,500 a month to "blast faxes" to supporters and media contacts. But beyond logistics the organizational behavior of campaigns also evolved. For example, Lynn Reed was one of the first chief information officers to be part of the senior management team of a presidential campaign. She took full advantage of this role in the Bradley 2000 campaign.

> Reed: It allowed me to be proactive, working directly with the field director... "Here's our field goal for the next three weeks and here's what we can do on the internet." When the different divisions of the campaign are communicating what their goals are, then I can be a part of the thought process in figuring out the role of the internet. If that never gets communicated to the Web person, then you are operating in a vacuum. (Reed 2001)

By the 2004 campaign season, the presidential campaigns had many different kinds of information officers, technology advisers, and Webmasters. Most of the top personalities in campaigns became involved in strategic e-mail communication with volunteers. However, the impact of new technology is felt not just in organizational structuring, but also in policy choices. "A strange thing is that the technology exposes holes in policy," observed Mark, who co-founded Astroturf-Lobby.com, "such that the tech team influences policy positioning strategy." In bringing information technologies into campaign strategy, senior managers were forced to concretize political choices that in the mass media campaign could be left unenunciated. Perhaps the best example of this was presented at the beginning of chapter 1, where two Republican women began receiving different messages about gun control and abortion. Given the choice between sending out a consistent message reflecting official party position or sending out different messages reflecting the diversity of opinion within the party, senior managers choose the latter. In the 2004 campaign, both Democrats and Republicans sent different kinds of e-mail content to people within their parties, based on the known spectra of opinion and on levels of party commitment. The hypermedia campaign takes full advantage of opportunities to narrowcast content.

While many of the largest PACs have their own specialized informational resources, consultants have helped the major political parties to develop proprietary systems – in the 2004 campaign the DNC had its DataMart and the RNC had its Voter Vault. Most candidates acquired their own data sets, but the national party committees made a distinct effort to facilitate the exchange of data. For the Democrats, state parties had to upload data to the DataMart in a specific format, whereas the Republicans converted any data format provided by their state parties into a common format. Through the internet, the DataMart could be updated dynamically by Democrat volunteers, but the data only covered two previous elections, and only thirty-six state party operations offices had access. In contrast, Republican state local and congressional campaigns in all fifty states had access to data covering four previous elections in their Voter Vault. The DataMart, Voter Vault, and other PAC information systems have common features, but all are distinct from the information systems of mass media campaigns. Information processes in the hypermedia campaign consist of smaller feedback loops, little information waste, and nontoxic data-gathering methods.

Political hypermedia are designed to turn a political campaign into a kind of news or service provider, user-centered and highly responsive. The customer is the voting constituent, and the products are palatable actors, icons, and arguments. Chris, from Voting.com, stated flatly: "I want to build a user-driven Web site that creates informed citizen-consumers." His business development plan makes an interesting parallel with eBay: "We need a self-reinforcing, virtuous circle of trusting relationships between buyer and seller that have made the auction site famous. This circle is to be brought to politics." Morris said something similar while on the campaign trail: "Consumers should be in control of markets, and the power of the internet is in transferring control." In this rhetoric, the competitive dispersion of political ideas and leaders can only lead to healthy deliberative discourse. The hypermedia campaign easily measures client satisfaction with strategy, where "clients" are either the citizens who ultimately vote, candidates who seek office, or corporations with political agenda. Larry, a specialist in data mining, made an explicit parallel between e-politics and e-commerce:

> The internet is a communications management tool. Politics is e-commerce. The supply chain management issues in e-commerce directly parallel those of politics. As you run a campaign, you have to manage resources, predict certain things, you have archived information, you have a production schedule, and the candidate has to be at certain places. There is a Web-based sell going on. Incremental sales count. You are building momentum and building your brand. The main difference is that in politics you have a distinct endpoint.

Given networked computing tools, many campaign managers reconceived the way information flowed within the organization, between like-minded campaigns, and between clients. E-politics consultants commonly followed three principles for reorganizing the flow of information within their campaign: They constructed small feedback loops, rarely wasted data, and collected data in such a way as to not threaten future supplies of data.

SMALL FEEDBACK LOOPS   The hypermedia campaign works with much smaller information feedback loops between citizens and the campaign, among different parts of the campaign organization, and among campaigns on affiliated issues. The hypermedia campaign can quickly and regularly study its constituents and its lobbying targets, reconnecting with these constituents and targets as if they were part of a panel survey. The information flows are decentralized, distributed, and versatile. With the growing need to coordinate multiple stakeholders around a campaign agenda, this kind of organizational innovation is increasingly necessary. Pollsters, telemarketers, speech writers, media strategists and spin doctors, direct mail writers, and TV ad producers report in some way to a chief information officer. In the political realm the hypermedia campaign is similarly a process of negotiation over the candidate's political strategies, a negotiation among community members, the candidate, campaign managers, the organization's formal employees, and affinity organizations. The opinion of constituents is continuously tested. In the old campaign structure, finances determined when and how often pollsters would be hired to conduct public policy surveys. In the new campaign structure, technologies maintain a constant watch on constituents' opinions. In contrast, the mass media campaign had a much slower turnaround time for information. Expensive television ad campaigns disseminated information, and polls returned information, but the feedback on campaign strategy was measured in days and weeks, not hours and seconds, as in the hypermedia campaign.

LOW INFORMATION WASTE   In the hypermedia campaign, data are not wasted and are always preserved. Data are either built into algorithms for predicting policy preferences or saved for a time when they might be worth selling to someone. The organization knows exactly who their members are, but the members may not know they are members. "People don't know that the groceries they purchase next week may have as much bearing on how they are represented in D.C. as the way they voted in the last election." The most constructive, policy-relevant campaign of the e-politics community has been toward online disclosure. Financial backing, voting history, candidate statements, and political affiliations are all things that help to define a political candidate and campaign, yet all are things that campaign managers like to refer to selectively, depending on their audience. Reed: "More important, there's unlimited message distribution at no marginal cost." Traditional pollsters rely on relatively blunt survey instruments, forcing respondents to choose between pre-selected answer options instead of revealing their preferences, and applying their own spin to make up for missing data. The mass media campaign did not have the same data-mining strategies, and a significant amount of data was wasted by the campaign.

LOW PROCESS TOXICITY   Collecting or disseminating information can have a toxic effect on public opinion polling if the process of gathering information makes future collection or dissemination efforts more difficult. Because data collection over new media can be innocuous, little about the process of collecting data using new media affects subsequent efforts to collect data. This is not so with mass media campaign methods. Telephone surveying is a toxic process in that the more telephone surveys are run, the more people get tired of participating in them. The error margin of computer-assisted telephone interview (CATI) systems is growing; three states have passed legislation allowing citizens to remove themselves from CATI databases; and similar initiatives are afoot elsewhere. Spam, negative campaign ads, and push polling are some of the toxic information processes of mass media campaigns: When a campaign negatively runs a push poll, the public gets discouraged and less eager to participate in subsequent polling efforts. The long-term problem of rising refusal rates and anti-solicitation technologies has had a clear impact on traditional polling efforts (Witte and Howard 2002). (See Table 4.1.)

As argued in chapter 2, the science of private opinion management is an important part of this new information flow. Recall that the scientific/technological method empowers the technical staff with important management decisions:

> Morris: Political positions are always full of contradictions, and we have to manage the paradoxes that become apparent when the party muckity-mucks decide to build a Web site. It comes down to me to juggle the party planks so that the paradoxes aren't as apparent or only appear to someone who does really deep surfing into the site. Before the internet the important political campaign managers had a kind of speechwriter's role, mediating between the different schools of thought that exist within a campaign. Now we don't have to mediate so much, we just organize the paradoxes so that they don't appear to clash.

The candidate or lobbyist used to exercise control over political communications, seeking a mass or targeted audience with a fixed message. The campaign managers sent messages and constituents received those messages. The campaign had time to craft and distribute messages according to its timetable.

The hypermedia campaign is agile and responsive, at once conducting opposition research, surveying constituents, collecting money, and directing public fervor. It is also true that in the hypermedia campaign, staff not taken on to develop technology must develop their own technology skills. Thus, adopting political hypermedia has required some organizational adaptation as well. But these adaptations occur not only in the flows and qualities of information, but also in the structure of the organization itself.

In the mass media campaign, the IT staff played the roles of speechwriter and archivist. In the hypermedia campaign, the IT staff is trusted for impression management and the organization of ideological paradoxes. Political consultants have long had specialized knowledge about polling techniques, rhetoric, opposition research, direct mail strategies,

Table 4.1A: *Information in the Mass Media and Hypermedia Campaign*

Attributes	Mass media campaign	Hypermedia campaign
Feedback loops	*Large and slow* Unidirectional media ads disseminate information out of campaign; polls bring data into the campaign; information is cycled in days and weeks.	*Small and fast* Information quickly moves along networks of friends and family; bridging and bonding occurs with affinity groups and constituents; information is cycled in seconds and hours.
Information waste	*High* Consultant instinct and experience drives campaign; information is monopolized; managers or candidates generate the cultural content for prime-time events and press conferences; data models are bivariate.	*Low* Data drive campaign strategy; membership generates content iteratively; information is decentralized; there is 24-hour instant publishing and nuanced, accurate, and deliberative polling.
Process toxicity	*High* Random sampling and telephone-based survey instruments, negative ads, push polling.	*Low* Purposive and noninvasive sampling through political hypermedia; spam; humor.

radio, newspaper, and television ad placement, and more (Friedenberg 1997). But now much of this raw information is available online, and many of these services are offered out of the box by organizations such as DataBank.com, Astroturf-Lobby.org, GrassrootsActivist.org, and Voting.com. These new information flows in political campaigns do not simply elevate the status of technology experts within the organization. There are consequences for the internal structure of the campaign and external relationships. Organizationally, these new kinds of power have both a bridging and bonding function, two powerful metaphors used by Norris and Putnam. The primary organizational adaptation to these new kinds of information flows has been new bridges to other kinds of affinity groups and tighter bonds to client groups. In this situation, bonding is

Table 4.1B: *Organization in the Mass Media and Hypermedia Campaign*

Attributes	Mass media campaign	Hypermedia campaign
Staff	*Organizational identity* Replaceable and defined by role; authority is monopolized with clear reporting relations among staff colleagues.	*Project-based identity* Incommensurate, and defined by need; authority is distributed among ideologue elites, *capo* managers, and coding generals.
Structure	*Administrative hierarchy* Vertical chain of command; financial or political basis of credibility is within the organization; vertical accountability and loyalty to the candidate or financial backers; organization is the source of cohesion; there is a clear division of labor, sequential production, and delivery of messages.	*Epistemic heterarchy* Lateral systems of accountability; epistemic and symbolic power basis of credibility; loyalties are project-based and given to membership or program; complex interdependence in division of labor; simultaneous production and delivery.
Content	*Content from managers* Functional disconnection between campaign executive and membership; campaign elites design mass standardized content. Citizens choose television, radio, or newspapers for broadcast content.	*Content from members* Strong bond between campaign executive and membership, strong bridge with other campaigns; elites may seed the campaign, but cultural content is individually customized. People choose content, which is narrowcast.

a process of recording the online researching habits of citizens, narrow-casting content, collecting private information, and modifying software settings on constituent computers.

The language of "getting it" helps to define the commercial and political niche of the e-politics community. Even though members of the e-politics community can quickly assess someone's technical competence, they frequently ascribe a more mysterious compliment of "getting it" to people with inspired ideas about how the tools can and should be used. People who resist the project obviously don't get it, and every member of the community has stories about how people and institutions resist ideas about putting content online. Most new media consultants have stories about institutional resistance to an open, interactive media environment. "Different departments within the AARP were asked to contribute to the public Web site," reports one professional campaign manager. "But the lobbyists didn't want to use it because people could find out what our strategies were and see who we were targeting. They tried to push us off all the time – they just didn't get it. It was one of the reasons I left." The organizational behavior of mass media and hypermedia campaigns can be contrasted on three points: the source of identity for staff, the structure by which staff resources are ordered, and the sourcing of cultural content that goes into campaign messages.

STAFF AND ORGANIZATIONAL IDENTITY Traditional political campaigns, especially the large national candidate and lobbyist campaigns, had very strict hierarchies. People were taken on for specific, well-defined roles and they could be switched out with other talent because skill sets for the roles were not highly specialized. There were clear reporting relations among staff, and information about campaign strategy and organization was monopolized at the top of the organization. Often, campaign organizations were clearly situated within the ideological framework of the Democratic or Republican party. In contrast, the staffers who work for hypermedia campaigns tend to affiliate for short-term projects. Skill sets are highly specialized in areas of information technology management, and people are more difficult to replace. Authority is more distributed, because IT staff makes seemingly technical decisions that also have an impact on the presentation of political information and shaping of policy, and older campaign staff depend on these IT professionals.

CAMPAIGN STRUCTURE Fundamentally, the heterarchy can be contrasted with the hierarchy. Whereas a hierarchical bureaucracy will fit a project into its structure, the heterarchical bureaucracy is fitted around the project. In their study of "green" firms, Pellow, Schnaiberg, and Weinberg found three important features of a pragmatist style of management, a style that contrasts with positivistic or practical management cultures of administrative hierarchies (Pellow, Weinberg, and Schnaiberg 1995, 12). Decisions are made by identifying problems and paradoxes that need managing, not solving. Rules are treated as working hypotheses constantly refined by the experience of what works. Respected organizational values include orderly thought, experience in empirical evidence, practical wisdom, and open dialogue. This style of management is used in the epistemic heterarchies of hypermedia campaigns. The hypermedia campaign is fluid, allowing active constituents and greater role in generating content, allowing the campaign executive more power in activating and manipulating less active constituents and flattening the overall campaign structure.

In fact, the hypermedia campaign is not unlike the agile, organizational form that many firms have taken since the arrival of the new economy, an organizational form termed "permanently beta" by Neff and Stark (2004). The permanently beta organizational form results from a constant process of negotiation among users, employees, and organizations over the design of goods and services. The permanently beta organization designs communication technology, and itself, for responsiveness.

CONTENT PRODUCTION A final point of distinction between mass media and hypermedia campaigns lies in the source of content for the campaign. In the mass media campaign, seasoned political consultants crafted political messages and generated most of the content that was presented on behalf of a candidate or special interest group. There was a functional disconnection between campaign executives and their members, and most members had few, irregular points of contact with campaign executives. Pollsters provided occasional feedback from constituents, and focus groups could be used to test particular messages and turns of phrase. While elite campaign managers have an important role in crafting messages for the hypermedia campaign, an immense amount of the work of generating campaign content gets transferred to volunteers and members. Members write blogs, submit photos, produce posters with their own printers, and append their social networks to the campaign network. Most important, they contribute personal data to the campaign, sometimes unwittingly. Testing messages and collecting feedback from constituents happens perpetually in the hypermedia campaign, through daily online polls, blogs, and spyware. Personalized Web pages allow users to prioritize campaign content, and information about constituents' purchases and research habits is used to shape the cultural content they are shown.

One of the advantages of these organizational and informational innovations is in more tightly binding supporters within the campaign. For example, Forbes supporters could pick from a selection of political ads to sponsor, and then sponsor the location and time slot. Supporters could contribute $1,000 toward a national airing during *Crossfire* or *Larry King Live*, or $75 toward an airing during *Wheel of Fortune* in Des Moines. In this sense, both political parties and issue publics try to encourage ideological binding when they adopt political hypermedia. Ideological control and filter management has been surrendered to political information consumers who can insist that their representatives more closely match personal preferences; consumers can choose other groups easily. More concrete is the deliberate attempt to draw the computing and networking resources of the private citizens who support an issue or candidate campaign into the campaign itself. The supporter can choose not only to support a candidate with a vote or campaign contribution but to extend the campaign's organizational reach by allowing the campaign to co-opt the supporter's e-mail networks and computing and printing resources. At the same time, the supporter may have the opportunity to promote a particular issue within a candidate's overall media strategy.

An important part of the organizational transformation of political parties and campaigns has been due to the demands of network partners, groups that may once have been peers, collaborators, or ideologically in the same camp but are now distinctly networked. The other part is a set of transformations that occurs through the information exchanges among their members. In hypermedia campaigns, the volunteer network is now such a formalized part of the campaign structure that campaign communications are generated and propagated by the membership.

A THEORY OF EPISTEMIC HETERARCHY

In important ways, the innovations of the hypermedia political campaign are logical extensions of decades of campaigning trends. But these trends – decentralization, targeted campaigning, managed paradoxes, and more – are so accelerated by hypermedia technologies as to make important qualities of the contemporary political campaign different from those of its mass media ancestor. The concept of epistemic community from political science and the concept of heterarchical structure from management help to explain the complex interdependence between communication technology and campaign organization.

As described in chapters 2 and 3, a small number of people from a diverse range of formal organizations collaborated on a significant number of complex new media campaigns. Even with shared norms, rules, and patterns of behavior, the community was not simply a casual or informal affiliation; it developed a complex organizational form design specifically for the peculiar demands of building political hypermedia. I call this form an *epistemic heterarchy*. An organizational heterarchy consists of actors or partners who are not equivalent or easily replaceable, operating in a system of complex interdependence toward the fulfillment of a shared normative project. Actors in a heterarchy have incommensurable roles and responsibilities. Each individual is caught up in multiple, overlapping associations with clients, bosses, and colleagues across government, private firms, publicly traded businesses, and charities. In particular, e-politics consultants receive paychecks from all of these sources in a given year.

The sociology of professions has been devoted to understanding how people enclose a profession, defining social boundaries and monopolizing information (Abbott 1988). Here occurs a hybrid profession with the mixing of ideas across professional categories, with the common currency being ideological commitment to direct, deliberative democracy. Only limited kinds of information are monopolized: Commercial firms rarely discuss the details of client behavior and attitudes; the better databases of voter profile information are proprietary and shared in fairly specific circumstances. IT campaign professionals are like other software developers, craftsmen who work in a cultural milieu of artisanship. Although others have written about the "culture of software," described as the community ethos of coders, it is difficult to translate the values of a group into the development patterns of their product (Carmel 1997). Many are also technicians who lived through, or are living through, the organizational crises that Barley has charted. Balkanized within traditional hierarchical firms and government bureaucracies, many developed relationships with other guild members across organizational boundaries or became managers themselves and forced their organizations to adapt to a control structure with a more horizontal division of labor (Barley 1996; 1997). Boczkowski, in his study of online newspapers, described the process of distributed construction used by people and organizations that "co-construct" content (Boczkowski 2004).

Certainly, the good feelings of generosity that the e-politics community began with have helped to keep things open. But all the managers know it is relatively easy to reverse-engineer any particular software innovation, and most campaigns are public enough that they, as experts, have a good sense of what is being done backstage in other campaigns. Finally, the conferences are used to create community bonds of trust, for inviting new members in, especially from cohorts of established politicians, pollsters, pundits, and other consultants who are seen either as dinosaurs for ignoring or underappreciating the role of hypermedia in politics or as pioneers for being political heavyweights who are forward-looking enough to grace the conference with their presence for an hour of speech-making.

Knowledge workers are highly portable, yet are also a project's real source of capital, which is why the knowledge worker is often treated as an associate or partner in the enterprise (Batt et al. 2001). Recall that many of the lowest technology staff in political campaigns are treated as an army of generals, because it is their technical ingenuity that is now a crucial source of innovative campaign strategy. Many workers have a single obligation that they consider full-time work, and then additional part-time, temporary consulting contracts. More interesting are situations where people are employees not of the organization for which they work but of an outside firm that agreed to lend personnel for specific projects. Most have a small set of senior executives, with highly decentralized working "committees," each with multiple roles in both innovation and sales. All components are well versed in each other's area of expertise, and they take advantage of the same knowledge base. The epistemic basis for community membership is as strong and in some ways is more pertinent a source of membership and allegiance than is any formal organization structure. The challenge is to create a professional working environment that facilitates informal interaction among creative designers, market strategists, venture capitalists, and technology experts. But the rhetoric they generate for journalists to feed to the public imagination also makes them an epistemic culture, creating and justifying the image of the digital democracy (Knorr-Cetina 1999).

Informal professional interactions can have different meanings, from saving time on formal contract writing to leaving room for a competitive edge (Macauley 1963; Uzzi 1997). But informal interaction in this context does not mean that authority is absent. There are, in fact, significant patterns of mutual monitoring as subgroups watch each other for parallel ideas in development or for a kind of internal competitive advantage for voice in shaping product design. In other words, authority disperses, rather than dissolves, as responsibility for research and design is distributed across the organization. Individual members may report to a team head or the company president, but they also report to other work teams whose own role in development may occur as a consequence of or in conjunction with a particular team's work. Mutually monitoring each other's progress makes it easy for creative ingenuity to flame into hot new ideas, but also leaves a command structure uncertain. Exercises of heterarchical authority occur in daily development meetings where both managers and developers propose new directions for each other's work but rarely enunciate an extended path-dependent development strategy. In fact, quite the opposite occurs: The development board meetings are about looking for ways to keep alternative development options open as long as possible.

The task of leaving options open often revealed patterns in lateral accountability. Lateral accountability occurs as a consequence of distributed authority. The organization as a whole appears to manage incredibly diverse roles, but the whole project is kept together by the legitimacy generated when teams have to share authority and accountability for production quality and production schedules. Rather than accountability following financial power or political power, it follows intellectual capital. For this reason, systems of authority and accountability may be stretched outside apparent organizational boundaries to bring in myriad consultants and experts into the heterarchy. This process provides legitimacy, especially for the team that becomes the "node" by which outside experts are brought in. For example, in April 2000, Election.com, in search of credibility, partnered with the Honest Ballot Association, the organization founded by Theodore Roosevelt in 1909 to combat corruption in New York's election system. Academic affiliations, such as those formed with the Annenberg School of Communications at the University of Pennsylvania or the Political Management School at George Washington University, also provided credibility.

Heterarchies are designed for short production cycles (Grabher 2001, 2002). Since many of the e-politics businesses were working toward inflexible political deadlines (the dates of conventions, the dates of elections), they had product cycles of months, not years. Many products went live only for short periods. In the 2000 campaign, for example, both the Pseudo.com's user-controlled Web cam on the Republican convention floor and Campaign Advantage's color-changing digital maps of voter returns used by news services did not live to see another election season. Moreover, the processes of designing and implementing a product occur simultaneously, not sequentially, as often the products are installed on a client's server and then tested or taken live before the design is complete (Sabel 1992). On any given day, staff members may confess to not knowing to whom they report, to being unclear about what their product is, or to feeling uncertain about meaningful deadlines.

Organizations that are internally heterarchical often become part of other heterarchical organizations and play a role in a kind of macro-heterarchy, as observed in the organization of firms in post-Communist states (Sabel 1990; Stark 1999). By constantly trading employees and looking for legitimacy with partnerships and contracted expertise, they redraw their own internal boundaries, move in complex alliances with other organizations, and keep their products ill-defined and their assets mobile (Sabel 1992). While organizational cross-talk can yield fruitful innovations, the rivalry that occurs in a system of distributed authority and accountability generates small epistemological battles. For example, labeling, interpreting, evaluating, and prioritizing problems becomes an exercise in generating nomenclature, and teams devotedly stick to their nomenclature especially if naming the problems (software bugs, client attitudes, etc.) can generate an analytical frame that reveals particular solutions. The more implications this analytical frame may have for the attribution of blame, the adjustment of work schedules, or the balance of power between teams, the more significant the labeling exercise becomes.

Because heterarchies are composed of complex overlapping affiliations, individuals often seek or create more neutral places in which to work. The task of work is spread throughout the day and across larger spaces. There is a formal office space, but work occurs at home, on the subway, or over the weekend, with tools that make conceiving ideas and work-related correspondence transportable. Work also occurs in the neutral territory for the e-politics community, the formal professional conferences and the informal happy-hour events and brown-bag lunch workshops. The conference network included events organized by others, within which smaller subgroups such as Democracy Row, Internet Alley, and Internet Avenue at the Republican or Democratic national conventions met to work. Other conferences, such as Politics Online and E-Voter events, were designed by and for the e-politics community. It was there that business plans or foundation proposals could be shopped around to the major players. Not everyone had the same business models, the same foundation proposals, or the same kinds of academic affiliations. But in these neutral places members of different organizations could use the same kind of language. For this community, the neutral ground of industry conventions and happy hour gatherings provides a place for discourse about how politics can and should be done, without the scrutiny of the traditional press or political elites.

Territorial dispersion does not threaten campaign heterarchies equipped with hypermedia communication technology and strengthened by occasional face-to-face contact among staff. While there is a community core in Washington, D.C. – where most of the organizations are physically based – there is also a periphery, the world outside D.C. where civic idealists are located (MoveOn.org, CalVoter.org, and Minnesota E-Democracy). They operate in other parts of the country but their projects' goals are indistinguishable from those based in Washington, D.C. Whereas contexts are structurally imposed, networks are individually constructed. In this sense, the operations that have sprung up in Washington and New York are primarily businesses with corporate funding and corporate clients. In contrast, the operations that have sprung up around the rest of the country tend to be civic projects of nonprofits. They operate together through the personal network that has been constructed by the individuals. Their physical location is a kind of contextual imposition on the organizations, but networked technologies are constructed to allow heterarchies to function despite territorial boundaries and distances.

Heterarchies function with as few formal professional boundaries and professional jurisdictions as possible. They are anathema to a firm's ability to earn a profit, since most of the profit is derived from extension services across jurisdictions. Project evolution is so unpredictable that firms must either be nimble enough to claim expertise should the client need something new or have enough friendly relations with other firms that they can subcontract and retain the role of project leader. They do adapt some of the strategies Hirsch observed in his study of cultural industry systems. He found that firms placed "contact men" at the organizational boundaries specifically tasked with maintaining networks; that firms overproduced and made subtle variations in new items so as to lessen the risk of complete failure; and that they co-opted powerful members from markets and industries in which they needed contacts (Hirsch 1972). In the new economy heterarchy, every employee is also a "contact person," and it is made clear that social capital is valued as much as technical skill. It is social capital that makes new deals possible. Projects struggle to postpone important architectural choices as long as possible so that they can repackage products on the whims of customers or new ideas for development. Projects certainly try to co-opt, bringing in traditional pollsters, high-profile pundits, politicians, and journalists to help them articulate the dream of a wired democracy.

POWER AND SOCIAL CONTROL IN THE
HYPERMEDIA CAMPAIGN

It is no longer possible to study the organization of politics without understanding the digital interface of political organizations. The design of political campaigns, and therefore the interaction between politicians, policy makers, lobbyists and citizens, cannot be separated from the digital interface. In one sense, political campaigns have always been network organizations, relying on networks of family and friendship to maintain political loyalty. But there is an important difference between the mass media and hypermedia campaign: Instead of voters choosing to support a candidate or campaign, now candidates and campaigns choose supporters.

Observing the political IT consultants of DataBank.com, Astroturf-Lobby.org, Voting.com, and GrassrootsActivist.org build political hypermedia revealed four particular kinds of political power. First, the technology staff has the power to define and extend an organization. Increasingly, the organizational Web site is an important source of identity. Not only do outsiders refer to the campaign Web site for content and cues about the organization's political goals, but the staff uses the Web site as a resource for learning about or confirming its political identity. Second, the technology staff has the power to filter, destroy, or protect information for the campaign organization. Since so much political campaign business now occurs in digital form, the technology staff simultaneously plays the roles of archivist, accountant, and confidant. They are the people who must be trusted to destroy information if need be, to protect information for either the organizational or public good, and to filter information so that the other staff is not inundated with "data smog" from the outside world (Shenk 1997). Third, the technology staff has the power to synchronize and network issue publics. It is usually up to the technology staff of a campaign organization to extend the electronic network to campaign constituents through creative new applications of political hypermedia. Since outreach and coalition-building are key strategies in contemporary campaigning, it is the technology staff that often maintains relationships with other campaigns through data sharing, opposition research, and Web site links. Fourth, the technology staff has the power to cause organizational deadlock, and sometimes the power of veto if small project goals come into conflict with policy that has been openly declared on the Web site. The code staffers write, the material schemata that take shape as they make hardware and software decisions, give their political organization an important performative power. Especially when it comes to Web site design, code reveals and conceals features of the organization to the outside world, enabling candidates or political parties to show different aspects of their ideologies to different people.

In sum, epistemic heterarchy occurs where people and organizations are tied up in multiple, overlapping affiliations, yet have many places that include neutral "thinking grounds." These structures also have to be full of people who are used to collaborative relationships and are not afraid of or restricted by the communication technology at hand. The last few chapters have analyzed important changes in the system of political communication in the United States over the last decade. First, a service class of professional, political technocrats with special expertise in information technology arose. Second, the political culture industry discarded mass media tools for targeting tools, primarily fax and direct mail, which let the industry tailor messages to specific audiences. Third, the engineers of political hypermedia made technical decisions that established criteria constraining subsequent decisions about political communication. In the next chapter, I discuss the implications of the hypermedia campaign for the meaning of citizenship, the process of forming political opinion, and the exercise of franchise.

FIVE

Managed Citizenship and Information Technology

Our contemporary system of political communication is built by information technology consultants whose design choices affect the exercise and distribution of political power or by technology-savvy citizens who have access to many of the same technologies and much of the same information that was once reserved for political elites. Political consultants, likewise, build their political values into the tools and technologies of hypermedia campaigns, and one of the most important normative choices they make is to value informational transparency and technological access over personal privacy. This has resulted in the proliferation of political information technologies through the consumer market and the collection of immense amounts of personal information that most citizens would prefer not to have surrendered. Hypermedia campaigns mine personal data for political inferences, redline particular communities for targeted campaigning, and implant campaigns with the hope of capitalizing on artificially seeded social movements.

I have presented evidence about how political communication is constructed through information technologies by the consultants working for some of the most important candidate and issue campaigns in national politics. In the Introduction, I provided quantitative and comparative data about how political information has been produced through new media technologies over the last decade, and in chapters 2 and 3, I went into richer ethnographic detail about the construction projects of four exemplary organizations. My argument is not that hypermedia might be used to manage and control political culture. My argument is that hypermedia *are* used to manage and control political culture. A growing number of single-issue campaigns, marginal political actors, and average citizens use information communication technologies that were once available only to elite political actors.

During the 1996 presidential campaign season, managers treated the internet as a publicity tool. During the 2000 campaign season, hypermedia became a crucial organizational tool. By the 2004 campaign season, hypermedia were deeply integrated into the system of political communication in the United States; they structured content not available in other media; they were used purposefully as organizational tools; and they were used aggressively for data mining. Between the 1996 and 2004 election seasons the organizational culture of campaign managers specializing in IT took shape; they were consistently producing technologies that simultaneously violated public privacy norms and empowered citizens for independent political action. Entrenched patterns of campaign strategy reveal the entrenched system of political communication through hypermedia.

THE WIZARDS OF ODDS

Over the last few years, IT consultants have played an increasingly important role in political life in the United States. They build technologies for political parties large and small, incumbent and challenger candidates, genuine grassroots social movements, and lobbyist-funded astroturf movements. However, most of the political information technologies seem to have been constructed with an eye to a kind of *managed* direct democracy, in which citizens have the capacity to generate political content, while campaign managers do their best to constrain the stream of collective interest. The new forms of campaign organization, and the new technologies, are deliberately designed to alter the structure of political communication in the United States by privileging narrowcasting tools and strategies over mass communication tools and strategies. They imprint their design values on political communication tools that all of us use, the most important being the priority of informational access and transparency over personal privacy.

Scholarship on the history of communication technologies suggests that there are two phases to the cultural composition of new tools. The first opportunity to imprint cultural values on the structure of communication technology comes when the community of architects make their designs and during the initial phase of technology diffusion. Initially, the cultural values of designers may inform some technical choices, and the designers themselves get to frame how they see their technology fitting into a social world. The second opportunity comes when social elites, usually equipped with significant financial capital, commit to a mass diffusion strategy through which they can imprint new values. However, the cultural frame of analysis also recognizes that technology designs get completed when they are used. In other words, users have an important role in defining how technologies will be used, such that the story of how a technology is intended to be used is incomplete without the story of how it is actually used (Suchman 1987). For example, the particular choices of individual engineers must in turn bear some contextual relationship to the norms of the professional community, the technical possibilities, the demands of the market, public expectations, and feedback from customers.

Teams of professionals with expertise in information technologies build the hardware and software tools for hypermedia campaigns. I presented four political management teams in chapters 2 and 3. DataBank.com and Astroturf-Lobby.org primarily work on tools for the production of political content, while Voting.com and Grassroots Activist.org primarily work on tools for the consumption of political content. In chapter 4, I revealed that despite different political ideologies and business models, the teams had a number of organizational similarities. DataBank.com and Voting.com served any client – lobbyist, politician, or citizen – willing to pay for access to rich data sources. In contrast, Astroturf-Lobby.org and GrassrootsActivist.org served primarily conservative and liberal activists, respectively. DataBank.com and Voting.com teams are opportunistic and for-profit, exploiting any prospect for making money, whereas Astroturf-Lobby.org and GrassrootsActivist.org are altruistic and nonprofit, looking for creative, though often problematic, ways to use information technologies to enhance political representation and public discourse.

DATABANK.COM AND VOTING.COM

Contemporary political campaigns have many powerful informational tools at their disposal. These applications are a significant improvement over traditional focus groups. DataBank.com profited most by selling access to its voter database. Computerization makes it easy for Larry and Dave to assemble data from many sources, including social science surveys, credit card purchases, grocery store sales, health-related expenditures, party registrations, charitable donations, and pollsters. They designed new software and hardware tools to allow them to merge more detailed and varied forms of information. More important, the quality of data has gone from being broadly demographic (information about class, race, gender) and attitudinal (policy preferences, political affiliations) to psychographic (political sophistication, research skills). Today, DataBank.com has basic information on 150 million voters and detailed profiles on four of every ten adults in the United States. Campaigns bought records for a state, congressional district, zip code, census block, city block, household, or individual. Dave and Larry are accustomed to news coverage and professional gossip that runs from admiration for bravery and innovation to condemnation for selling democracy, violating privacy norms, and collaborating with credit card companies. However, they have the gratitude of several U.S. Presidents, many congressional seat-holders, and many more lobbyists. Recently, they have made their service available over the World Wide Web, so that customers can directly access and pay for the data they want.

During the election, they offered a specialized service for political campaigns wishing to test public tolerance for negative campaign ads. Attack ads are risky, but with this new technology, DataBank.com showed different people a range of campaign ads, each with slightly different text, audio, and video stimuli. The campaigns that used the service felt they could better manage their images because they could tell which ads showed strength and leadership without showing bullishness and negativity. DataBank.com's multimedia surveys were more cost-effective and less time-consuming than traditional focus groups, with greater statistical purchase due to purposive samples and smaller costs with digital distribution of video actualities and electronic press kits. In sum, the MessageTester let campaigns strategize around constituent desires, estimate policy preferences, and adjust campaign strategy accordingly. There is a fine balance between going negative and showing strong leadership, and the MessageTester allows candidates to negotiate these perceptions by testing a range of possible messages and airing the one proven to elicit public sympathies.

Voting.com, now defunct, was a complex organization. A company with many generals, the staff was often uncertain about how reporting relationships were organized. Moreover, there was constant tension between the avowed goal of helping democratic discourse and the necessary goal of making money. "The whole business model was designed to get people interested in politics to use the Web site," reported Sarah, one of the company's data experts. "And from that use, they hoped to get personal information for a database that they would sell to marketers." Voting.com's business model attracted investors with the lure "imagine selling guns and ammunition to those who oppose gun control or contraceptives to those who are pro-choice." Troubled by the work she was being asked to do, Sarah quit even as the company was growing:

> I left because it was so distasteful. That campaigns draw out of peo-
> ple their cherished political beliefs and private perspectives on gov-
> erning their country and running their lives – and their children's –
> lives and using that information to hawk products to them.

One particular information technology bothered Sarah most. The OpinionBot was a software program for summarizing and cataloguing media
content. Not only did the company tailor OpinionBot to crawl over Web
sites and through Usenet postings, it was designed to watch over specific
discussion groups set up by clients who want to seed political dialogue
online and then sift through the text, images, audio, and video content.
Moreover, OpinionBot functioned like a push poll, recording names and
addresses as it worked, sending messages asking for financial contributions, volunteer time, or other forms of participation to people who
were predicted to be sympathetic. The OpinionBot also behaved like
an avatar, visiting chat rooms to express an opinion, drop some gossip,
or draw attention to a Web site, without letting the participants know
that the content was generated by a program. "Not only does this allow
like-minded people to meet and share ideas," said Chris in a pitch to
potential clients, "but it captures, analyzes, and reports political views of
OpinionBot users in a format useful for politicians making policy decisions." Since the internet provided such a large sample frame of users,
Voting.com claimed that OpinionBot kept track of the top 20 percent of
the opinion leaders on key issues, anticipating broader changes in public
opinion.

The CandidateShopper was Voting.com's utility for helping people
decide which candidate to support. Users were asked to provide their
political preferences and their home addresses. The Web site coded political candidates for their issue positions and would show users which candidates matched their political preferences most closely. The Web site also
used these profiles to customize news content and political messages to
the user. These profiles were studied and sold to political campaigns.
After the company had folded, Chris met me in one of his more cynical
moods:

> The Voting.com and sites like it have business models based on an
> element of fraud. "Come to us for information that will help you
> be better citizens. We'll help you pull together information, show
> you things, keep you updated, make you a smart voter and make

democracy stronger." At least Amazon.com admits that they have products to sell you. Voting.com had a shell game about what we wanted and why we existed. I don't think the average American internet user understands.

Ultimately, 170,000 people surrendered detailed profiles about their demographics and political preferences in exchange for access to Voting.com's information on candidates. When the company went bankrupt, this data and its e-mail list were some of the assets auctioned off.

GrassrootsActivist.org and Astroturf-Lobby.org

With one of the most detailed relational databases on voter preferences in the country, Astroturf-Lobby.org built complex strategy models for clients that predict legislative or electoral outcomes based on practiced formula for public opinion management. While Voting.com was a business seeking profit, GrassrootsActivist.org is a nonprofit organization seeking creative ways of using technology to improve political discourse. The founders of GrassrootsActivist.org built a "citizen-centric" Web site, and they decided early on to work as a nonprofit organization because they felt that "people would trust a dot-org, but not a dot-com." They became friends while working at e-marketing firms in Silicon Valley and believed strongly in consumer-centric interactive marketing. In their conception, the expectations that consumers have for e-commerce software are the same as the expectations that citizens have for e-politics software. Even though they had the legal tax status of a nonprofit, they thought of themselves as service providers accountable to political information consumers, not as leaders of social movements.

> Morris: The power of the internet is in transferring control to the user. We wanted to give people a real role in political dialogue, and as a commercial entity, the best business model would be one that restricted people's choice and tried to direct them towards established political powers. We knew we could more easily raise money in the private sector, but the urgent opportunity to raise civic participation would be sacrificed.

The project's founders, Morris and Sam, said they never had an agenda. "We want to empower for the sake of empowering, and the foundations called us dreamers." But even though they saw themselves as altruists, they used marketing language from the world of e-commerce: "You let consumers tell you what they want, and you respond with products suited to their demands." Morris and Sam had difficulty raising money from charities and marketing their Web site. "I'm a little disappointed in the site in that it isn't as big as we dreamed that day Sam and I sketched out our plans on a white board. The foundations just weren't accessible."

GrassrootsActivist.org has a tag line of "Building a competitive marketplace for political ideas and leadership," and even though they use the language of the marketplace, they remain critical of the political hypermedia projects that are obviously run for profit. "The hooks you put into your organization or Web site in order to make money compromise the civic goals of any for-profit site. Investor pressure for profit challenges the dedication that staff has to the publicly espoused goals of the site." Part of Mark's solution to the democratic malaise is a tool to help lobbyists from any part of the political spectrum get satisfaction from any legislative body, through a complex system of algorithms in a management software called VoteMover. Their formulae predict success at different stages in a political campaign. By constantly testing the formulae, they made increasingly accurate models of how to win legislative votes. "We do grasstops, not grassroots," joked Mark when he described the algorithms of his VoteMover program.

There are many studies of the difference between insiders' perceptions of their work as noble and outsiders' perceptions of the same work as deviant (Silver and Geller 1978; Jackall 1988; Vaughan 1996; Perrow 1999). The culture of this community of political consultants, consistently formed across these organizations, holds that it is acceptable to sacrifice personal privacy for political transparency. There was dissent from this opinion, dissent that took the form of *pro bono* projects and after-hours hacktivism. But this accepted opinion became institutionalized through technologies that both sought to assemble accurate data on our political preferences and make it *less* necessary for us to be attentive to our political lives. In this way, the trade-off between privacy and transparency became acceptable and couched in the engineering language of information technology development. Across many different kinds of political campaigns the same pattern of decision-making turned deviant behavior to acceptable campaign strategy.

DEVIANCE AND DECISIONS

An important part of political communication is the process by which someone with power makes choices about technology that affect the way the rest of us exercise power and make choices about technology. Chapters 2, 3, and 4 revealed many of the important kinds of political strategy choices made by campaign managers. First, political information technologies distribute political data through market mechanisms. For little cost, a citizen accesses most of the informational tools of the largest, most well-funded and well-staffed political campaigns, and evidence suggests there are many people who take advantage of this accessibility. Second, political hypermedia have been designed by political consultants to make it possible to manipulate data in radically new ways, such as scaling data across geography, time, and units of analysis, while reducing error, including more people in samples, and building sets of psychographic variables and nuanced opinion models. Third, many hypermedia tools have been designed for use on personal computing equipment, so that almost any computer-savvy citizen with access to the internet can manufacture political campaigns with low production costs and significant organizational reach. Fourth, political hypermedia have been designed to project such campaigns across communication networks that link multiple media across the country in seconds.

Hypermedia campaigns constrain individual political choice by denying access to some content and preventing some courses of political engagement or activism. Moreover, hypermedia campaigns establish the routes by which people discover new information, form their opinions, and express their preferences. They are material schemata for our political culture, the exoskeleton that structures the distribution of political content. They have become instantiations of our political culture. Aspects of the technology, their methods of development, the language of the political consultants who designed the technologies, and the processes of political campaigning are essential to understanding changes in our system of political communication.

Many of the design choices made in recent campaigns will pattern the way political information technologies are used for decades to come, and understanding the normative structures and social assumptions of a campaign's designers will have both theoretical implications for our understanding of how culture is built as well as policy implications for the conduct of the social sphere online. Examples of data mining, political redlining, and implanted campaigns can be found before many political hypermedia were designed, but they are a significantly more prominent feature of the contemporary system of political communication. Three particular decisions, taken in most hypermedia campaigns, set precedents for subsequent decisions about how particular applications were to be designed, entrenching seemingly abstract norms in material technology.

The first common decision was to mine personal data, merge information, extract direct and indirect political inferences, and then sell the data. The process of mining data was described in detail in chapters 2 and 3, and the targets of data mining include voters, political candidates, and special interest groups. Data mining is research into the implicit and emergent information within multiple, compiled records that were originally collected for other, explicit purposes. For the most part, Voting.com and DataBank.com sold data about citizens to political campaigns; and for the most part Astroturf-Lobby.org and GrassrootsActivist.org gave away data about political campaigns to citizens. Data mining collates rich supplies of political information, and openly selling such data at competitive prices ensures that most of the supply is not monopolized – it could be bought and sold by powerful political actors and average citizens alike. This is problematic because so few of us have given informed consent to have the information on us collected and merged, much less used to draw political inferences from. The hypermedia campaign may or may not be well funded, but it is rich in mined data.

The second common decision was to redline particular political communities, using mined data, to concentrate campaign resources on only the most likely voters or the people most likely to be susceptible to or inspired by a campaign message. It produces political content only for mass consumption over broadcast technologies, but also for private consumption over networked technologies. But communities of voters are not the only ones who are fed tailored political messages. When lobbyists and grassroots movements are equipped with hypermedia campaigns, elected leaders and their staffs are also susceptible to the same kind of intelligent targeting that shapes the kinds of information coming into their offices. The employees and advisers or Presidents, governors, senators, and representatives are also profiled, so that the flow of information into their offices can be shaped. The hypermedia campaign does not operate on the principles of mass communication; it is built to send narrow messages to communities that have been politically redlined.

The third common decision was to implant campaigns wherever extra political clout was needed. This is problematic because of the range of deceptive practices needed to maintain an implanted campaign. Sometimes constituents are not told that they are being represented and are unaware that they are members of an issue public. Often, the constituents of an implanted campaign are not aware that the leaders of their movement – whom they think of as representatives – are employees of a sympathetic industry lobby group. Other hypermedia campaigns do not appear to have members but promote a message with a viral marketing strategy. Herein lies one of the key differences between mass media and hypermedia campaigns. The mass media political campaign develops policy positions to reflect the opinion of the constituents or leaders it courts; the hypermedia campaign presents appealing features and conceals less appealing features according to the audience being addressed, leaving the true core policy positions strategically ambiguous or sheltered from public view.

THE ORGANIZATION OF NORMATIVE DEVIANCE

The premise of this book is that the role of technology in political communication cannot be understood without taking into account the organizational context in which individual political consultants make design choices that provide both capacity and constraint over how the rest of us participate in this democracy. Why, over the last decade, did political campaign consultants continue to develop political hypermedia that violate privacy norms? As revealed in chapters 2 and 3, we do not always know we are contributing data to a political campaign. We may agree with the campaign agenda while knowing little of its motives and leaders, or we may begin a campaign that competes well against those of larger, well-financed lobby groups. Why did many of these political campaign consultants also develop political hypermedia that reduce the control of candidates, senior campaign mangers, and lobbyist funders over their supporters through tools that actually empowered citizens? Political campaign consultants deviated from public mores about privacy, but normalized this deviance through the socialization of professional conferences. The problematic work of data mining was done through projects with a primary goal of using information technology to improve democracy. Often the problematic work of violating privacy norms was rhetorically described as part of the process of bringing more transparency to political life.

Many designers of political information technologies share norms that might be considered healthy for a vibrant democracy. Their projects seek to bring transparency to politics by providing information about policies and policy alternatives, candidate histories, and records of financial contributions. They make this information immediately available online, through press releases and interactive databases, from entire copies of the Starr Report to campaign budgets reviewed by the Federal Election Commission. Raw political data, such as public opinion data, is competitively priced so that both big budget campaigns and neighborhood activists can purchase the same intelligence. Political information technologies should be convenient and accessible, such that people with internet access can express their opinions, learn about issues that concern them, and contribute to the political groups with whom they find affinity. An important part of making political data marketable is making the data modular, such that the most relevant attributes of a constituency can be easily extracted for analysis. But these values about information technology design – transparency, immediacy, price competitiveness, convenience, and modularity – also lead campaign designers to make a series of design decisions that change the character of democratic deliberation for the worse.

How can the surreptitious activities of these political campaign consultants remain so clandestine? It turns out that their activities are clandestine only during a campaign, and the community has an evolved process for discussing their work more collegially after a campaign. There is little public interest, much less participation or oversight, however, in this evaluative process. Even during each campaign period, journalists cover news stories about the importance of new information technologies to democracy while simultaneously breaking stories about appalling privacy violations. Why don't companies expose each other's abuses if doing so might help their competitive advantage during a campaign? It turns out that there are occasional acts of whistle-blowing, but understanding the implications of how political hypermedia are designed is as complex as understanding campaign finance reform. It turns out that these ethical violations are socially organized: During a campaign, there is an *external* organizational process for evaluating the possible consequences of design options that managers have available. After a campaign, there is an *internal* professional process for evaluating the consequences of managers' ultimate design decisions.

It would be intellectually lazy to say that the decisions to mine data, to redline key political communities, and then to narrowcast information were a hazard of groupthink or were taken because of innate properties of technologies such as the internet. The first is organizationally deterministic, while the second is technologically deterministic, and either conclusion wrongly absolves agency and responsibility for key decisions in campaign management. The evidence in chapters 2 and 3 illustrates clearly that it was a sequence of decisions – individual and collective – that deliberately and specifically changed the way political content was produced and consumed.

Over the course of observing many different kinds of contemporary political campaigns, such as those organized by DataBank.com, Astroturf-Lobby.org, Voting.com, and GrassrootsActivist.org, it becomes clear that there is a pattern to the way campaign decisions are made to justify campaign strategies that even many campaign managers consider unethical. This process cycles between informal signals that inappropriate campaign strategies are being formed and official recognition that such strategies are necessary.

During the initial stages of strategy development, the low-level designers, coders, and data miners – described in chapter 4 as coding generals – expressed reluctance to design tools that violate privacy norms. When campaign managers pushed designers to build these kinds of hypermedia tools, staff reacted ambiguously and were neither enthusiastic nor critical. Even when designers expressed their reluctance to pursue problematic campaign strategies, they did so with peers, and their reservations were only weakly signaled to senior managers. From the vantage point of campaign managers, it was difficult to measure the significance of the normative violation against the potential benefit to the campaign. Persistent signals that an aspect of campaign strategy was unethical eventually triggered acknowledgment from a senior campaign manager, but the response was that the long-term goals of informational transparency and campaign victory were more important than the immediate concern about an unethical political strategy. Whatever the nature of the reservation, it was rhetorically reframed as irrelevant (the designer was wrong about its implications) or a casualty of the campaign's broader goal (a necessary deviation). This reframing was done while implementing the problematic strategy.

Once the strategy to mine data, redline communities, or narrowcast political information was in place, campaign managers rarely forgot about the ethical reservations expressed during the development of campaign strategy. As the campaign progressed, any advantage brought by a deviant strategy was normatively weighed against the severity of privacy violations. The grievances were reframed, but this time with evidence about the benefit to the campaign. If the campaign was doing well, managers described the ethical concern as misplaced and naïve, disqualifying it as wrong. Externally, successful political managers are invited to lecture others on innovative tactics, so deviant strategy is validated. In this way, a normatively problematic campaign strategy becomes an acceptable risk. Once the campaign is over, senior managers make an official, internal statement that the violation is worthwhile. Campaign managers begin discussing the strategy in conference panels, and the rest of the campaign management community learns that a normatively suspicious strategy worked for a normatively noble goal. In this sense, the strategy gets "laundered" because open debate about the problematic strategy is conducted during an industry conference after the campaign, with peers. These industry conferences are semi-public in that managers lecture or gossip freely, but there is a collective understanding that no one will be publicly chastised. The candidates, or campaign sponsors, are the bosses. Campaign strategy is secret while the campaign is on and is discussed publicly only after the fact. As with Vaughn's study of NASA engineers:

> Unfavorable information is lost, not by malicious intent, pur-
> poseful concealment, or reluctance to say something superiors
> do not want to hear (all psychological in origin), but as a col-
> lective and systematic consequence of organizational structure and
> roles: people deliberately do not seek out unfavorable information.
>
> (Vaughan 1998, p. 273)

Political campaign managers have their own analytical frames, which allow them to neglect ethical norms that conflict with commitments to more immediate political objectives. Hypermedia campaign strategy is a collective project: decentralized and distributed; creative, collaborative, and competitive; developed in an system of epistemic heterarchy; structured by a process of normalizing deviance. Most important, it is the source of technical and organizational changes in the way we learn about politics and communicate our preferences, changes that are made manifest in new capacities and constraints on us as citizens.

CITIZENSHIP IN THE DIGITAL DEMOCRACY

Theorists such as Tarde, Habermas, and Anderson have helped to define a healthy public sphere, a space where people exchange ideas and challenge one another's opinions. First, it requires the fact of shared text, regularly published and generally accessible; citizens must be confident that the text is indeed shared across the polity so that everyone has access to the same quality of information. Second, it requires the act of conversation, through which we constitute the public sphere when we discuss the affairs of state and share the floor without discrimination. For practical reasons, we agree to mediating institutions, such as pollsters and newspaper editors, who assist the act of conversation by helping to distill opinion and present distinct, coherent policy options. Third, it requires the space for action: legislatures, courts, voting booths, and places of administration where decisions are made and enacted (Tarde 1898; Anderson 1991; Habermas 1991; Katz 1992). The more of these spheres the better, says Calhoun (1998), so that different people can communicate their needs to one another.

Political life in the digital democracy has some of these attributes. But in redlining some constituents and communities and then narrowcasting political content, hypermedia campaigns diminish the amount of shared text in the public sphere. Even though new media technologies have diffused quickly, there are still significant portions of the population either without the technology or without the informational skills to participate in the public sphere online. Those with the technology and skill set have access to vast quantities of political information, of varying quality. They join political chat groups, start their own hypermedia campaigns, and sign up for listservs. Sometimes this online political communication is imbued with few of the race, class, and gender status cues that can encumber or enrich political interaction offline. The internet mediates communication, but as we become more familiar with the technology, we learn to make our own editorial choices about political content. Indeed, it is easy to find unedited political information if need be; entire speeches, drafts of legislation, financial contributions, voting history, and other records are all there for those interested in deep research. People who want to do their own recount of the 2000 election can even view online images of ballots cast (and miscast) in key Florida districts. The internet is only nominally a space for action in the sense that hacktivists – hackers with a political agenda – do their work online. Only the most rabid pundits have imagined that political life online would succeed political life offline, but we are still left with the broad question, similar to the interesting query taken up by Merton and Lazarsfeld fifty years ago. What are the implications of these significant new communications media for the health of the public sphere?

The political content produced by individual citizens is particularized. A million people may view an official party Web site, imagining that the text is shared (as Tarde would hope), but they do so in physical isolation from each other, without knowing that the text is almost exclusively theirs and something of their own creation. At least with the presentation of political content on the television, the viewer knew that everybody else was seeing the same thing. The issue publics that grassroots activists created with data and tools from DataBank.com and GrassrootsActivist.org allowed members to learn a lot about each other's grievances. Members built empathy and participated in forming campaign strategy. In contrast, the issue publics that lobbyists created with data and tools from Voting.com and Astroturf-Lobby.com tended to prevent members from learning much about each other, or even from learning of their membership. These members were deliberately chosen and channeled as needed. In this sense, political hypermedia are designed to organize political information for us, on the basis of either our consciously surrendered preferences or inferred preferences from records about our habits. The schematizing then gets done for us, whether we are political leaders or average voters, and both congressional leaders and citizens can be manipulated by hypermedia campaigns with bad intentions.

THIN, SHADOW, AND PRIVATIZED CITIZENSHIP

The production of political content through hypermedia technologies is a process of tailoring content not for mass consumption but for private consumption. Knowing what we now know about how contemporary political campaigns are organized, what might we theorize as the significant impact on democracy? Lupia (1998) asks the sensible question about information and citizenship: Can citizens learn what they really need to know? Every citizen cannot know the details of every policy option, and a close look at the history of deliberation suggests that it is always a small community of people who learn about policy options and engage in debate. Public discourse is rarely egalitarian, and often a truly public discussion involves a large group of wildly divergent interests, rarely civil and rarely productive enough to earn the label of deliberative democracy. Thus, as Schudson (1998) points out, our vision of democratic ideals lags behind our changing practices. The United States has actually had several different kinds of citizens, each with different informational needs. For the Founding Fathers, a citizen was a property-owning white male, imbued with the natural virtues of leadership and the *noblesse oblige* to govern over poorly informed populations. The citizen of massive nineteenth-century political parties was not especially informed but voted with the expectation that party patronage networks would distribute the resources of government-led economic development. Beginning in the twentieth century, citizenship was both an obligation to vote at a polling station and an assertion of rights in the courthouse. With the rise of political hypermedia, the information-based model of citizenship assumed that voters are willing and able to process vast amounts of information simply because this information is accessible online. This analysis of hypermedia campaigns helps us to move beyond the model of individually informed citizens. But to move beyond the model of informed citizen we must also move beyond the analytical frame of mass media political communication, and the theories about hypermedia campaigns developed here suggest that we also need to evaluate the meaning of citizenship in contemporary political life.

First, citizenship roles are thinned by hypermedia technology that remove the burden of being informed while expressing political opinion. In fact, the technology is designed to give prominence to selected voices, favoring the opinionated over the informed by giving the former representation through opportunities to express outrage. The metaphor of *thin citizenship* is borrowed from the computer science jargon for "thin clients": computers that have very little resident software but remain connected to a large memory resource in which all the organization's software and documents are archived. In the same way, political hypermedia are designed for thin citizenship, a role that does not require individuals to have their own active, engaged political memory because they can quickly respond to poll questions that present simplified policy options. The thin citizen can respond quickly to political urges and need not spend significant amounts of time contemplating political matters.

Thin citizens do not need to expend much interpretive labor in their political lives, because they use information technologies to demark political content they want in their diet. They choose which editors and which issues take priority and minimize their exposure to random or challenging information. "This is not a democracy," said Rob Arena, from the Dole 1996 campaign. "These people do not think about this stuff 24 hours a day, seven days a week. They want to have a life. They want to go out. They want to go out to movies, hang with their friends, and go home. They don't want to spend Friday night sitting in front of a computer screen figuring out George Bush's Social Security policy" (Jagoda 2000, 96). The thin citizen participates in five-minute protests through the computer, by signing electronic petitions forwarded by friends and family, for example. Political hypermedia have been designed to permit, and promote, thinned citizenship roles.

Deliberately thinned citizenship makes it difficult to proscribe broad institutional means of servicing individual grievances. Indeed, since democratic governments are designed to redress collective grievances, thinning citizenship leaves fewer generalizable cues and minimal moral benchmarks. Political hypermedia are designed to deny universal, collective needs and to accept diverse individual needs. Moreover, the internet allows a campaign to measure and weight levels of political commitment, especially fractional levels of support that never translate into financial contributions or voter commitment:

> Mark: There's a big difference between the person who casually cares about the environment but does little, the person who cares enough to write a $100 check but forgets about it the rest of the time, and the person who goes to the local chapter meetings and does beach cleanup in the summer.

The first person might respond to a polling question about the environment as a political priority, but do little in her or his own life for the environment. The second person might contribute financially to an environmental cause, but invest no personal time in joining a civic group. The third is the traditional activist, the self-motivated participant that a civic group can count on. However, this latter type of person is rare, so hypermedia campaigns make the best of fractional support. For example, during the 2000 campaigns, the Sierra Club was particularly excited about getting more "light greens" through its internet strategies. These were new members who passionately wanted to preserve a local species but did not think of themselves as environmentalists or subscribe to a larger environmentalist agenda. The Sierra Club found these people through a hypermedia campaign.

The thin citizen values the internet for quick access to information and the easy opportunity to register opinions on a political Web site. The internet allows citizens to manage their distance from political issues. Candidates must remain ideologically competitive, and they use hypermedia to present different and sometimes conflicting ideological packages to different communities or supporters. The thin polity may have an immense total supply of information that is only sparingly shared among citizens. Information is unevenly distributed among communities, except for citizens with good search skills or those who can hire consultants with good information management skills. Conversely, a thick public sphere would have consistent, rich sources of political information in which all citizens can be immersed.

While political hypermedia can be used by social movements to organize or by organizations to build a social movement, hypermedia can also be used to form more thinly veiled forms of issue publics: small groups of like-minded people specifically interested in advocacy more than expanded membership. One of the peculiar phenomena of the recent campaign are the IRS-classified 527s, charities that accept money and spend it on behalf of a candidate or partisan issue but have no palpable membership. The corollary to a social contract with thinning citizenship responsibilities, however, is that some way of collating and anticipating public opinion is necessary. Thin citizens irregularly connect to contribute to a policy discourse, and when they do, it is for a brief, considered contribution on a selected issue. The rest of his or her formal contribution is made by his or her digital shadow.

Whereas the exercise of thin citizenship is at least a direct and deliberate activity, there is an indirect expression of citizen preferences through our *data shadow*. I described the new mechanisms of representation that work in hypermedia campaigns, a system of shadow citizenship in which lobbyists represent public interests but rely on our data shadows to model and predict our opinions. Whereas public opinion was once bluntly measured with polls, today it is modeled and predicted with surprising accuracy but not always with our informed consent. As we go about the business of our lives, we leave a data trail that is increasingly referenced by political actors, data from which our individual political preferences are extrapolated.

As this book has explained, we now have the power to have our interests represented without behaving as a traditional citizenry. Data profiles, some of which we generate knowingly and some of which is collected without our informed consent, are our true representatives and, in fact, what are truly represented. "Nothing is more dangerous than the influence of private interests on public affairs," wrote Rousseau in Book III of the *Social Contract*. Through active engagement in a political community, the citizen evolves "a second life, a moral life, which is not his sole possession, but whose reality depends on the continued existence of his fellow-citizens and of their association." Political hypermedia create this second life for us, and it is not our possession. It is a silhouette of our political selves, composed of raw data about how we think and act in our private worlds.

In their study of popular culture systems, Horkheimer and Adorno (1972) concluded that "individuals have ceased to be themselves and are now merely centers where the general tendencies meet" (p. 155). This might have been true for the mass media systems they were observing, but internet systems are designed to track and locate much more specific tendencies. Calhoun (1998) echoed this by later arguing that electronic technology may do more to foster "categorical identities" than complex personal relations. The identities, however, are not quite as categorical as he predicted. First, the categories into which we are put as citizens are ideational, not just demographic, and so complex and subtle as to be epistemologically distinct from the bivariate polling categories used before hypermedia campaigns. In other words, the traditional polling sciences were founded on a theory that we can know something about a person based on direct inferences from a few key demographic labels. In contrast, the hypermedia campaign relies on both direct and indirect inference and constructs highly nuanced categories of constituents.

> Larry: The American public has outsourced their democracy to a class and elite that is active in politics: politicians, members of the media, think tanks, and political consultants. The people renew this contract every two years for a third of the Senate, and every four years for the President.

Between these formal elections, political leaders and lobbyists consult with our digital shadows. The technical solution provided by the e-politics community, arrived at during conferences about democracy and new technologies and through campaign work, was to direct as much political discourse as possible through the new tools of political hypermedia. The problem with the democratic institutions set up by the social contract is that the parties to the contract – the governed and the governing – did not have suitable tools for supervising compliance.

The data shadow follows us almost everywhere. We are not always aware of its appearance, but others can observe our silhouette. The data shadow has become an important political actor. It is the silhouette created by our daily activities, and it is one of the parties to the new digitized social contract. Some people have more crisply defined data shadows, depending on how many political hypermedia they interact with on a regular basis. Credit card purchases, voter registration records, polling data, magazine subscriptions, and the other resources identified in chapter 3 help to create the data shadow. Increasingly, our data shadows represent us in political discourse. Political candidates and organizations also cast data shadows.

Today we cannot help but create a data shadow. So many hyperme-dia technologies get mined for data, even those not expressly designed to collect political information, that our data shadows inevitably gener-ate political information. Political lives are constructed from the bytes we leave behind us, for use by a range of political actors who claim to represent us, regardless of whether we consider them legitimate. For most citizens, voting is an opportunity for political expression with few barriers or costs of participation. The internet significantly lowers the barriers to entry and costs of participation for a wide range of other political activities. Hypermedia campaigns give very thin citizenship roles to their members and constituents.

In a grassroots campaign, members of a social movement select politicians and lobbyists as representatives. The purpose of a mass media electoral campaign is to offer political content that helps citizens choose politicians. In contrast, in an implanted campaign, lobbyists and politicians select voters to represent them. Whether voters do so unconsciously with their data shadows, consciously but rarely as thin citizens, or as active information consumers depends on the individual's commitment to participating in the marketplace of political ideas. Hypermedia make it possible for lobbyists to reverse these roles. The purpose of a hypermedia campaign is to have lobbyists and politicians choose voters.

Political hypermedia collect more data on voters and candidates. They reach a growing number of people and subsume television-based politics by redesigning the public's expectations of television. Political television ads themselves must now call to online identities. Today's political television ads must identify a Web site for more information or must be produced and designed by intelligent voter data collected over hypermedia. Not only do many political television ads take on the aesthetic of hypermedia art, but they are written using intelligence gathered by hypermedia campaign, are narrowcast to particular television markets (as dictated by this intelligence), and are then stored online for easy access at other points in the campaign.

What is meaningfully represented in contemporary political institutions is not you but your data shadow, the political personality deduced from data about you. Sometimes your opinion diverges from what statically derived models say your opinion is, and some of us know how to manage our data shadows while others do not. Some of us know what our data shadow looks like, while others do not. However, the data that constitutes our political personalities, including explicit citizenship acts and the implicit political meanings of consumer behavior, are bought and sold in the market. In this sense, hypermedia campaigns have "privatized citizenship."

Third, by *privatized citizenship*, I mean that informational duties and responsibilities once provided by the state are commodified and provided by independent businesses, that the deliberative and decision-making environments of citizens engaged by political hypermedia are individualized and intimate. The incentive to participate is not that of public service but relief from private wrongs, as framed by hypermedia campaigns. Political hypermedia are designed to move democratic conduct from the public sphere of rallies, town hall meetings, newspaper editorials, and coffee shop debates to the private sphere of screens, key strokes, and highly personalized news services. For campaign managers and policymakers, commercial data about voter preferences make it easier to evaluate and push both public and individual sentiments. I argue that political hypermedia are deliberately designed to privatize in multiple senses of the word: to move the logistics of citizenship from the public to the private sector, into the private world of home and work space, where individuals act more out of private discontent on select issues than out of public duty for collective welfare.

In the late 1990s, many companies discovered the value of building online communities within their consumer bases. They found that word-of-mouth marketing, which relied on personal networks of family and friends, provided valuable conduits for information about products and services. These consumption communities of political actors, icons, and arguments are structured like those subcultures of e-commerce. Rather than product or service loyalty as the primary basis for affiliation, loyalty to the issue position or candidate is the primary basis for affiliation (Rheingold 1993; Canter and Siegel 1994; Hagel et al. 1997; Rosen 2000). Deliberately seeding such communities had a number of advantages to companies. They tracked customer opinion, made customers more loyal through community bonding, increased sales, reduced marketing costs, and encouraged brand loyalty (Wenger 1998; Brown 2000). Seeding political consumer communities is no different in this regard. Nevertheless, in the hypermedia campaigns studied here, consuming political information exclusively through hypermedia led to fragmented perceptions, individualized media experiences, and fewer random encounters with new, unfiltered information. To meet the needs of the privatized citizen, the political consulting industry imagines a market for political information and puts the consumer at the beginning of the design process of political hypermedia.

Hypermedia campaigns allow us to be thinly engaged, allow political actors to construct constituencies based on our data shadows, and, when we choose to be engaged, make the exercise of engagement more private than it was in mass media campaigns. There are two contradictions in how the hypermedia campaign has been presented to the public by political consultants. The first is the *contradiction of hypermedia choice*. On the one hand, we are offered tools that give us the capacity to make better decisions, while at the same time so much of the data gathered about us constrains our future opportunities to learn political information on our own or constrains our random exposure to new political information. Hypermedia make this structured form of choice seem palatable through the empowerment rhetoric of digital democracy. The second is the *contradiction of surveillance as franchise*. Hypermedia campaigns collect immense amounts of data on our habits and preferences, often in the name of making democracy more direct through communication technology. In the process of evaluating their decisions to mine data, redline certain communities of constituents, and narrowcast particular messages, campaign managers often argued that surveillance was the best way to represent a constituent or member fairly. Sometimes this membership is part of an endogenously formed social movement with a leadership that collects intelligence on its constituents, but more often this membership is an exogenously formed social movement with an implanted campaign structure. The membership is really a small community of lobbyists who have proactively assembled data on a large number of like-minded yet disconnected people. This disconnected population has little collective consciousness and has not experienced the meaningful cognitive liberation that comes from being aware that other members share grievances (McAdam 1982).

POLITICAL SCHEMATA RATIONALIZED IN CODE

From the outside, campaign politics may seem wild and unpredictable. However, the hypermedia campaign brings an increasing amount of rationality and structure to the battles on our political landscape. Several of the new media working groups within DataBank.com and Astroturf-Lobby.org used the language of technology to describe the structure of political communication in a democratic political system. For the engineers of political hypermedia, the technological rationale became the rationale behind democracy itself, to echo Horkheimer and Adorno:

> It has made the technology of the culture industry no more than the achievement of standardisation and mass production, sacrificing whatever involved a distinction between the logic of the work and

that of the social system. This is the result not of a law of movement in technology as such but of its function in today's economy.... No machinery of rejoinder has been devised, and private broadcasters are denied any freedom.

(Horkheimer and Adorno 1972, 121–122)

But whereas the mass culture industry was geared to standardized content production, this industry was geared toward particularized content production. Moreover, whereas Horkheimer and Adorno mourned that the technical system of culture industries broadcast monotony and allowed no "machinery of rejoinder," the political hypermedia were designed specifically as a mechanism of rejoinder, with different capacities and constraints. When the campaign teams of DataBank.com and Astroturf-Lobby.org met to organize a political campaign, they rationalized political life with a shared understanding of how political communication is structured.

Campaigns often have an instrumentalist view of purposive and rational action in the public sphere and they impute reasoning, if not reasonable, voters. Consequently, one aspect of the rationality of hypermedia campaigns is not simply that providing information will help to win public approval, but that a public can be constructed for the purposes of the campaign. Weber would not be surprised to find rationalization in political life, a process defined both by scientific public policy-making, political campaigns equipped with tools for systematic data analysis, and a professional cohort of consultants who build the instruments of political rationality. Habermas – and Marcuse – interpret Weber's concept of purposive-rational action not just as a means of transforming old social institutions but as a potential form of political domination:

> The controlled translation of technical into practical knowledge and thus the scientifically guided rationalization of political power is possible. Political rationalization occurs through the enlightenment of political will, correlated with instruction about its technical potential. (Habermas 1970, 80)

But what does it actually mean to "rationalize" politics? When campaign staffs discuss their work, they share an understanding of order in politics, an order they restructure – in Gidden's sense – with their work. Of course their work is often about contingency planning and recovering from political intrigue and disasters. But underlying the specific dynamics of an issue area is a shared understanding about the "rationality" of political communication. In this way, the technical language used in specific project meetings became a system for organizing cultural content for the rest of us.

Media have often been treated as having a rational social function. For example, Lazarsfeld and Merton (1948) described mass media as having three functions: status conferral, enforcement of social norms, and the "narcotizing dysfunction." Whereas exposure through mass media tends to confer status on individuals, exposure through political hypermedia tends to confer status on issues. Political hypermedia do not allow political candidates to legitimize their status the way mass media do: Users can question and research political statements over the internet in a way they are not able to do when they see the same statements made over television. Second, the pattern of norm enforcement differs. Both mass and hypermedia help to close the gap between private attitudes and public morality, but the exercise of leadership in the political/moral realm is easier through mass media, which allows one leader's voice to permeate through to all citizens. Through hypermedia, political and moral opinions have many sources and many small audiences. The room for declarative public leadership is smaller. In contrast, because political hypermedia improve social memory and recollection, campaigns are more likely to expose corrupt or immoral practices of their competitors. Since hypermedia polling makes the refined measure of opinion possible, political and moral leadership is more likely to come from citizens expressing outrage at the conduct of individual leaders than from politicians taking moral positions. Whereas it used to be up to journalists to bring normative deviations to the public's view, private citizens can now conduct the same research themselves. Third, the narcotizing dysfunction is the application of mass media's discursive influence for either special interests or to keep the people politically apathetic and inert. Here the contrast is more marked, as political hypermedia are deliberately designed to activate issue publics, whereas mass media are designed to convert our political energies from active participation into passive knowledge.

Some campaigns thought a particular innovation would help their candidate or issue campaign defeat opponents. Others acted altruistically, thinking it would help their specific campaign but also improve the quality and quantity of political deliberation. Still others acted reluctantly, preferring to imitate technologies and techniques only when necessary to keep up with opponents. Whereas the founders of Voting.com and DataBank.com saw opportunities to make money selling information and tools to political parties and candidates' campaigns, the founders of Astroturf-Lobby.org and GrassrootsActivist.org started nonprofit organizations to provide information and tools to citizens, activists, and lobbyists. Cut another way, DataBank.com and Astroturf-Lobby.com offered tools that help campaigns and leaders to produce and transmit political messages, whereas Voting.com and Grassroots-Activist.org offered tools to help citizens – called "political information consumers" – understand and organize political information.

Regularized political communication is no longer an elite, exclusive act. This is not just a shift in political communication patterns or in the effect of media. It is an important evolution in the structure of political culture: scientific rationalization of the process of manufacturing public opinion; evolution in the structure and behavior of large political campaign organizations; and the ascendancy of small campaign organizations. To evaluate these structural shifts, we can revisit the rubric of political campaign managers themselves and build theory around their definitions of the components of political communication systems: objects, events, processes, and memory.

Political culture has classically been described in terms of a collection of "objects," such as legislative bodies, bills and acts, politicians, interest groups, corporations, parties, and the media. Of course, citizens themselves are objects when they are active in the public sphere (Almond and Verba 1963). As political objects, citizens use communications media, especially hypermedia, to manage not only organizational logistics, but also their own identities. Through the hypermedia campaign, all of these actors present different aspects of their characters to each other. For example, the mass media political communication strategy of the National Rifle Association promoted a singular identity of the "NRA," but its current hypermedia campaigns promote "MyNRA." Such a Web site provides general news, including sports and stock quotes, membership news, and researched content skillfully excusing gun-related violence. Redlining forces different groupings of objects, such that lobbyists can demark which citizens will be suitable activists and which political opinion leaders or political leaders will be sensitive to perturbation. There are many more competing actors, each with powerful communication tools. These actors can cultivate different aspects of their political personalities, preparing character attributes and policy positions for ever more narrowly defined communities. It is not only that the process of managing public opinion is being performed by new actors but that the process of managing public opinion is fundamentally different. Traditional polling tools are blunt instruments compared with the tools of hypermedia campaigns. It is still possible for political elites to manipulate public opinion, so non-elites have access to the same tools of manipulation, and the tools needed to expose the manipulation. Campaigns are more logistically agile and more often rely on their user base to provide content for an agenda that has already been composed in some way.

In mass media campaigns, a political event is both spatially and temporally specific. The place and date of the event is well advertised and sometimes recorded for later use by the campaign or by journalists. Now the technology to record and distribute content about events is itself distributed such that nontraditional actors can record events from their own point of view and provide that content online, making it accessible anywhere, anytime. Not only do political events in the hypermedia campaign lose their territorial and temporal boundaries, not only are events themselves mobile, but political events are multisited. Virtual participation technologies make it possible to extend the site of political events well beyond the physical stage built by the campaign. It is still something of a staged event, because the campaign does as much as possible to manage the conditions of those participating virtually. In this very concrete sense, political events can have much more complex organizational logistics in the hypermedia campaign. An election event, a state of the union speech, or a court decision can provide a very focused target for all participants. In this way, the campaign was an organization bounded by specific goals, and once these goals were met, the campaigns were dissolved.

Objects and events, however, are no longer the most important structural features of political communication. Campaigns no longer dissolve; they evolve along with their technical capacities, where defining and redefining both goals and technologies is a perpetual process. Through hypermedia, there are often multiple sources of records about the event itself, records that are widely available and play an important part in defining our collective memory. Representation is no longer a singular event occurring in the act of electing a representative on election day but a continuous process of feeding data, sometimes unwittingly, to organizations that claim to represent us. This flow of data to political representatives is greatly accelerated over the polling techniques of the mass media campaign. As discussed in chapters 2 and 3, the process of political campaigning co-opts volunteer resources and social networks.

Some political campaigns exist to write or rewrite our social memory of actors, events, or processes. This can be done by preserving or destroying content or making it more or less accessible, now and in the future. Traditional campaigns are about making facts – or a particular set of facts generated by the campaign's experts – available to the public. Today, memory campaigns are numerous, especially those seeking to make "simple facts" available. Thus, the Starr Report is available; campaign financing decisions are available; voting histories are available. We can remember more about political figures' pasts, and campaigns battle for these memories just as hard as traditional mass media campaigns used to battle to spin today's news. Online, we find doctored photos of young Senator Kerry going to radical antiwar protests and doctored documents about young President Bush going AWOL from National Guard service. Whether they are consulted by the public is an important question; but the clarity and corruption of political memory is an important new feature of our political culture.

Indeed, there are multiple memories, digitally etched. People store different perspectives on the same events. Singular memory streams of information no longer dominate the narrative of political events. There are also multiple ways to retrieve information about the same objects, processes, and events in political life. The political memory is neither temporally nor spatially bounded. The mass media political campaign had the advantage of working with technologies that did not allow individuals easily to recall cultural content from years gone by. Newspapers and television are archived in some ways, but the social memory for political character and lobbyist positioning was relatively short. Now our political memories are digitally preserved; not geographically fixed in one city or one archive, they are accessible around the country if not around the world. Digital materials may be sited on specific hard drives, but they have a global span (Sassen 2004). The thin citizen may not know all of the prominent figures on the political landscape but can easily access archives, histories of financial backers, texts of speeches, legislative mistakes, and even inconsistencies in campaign messages.

RANDOMNESS AND DISENGAGEMENT IN THE PUBLIC SPHERE

In rationalizing political communication through hypermedia technologies, we diminish our exposure to random political content, and it becomes increasingly difficult to disengage from the public sphere.

Less of the information circulating in the public sphere gets randomly distributed, and ever more private data are read for political implications. Social movements arise as individuals encounter new information that inspires their activism. The public sphere itself is predicated on the notion that all issues are being debated. Not every person is following every important political issue, but altogether, we hope that someone somewhere is debating each possible issue. Of course, everyone thinks their favorite issues are important. The public sphere works when we assume that if an issue is urgent, it will come to attention deliberately through friends and family or randomly through an accidental encounter with an unusual source or personal experience. More than that, we have *faith* that our political communication system will bring the truly outrageous issues to our attention.

Traditionally, a large portion of the political information we had digested each day was through random encounters with newspaper headlines and other opinions, but political hypermedia are designed to remove the risk of random exposure to political content from our lives. Hypermedia provide political content in sequence, in context, in patterns determined either by the set criterion of users or by campaign managers. Hypermedia campaigns are designed to present information in a largely unmediated form or in a form that is mediated by the citizen's own filtering preferences. These privatized public spheres are self-selected, nonrandom groups of people deliberately producing and consuming political content. In chapter 3 the process of political redlining was exposed. Redlining referred to the campaign practice of declining to serve a community if it was not part of a sensitive electoral district or declining to serve individuals if they are perceived to be less sensitive to the political issue. In other words, if a community is not in a politician's service area, it is not targeted by a hypermedia campaign, and if a person is not an engaged citizen likely to feel sympathetic – a suspected nonvoter – he or she is not targeted by a hypermedia campaign.

It is not a truism to say that all information is political, because a significant amount of the personal information about us now feeds both direct and indirect inferences about our political opinions. However, the way the new technology is designed, citizens have little choice over the lobbyists who claim to represent them. Our data shadow becomes a constituent of campaigns we know little about. Before political hypermedia, the citizen could choose to leave a political district or to disengage from the consumption of political content. But today, even if you want to disengage from political life – that is, stop consuming political content – turning off the television is no longer enough. You would have to stop using credit cards, the postal service, e-mail, the internet, and the telephone, and you would have to stop buying newspapers, books, and magazines. To disengage from the politics of health care or energy, for instance, you would have to stop buying medicine and fuel. It is almost impossible to stop casting a data shadow.

Distributing political information through the market requires that there be different qualities of information available, at different price points. Richer campaigns purchase higher quality political information or better informational services. Individuals purchase technologies that guard against surveyors calling on the telephone or spyware being installed on the home computer. Therefore, even though the market is now structured to allow the individual political information consumer to shop for more nuanced policy and representative options, citizens need the research skills to do so smartly. Even with research skills, customizing political content diminishes exposure to random news stories or life encounters that help to build empathy.

The healthy public sphere requires shared text, the act of conversation, and organizational room for political action. However, the healthy public sphere should also be defined by some degree of random exposure to new people and ideas. It is this random interaction that allows us to build empathy with the unfamiliar grievances and predicaments that people in other communities have. How can we share information, converse, and act, while sensibly distributing these activities in a socially equitable way, and while preserving peoples' right to manage their own data or disengage, if they so desire?

POLICY AND PROCESS FOR THE HEALTHY
DIGITAL DEMOCRACY

How can we build a safe digital democracy, with an information technology infrastructure that both brings transparency to political institutions and respects individual privacy? Currently, the supply and demand for political information is organized under an open market system with little public oversight. More important, with the spread of hypermedia campaigns and the thriving market in political data, the opportunity to make collective decisions about the architecture of political hypermedia is passing. The answer, in part, is that some kind of deliberate public oversight needs to be extended to cover the use of information technologies in political campaigning. There are few reporting practices for a particular campaign's information management practices. There is no whistle-blowing protection. Political campaigns are required to submit their financing records, and they should be required to submit details about their use of hypermedia technologies relying on voter data.

What would a safe digital democracy look like? To answer, we must refer both to the condition of individual privacy rights and to the condition of the public sphere. Individual privacy rights in the United States could be better protected with a stronger directive from government, one that would guarantee control over personal information as a right, governmentally enforced. Both private firms and government agencies should be required to obtain the full and unambiguous consent of citizens before data mining, and citizens should be able to track the use of information about them – their data shadows – to see whether and how they have been redlined. The benefits of public policy oversight include legal coherence, citizen and consumer confidence (since so much consumer information now has political implications), and a clear allocation of responsibility to political campaign managers. In theory, political campaigns would benefit from more public trust and more accurate information from those who opt in and agree to contribute information to the public sphere.

The prime benefits of such a system would accrue to citizens. We would reserve the right to choose to participate in the collection and aggregation of political data about them, increasingly the ability to control personal information. A policy regime could provide both public education and legal enforcement. Of course, there are number of costs to this kind of policy oversight. Politicians and policymakers would lose information about those who do not wish to provide data, and political campaigns would have to bear the financial cost of complying and managing consent. For some consulting and data management firms, there would be lost business opportunities, as any restriction on the aggregation and trade of political data is a threat to profit.

There are risks to such a scheme, and publicly evaluating both the benefits and risks should be the first step in a policy regime that extends into the area of political campaigning. If citizens opt in and agree to share their information, should they have the right to access their data and see how that data are being used? What kinds of liability and legal consequences should there be for privacy violations? There are many questions about what such public oversight might mean for the political process, but it is clear that we must now begin to debate the advantages of different models of public oversight.

In terms of the public sphere, we should begin to imagine ways of turning the abstracted principles of ideal public sphere institutions into concrete forms of political organization. Recall that we needed shared text, the act of conversation, and the space for action. It should be possible to promote public collections of information about candidates for office, public policy options, and issue-specific campaigns lobbying government. Many public agencies such as the FEC and FCC have accessible Website content, and agencies such as these should be given the financial support necessary to quickly turn informational accounts from political campaigns into publicly accessible information. We developed straightforward rules for local campaign behavior about posting signs in yards. Why not also create standards for behavior of hypermedia campaigns with respect to personal data?

Like many other arenas in which public policy is warranted, industry "self-regulation" has not met, and is not likely ever to meet, our expectations for a safe digital democracy (Starke-Meyerring et al. 2004). Regardless of the size and ideology of the political actor, computing technologies have taken an ever more important role in campaigning. The sacrifice of individual privacy for democratic transparency has been a discernible goal of the political consulting industry. This sacrifice was openly negotiated in public conferences by political campaign managers with expertise in information technology and was methodically implemented across different campaign projects of different sizes and ideologies.

Evidence suggests that it was a careerist congressman looking for opportunities to serve constituents who turned the post office from a patronage network to a public service (Kernell and McDonald 1999). Could the same be done for political hypermedia? The public is largely uninformed and disinterested in how political information technologies are used by political campaigns. It is unlikely that the public wants its information collected and shared in such a way. Survey research consistently shows that people are very concerned about maintaining their privacy rights but understand very little about how those rights get violated on a daily basis. We are very concerned that information about us might fall into the wrong hands. Perhaps we should not expect everyone to understand all of the mechanics of cookies, spiders, and spyware technologies that capture information about us, since a surprisingly small portion of internet users consciously manage their browser security settings (Rainie 2000).

Perhaps we should not be surprised that some campaign managers have inscrutable practices, but we should still be surprised that the practices are organizationally managed and that we, the public, share in providing a context of disinterest. We can change this to a context of interest. The choices of campaign managers were made in a context of an institutional vacuum. By default, the firms that are designing technologies for political life have done so using themselves as sounding boards for definitions of deviance and sources of validation.

Deviant decisions were made by many types of political actors and reproduced across many kinds of hypermedia projects. There is a myth that bad political campaign practices come from individual bad actors: the most desperate politicians, the richest and most conniving lobbyists, or the most underhanded consultants. Instead, I have found that the deviance is organizationally managed within campaigns and that campaigns operate in an institutional context that leaves practices unsupervised and normative expectations unclear. The proscription and instructions for change must come from outside the campaign organization. Privacy norms are rarely enunciated and articulated for the consultants. Deviance was defined by the group, but we need to define it for them. The political consulting industry has data on how the public wants and uses political hypermedia tools; they have data on the privacy norms of the public. But they have had no signals about how we value one over the other, or the conditions under which we would tolerate violating one for the other.

We must act now. While political hypermedia are an ever more important part of our system of political communication, specific applications are perpetually in development and can certainly be changed with public instruction. Design decisions were incremental; deviance was defined by the group and routinized through the rhythm of campaign cycles. Ethical violations were socially organized, but the technological possibilities and absence of policy oversight mattered. Technology mattered because primary decisions (placing data on the open market) patterned subsequent options. Campaign strategy is secret while the campaign is on and is discussed publicly only after the fact. Given that the process of campaigning is competitive and secretive, few consultants resisted senior campaign managers who encouraged privacy violations in the name of transparent democracy. In a sense, the secrecy of campaign practice is institutionalized by the way organizational structure, information processes, market transactions, and regulatory regimes of the FEC and FCC undermine most attempts to critique the use of political hypermedia by campaigns.

We should not be deceived by the myth that designing political information technologies is an apolitical engineering project. As revealed in previous chapters, there are few rules to guide engineering decisions that fundamentally affect cultural schemata and the structure of political communciation. There are formal rules about reporting campaign finances and informal rules of professional associations about how to collect and report data. The informal norms should be formalized, and the standard of allowing citizens to opt in to information-gathering schemes should be entrenched in clear public policy.

By now, many of the campaigns, lobbyists, candidates, and political consultants I studied have come and gone. Other political consultants with expertise in hypermedia have taken their place: Voting.com went bankrupt in 2001, but CompleteCampaign.com started up in time for the 2004 election season. No good ethnographer would ever be able to say that all new examples of a social phenomenon are the same as those already studied. The four organizations described here are based on a careful selection of cases from my field site of hypermedia campaign consultants, and I am confident that they can still represent many of the organizational newcomers that try to serve them today. Moreover, since I know that many of the players in my field site work for political campaigns in advanced democracies around the world between U.S. presidential campaign cycles, I am confident that the organizations profiled here will be reproduced in other countries in years to come.

The internet is a conduit for financial contributions from foreigners in the United States to political campaigns in their home countries. Émigrés increasingly use online services to send money to their home countries, sometimes for family use, sometimes in support of favored political causes. Candidates for the Mexican presidency actively campaign in the United States; the Cuban government provides an easy portal for overseas Cubans to make credit card contributions to their relatives' income; and today most of the world's social movements have some kind of online identity and physical presence in the United States. But hypermedia are also used in different ways in other countries. In an important sense, political content fills in wherever technologies permit. Cellular telephone technologies are particularly advanced in Asia; Japanese and South Korean campaigns are particularly adept at sending text messages over cellular networks to poll public opinion and remind supporters to vote.

As with many other professional consultants today, the work of campaign management increasingly takes managers overseas. There is a rhythm to the business of campaign management in democracies, a rhythm set by the flow of money in politics. Cycles of innovation begin in the United States during the presidential campaign season, when campaigning and lobbying budgets are largest. In the subsequent year, many hypermedia campaign managers take their cutting edge technologies to other countries, usually Canada and the United Kingdom. Two years after a presidential election, they take their innovations to Australia and Europe. Three years later, they take on contracts in Korea, Japan, and the Scandinavian countries. Some will take contracts in Russia, Mexico, and other countries with a growing demand for political consulting services. In this way, hypermedia innovations of the high-stakes, well-funded political campaigns in the United States diffuse across other polities, democracies or otherwise. In many spheres of law, preventative policy strategies in the United States have an impact on the rest of the world. With some regulatory oversight of hypermedia campaigns, for the good of individual privacy and health of the public sphere, the United States would have a positive influence on the way new information technologies are used in political life around the world. Responsible innovation, by being guaranteed in this advanced democracy, has a better chance of guaranteed everywhere.

The hypermedia campaign takes advantage of the norms and values that have been entrenched in technology when designer choices embedded attitudes about how democracy should work into code. The tools of a political campaign, the choices that campaign managers make about manipulating data, ideas, and people, reflect their own political norms. In this sense, the code in software has become embedded with the normative choices of designers. Some campaigns choose to obstruct real learning about political issues, manipulate their membership, and prevent too much interactivity. Other campaigns allow a range of interactive tools, adapt their organizational behavior to allow members to both produce and consume political content, and give such members the capacity to seed their own campaigns.

The system of political communication in the United States changed significantly over the last decade. Information technology now provides the skeletal support for our democratic political culture, but in interesting ways this infrastructure was designed by a small group of campaign managers with a specific vision of how it should work. We do not regulate the informational infrastructure of two important political institutions:

the political party and the political campaign. These technologies are built by groups of people working in concert, and they embody value choices of their designers. These technologies are incarnations of cultural schema that provide capacity for some kinds of political communication and constrain other kinds of political communication.

The political campaign is one of the most important organizations in a democracy, and whether issue- or candidate-specific, it is one of the least understood organizations in contemporary political life. Evidence from ethnographic immersion, survey data, and social network analysis revealed the changing organization of political campaigns over the last five election cycles, from 1996 to 2004. Over this time, both grassroots and elite political campaigns have gone online, built multimedia strategies, and constructed complex relational databases. The contemporary political campaign adopts digital technologies that improve reach and fund-raising, and at the same time adapts their organizational behavior. The internet is used for unique content not found in other media, it is used purposefully as an organizational tool, and it is aggressively used for data mining. Such close management of citizen information supplies is risky, however, resulting in implanted "astroturf" campaigns, political redlining, and the data shadow of contemporary citizens. The production of political culture is increasingly the purview of technocrats, whose choices about technology design affect the distribution of political power, or nontraditional actors who, equipped with political hypermedia, exercise the same marketing capacity as traditional political actors. The new system of producing political culture has immense implications for the meaning of citizenship and the basis of democratic representation.

Political philosophers have long warned us about the rule of public opinion and the possibilities of tyrannous majorities. The stronger the authority of the majority, the less frequently energetic minorities will arise, and the more time political leaders will spend not in forming their own opinions but in discovering and hastening to obey public opinion. If we should be worried about the health of our advanced democracy, it should not be for this reason. Organizing citizens through information technology has made it easy to discover public opinion. Political leaders, lobbyists, and campaign staff have proven quite adept at creating minorities, rather than just following majorities, directing public opinion, not just obeying it, and managing the contemporary performance of citizenship.

Appendix: Method Notes on Studying Information Technology and Political Communication

What has studying communication systems of political schemata, over media effects, meant for my method and findings? First, I treated technological innovation as evolutionary and contextual, not revolutionary and causal. The literature on media effects is occupied with either claiming or debunking the technological revolution in politics. I argued that a more sensible analytical frame treats technological innovation as co-evolutionary with organizational behavior. I still made arguments about what is new, and old, and different, but I did so with the language of evolution in technological systems and social institutions, not with the language of revolution. Second, I treated politics as a set of public discursive phenomena and private strategic choices. The discursive phenomena of digital politics were revealed in the Introduction through the images of digital democracy, and in chapter 4 through the rhetoric of e-politics industry ideologues. The private strategic choices of campaign managers were revealed in chapters 2 and 3 through ethnographic experience with four campaign consultancies. The images and rhetoric tantalize public imagination about how technology might be used to improve democracy; the private strategic choices of campaign managers actually brought information technology to political life, both improving and denigrating democratic norms in complex ways. An analytical frame that treats politics as culture pre-empts the quest for simple media effects and enables exposure of the subtleties of life a digital democracy, particularly with regard to the means of citizenship and representation and underlying logic by which political communication is organized. I started with more inclusive definitions, treating social practices and institutions as example of political culture, and treating multiple technologies with similar properties as part of a larger system for collecting and distributing political information.

When it comes to studying the role of information technology in political life, investigating media effects has often meant studying how technology is used. This research into impacts and outcomes usually takes news consumption as a proxy for the input of political information and voter turnout or sophistication as the outcome. I have argued here that it is important to study both how the technology is used and how it is designed, how political campaigns are produced and consumed. We have a better understanding of the practice of political life, not just political outcomes. Whereas the media effects research is primarily aimed at explaining voting outcomes, the cultural method gives us more theory about how those votes are actually earned or discouraged.

In studying the role of new media communication technologies (such as the internet) on political communication, the traditional media effects approach has been most concerned with news consumption habits and the prevalence of chatting about politics online. Most studies have looked for a direct causal connection between kinds of media use and degree of political sophistication among users, or prevalence of voter turnout among users. In this sense, the media effects approach is concerned almost exclusively with the consumption patterns of political content. I argue for a different analytical frame, one concerned with the organized system of political communication. In this sense the political culture approach is concerned with both the production and consumption of content. Information technologies themselves are being constructed as a part of our democratic institutions, resulting in important cultural shifts. Tracking individual opinion allows lobbyists to manufacture protest movements of individuals who have never consented to the collection of information about their political preferences. Several scholars have observed that public opinion is constructed. I have revealed the techniques and technologies of this construction. To understand the role of new media information technologies in politics, we must look beyond the reductive studies of "media effects" that model patterns of technology use among the citizens. A more cultural analytical frame allows one to treat singular innovations and acts as conditions and symbols of important structural change in the way we conduct our politics.

Social scientists often apply multiple methods to study unusual forms of organization, but a growing number of social groups constitute hypermedia organizations: They have adapted in significant ways by using new communication technology to conduct the business of social organization over large areas and disparate time zones and at all hours of the day. The internet, cell phones, personal digital assistants, private networks,

and databases all help to extend traditional organizations into hypermedia organizations. This conjoined superstructure of fast, high-capacity
hardware and software communication tools lets people transmit, interact with, and filter data. Significant differences exist between the traditional media and new media now employed in firms, state bureaucracies,
civic groups, recreational communities, and political campaigns.

Few social scientists would label a method "ethnographic" if it were
conducted using telephone or conference calls with subjects, and most
would not acknowledge an ethnographic project if it were done primarily using e-mail, listservs, or other chatting technology. Still, researchers
struggling to study communities and organizations structured around
new communications technologies with the depth permitted by qualitative methods have tried to develop a kind of "multimedia cyber-
anthropology" (Paccagnella 1997). Some of the richest theory building
about democratic practice comes from political ethnographies where
scholars have immersed themselves in a small, carefully selected community that can teach us about political culture more broadly (Mansbridge
1983; Eliasoph 1998; Doppelt 1999). Moreover, several good handbooks
on doing qualitative research over new media now exist (Markham 1998;
Hine 2000; Mann and Steward 2000; Miller and Slater 2000). Since this
is a relatively new means and subject of research, these authors take on
the important task of justifying the use of qualitative methods and of
thinking reflexively about the role of researcher in studying life online.
While they identify the promises and pitfalls of doing qualitative research
online, we still have few specific research strategies for working around
a challenging problem in the social sciences: sampling with qualitative
methods. I argue that even though many wired communities and organizations are structured in such a way as to make qualitative investigation
difficult, we need to develop more rigorous methods in order to obtain
generalizable qualitative data and transportable theory in the study of
new media and society.

Political hypermedia, as defined in chapter 1, have three design features. First, they are structured literally over and above traditional media
in a network of satellites, relay stations, and databases that coordinate the
retrieval and delivery of public and private information. Second, these
media operate at greater speeds and with greater amounts of content
than do traditional media. Third, they make socially significant symbols
more transient by permitting simulations of offline interaction, speedy
circulation of social signs and meanings, and rapid decomposition and
recomposition of messages. From e-commerce firms to state agencies

and news media, organizations that employ these hypermedia technologies are growing in number and social significance. How can a researcher study an organization whose most interesting attributes make it difficult to do so in a rigorous, qualitative manner?

Researchers tend to adapt methods over the course of research, and I adapted several research methods to study several hypermedia organizations working in politics between 1996 and 2004. First, I assessed some of the problems common to studying hypermedia organizations, from online fan communities to dot-com firms and wired political campaigns. Then I evaluated ethnography and social network analysis, and, after unpacking their relative strengths and weaknesses, I repackaged a method – network ethnography – that was better suited for studying hypermedia organizations. Network ethnography is not simply the sum of two traditional methods, however, and in conclusion I discuss the synergy between methods, identifying network ethnography's unique aspects, critically assessing its strengths and weaknesses, outlining how it was used in collecting evidence, and illustrating its purchase in developing an argument.

METHODOLOGICAL CHALLENGES IN STUDYING HYPERMEDIA ORGANIZATIONS

Ethnography is the systematic description of human behavior and organizational culture based on first-hand observation. As new forms of social organization and communities appear, researchers must adapt their methods in order best to capture evidence. Researchers in several disciplines are navigating a range of methodological challenges in studying essentially the same social phenomena: physically decentralized social networks made up of individuals who form a community but are not members of the same formal organization. These organizational networks are called "epistemic communities" in political science (Haas 1990; Young 1991), "communities of practice" in sociology (Latour 1981; Bijker et al. 1987; Abbott 1988), and "knowledge networks" in management (Uzzi 1996; Podolny and Page 1998). Scholars have been studying this kind of social interaction for some time, but it has proliferated in recent years with the advent of new communication media.

Certainly, some challenges of studying hypermedia organizations are the same as they would be for the study of more traditional groups: entry, exit, and membership roles have to be negotiated whether the field site is a café, privately held firm, or white supremacist group (Adler and Adler

1987). But the most common challenge in studying the culture of hyper-media organizations lies in avoiding a flavor of either organizational or technological determinism, and one advantage of qualitative methods is that they allow researchers to expose how people build culture from the bottom up.

Organizational determinism occurs when the researcher imputes community culture from the formal structure of its networks and hierarchies. For example, it is rare that the importance of individuals in an organization can be determined by their use of new media such as e-mail. The campaign manager who does not adopt e-mail may be isolated in an e-mail network while retaining a central role in the campaign, and information exchanged in face-to-face executive meetings will not reach lower-level workers or volunteers (Garton et al. 1997). Interviews conducted by the researcher or the researcher's participant observation alone may not capture the dynamics in which managers may retain power, despite their limited use of e-mail. The problem lies in an analytical frame that equates the particular structure of an organizational field site with broader social phenomena. For example, we could study a group of mushroom pickers in the hope that they would teach us something about political communication. Unless this wild mushroom picking club is made up of former U.S. Presidents, such a study would probably teach us only about the social organization of mushroom pickers. In other words, the boundaries of the organizational field site are so constraining that the explanation for a phenomenon can be only the organization itself.

Technological determinism occurs when the researcher imputes community culture from the formal structure of communication tools. Some scholars in the history of science and technology insist that technological systems are socially constructed and try to deny any technological determinism in their writing (Bijker and Law 1992). At the same time, some acknowledge that it is difficult to study the social construction of technology without also speaking to the technological construction of society, and blame their methods (often historical or archival) for yielding a kind of evidence from which it can be difficult to isolate the former. For example, we could study a listserv about presidential politics or the content of the presidential Web sites. We might be excited by the fact that restricted gender and race cues make debate balanced and fair or disappointed at the manipulative rhetorical devices and paucity of useful information on a campaign site. But such a study would not teach us about how the rest of the country experiences political content, especially those not on the listserv and those without training in rhetoric. In other words, the boundaries of a technological field site are so constraining that the explanation for a phenomenon can only be the technology itself. Thus, the method that a researcher chooses can strongly affect the language used in the researcher's observations; usability studies alone tend to yield technologically deterministic language, and fieldwork alone tends to yield organizationally deterministic language.

UNBUNDLED SOCIAL CUES AND TERRITORIALITY

Some of the problems of organizational and technological determinism have common root causes. These result from the application of traditional ethnographic methods to the study of patterns of social interaction that are essentially aterritorial or that take place over communication technologies that reduce social cues. Traditional methods were designed for the study of physically centralized, territorially specific social interactions. Territorial interactions are bundled in fixed, enclosed spaces in which people order and administer themselves, their resources, and their relationships. The territorialization of space is the dominant means of social organization, and the demarcated space serves as a container for political attributes, enforcing cartographic boundaries as social boundaries. Space lacks content until participants collectively define objects and relationships, and administration itself is a process of planning for change by separating and recombining the objects and relationships within the space. A good example is that of the "empty" city lot – a place with only trees, weeds, and rodents that is devoid of socially valuable content until it is integrated and made socially functional through urban development. These "full" social spaces, or the process of filling them with cultural meaning, are of particular interest to the qualitative researcher.

If there are reduced social cues between subjects who communicate with a particular medium, there are reduced social cues between the subjects and the researcher who joins in the use of that medium. E-mail may appear to reduce social differences and increase communication across organizational boundaries (Sproull and Kiesler 1986), but the ethnographic perspective cannot do without some sense of the broader social environment in which these changes appear (Spears and Lea 1994). These new ways of working also increase social interaction between territorially and organizationally distant individuals, but distance should not become a methodological reason for excluding them from ethnographic study (Sproull 1992; Constant et al. 1996). In other ethnographies of modern work forces, engineers or other technicians are based in field sites that have a distinct workplace. From the researcher's point of view, the advantage of having a workplace as a field site is that cultural peculiarities can be attributed to a distinct *in vitro* effort to create and manage norms in a group of people bounded by the hierarchy and location of the firm (Kunda 1992). In contrast, many hypermedia organizations have a less territorial basis, and this is not a methodological oversight or a problem of site specificity. It can be especially challenging for a researcher to interpret the content of messages sent over new media, since many are text-based and can mean different things to different recipients. Researchers can easily reinterpret or misinterpret these messages if they lack deep knowledge of the individuals and relationships involved. Moreover, it is difficult to reach this depth of knowledge with computer-mediated communication between the researcher and subjects. Rich and complex communities can still evolve over communication tools that reduce social cues, but these social worlds exist somewhat independently of the social worlds in which we spend most of our time, and it takes extra care to connect sensibly an online world of limited social interaction with everyday lives.

Interestingly, many ethnographies of the new media experience carry auto-ethnographic features, introducing the researcher as one of the subjects in narrative (Turkle 1995; Markham 1998). This may result from the fact that researchers who call their explorations of life online an ethnographic journey, but work only with online text, must work with the same diminished social cues as other users. The experience of the researcher becomes most of the content of this kind of ethnographic project. Virtual ethnographies that do not become auto-ethnographic may still produce elaborate discussions of the meaning of self and of human cyborgic qualities (Hakken 1999). Some of the more popular readings about life online tell fascinating stories of intrigue and entrepreneurship (Borsook 2000; Bronson 2000a,b; Lane 2001; Lessard and Baldwin 2003), but they are rarely generated by extended fieldwork with systematic participant observation. Some kind of qualitative method feeds discourse about cyberculture, from the earliest accounts of life online to the latest case studies of wired communities (Dibbell 1993; Correll 1995; Baym 2000; Silver 2000).

Since new communication technologies permit ever more nuanced human interaction over large areas, researchers are increasingly faced with a new challenge: How can we qualitatively study culture produced in situations of decentralized human interaction with the high ethnographic standard of first-hand experience, and how can we produce generalizable theory about that culture? How can we qualitatively study culture in such a way as to strike a palatable balance between macro-structure and micro-agency, while avoiding the pitfalls of organizational or technological determinism? Research into the role of computer-mediated communication in management structure is vast, but it is rarely ethnographic and rarely able to speak to problems of organizational culture (Pickering and King 1995). Thus, the field of communication studies covers the role of e-mail in altering organizational hierarchy (Marcus 1995) and organizational learning and innovation in firms and governments (Kiesler and Sproull 1988; Huff et al. 1989; Contractor and Eisenberg 1990; Kiesler and Sproull 1992; Constant and Sproull 1994; Contractor and Monge 2004). In contrast, research into the organizational culture of wired neighborhoods, fan groups, and online communities is less equipped to connect these cultures to off-line spheres of social interaction. On some occasions, these communities do not even form around a central person, place, corporeal organization or with the benefit of face-to-face interaction between members; the better ethnographies of hypermedia organization do take the extra methodological step to look at members' lives off-line, even though many of these have been interested in microcultures and have not justified case selection with the goal of broader comparisons.

For example, in *Tune In, Log On*, an ethnographic study of a Usenet newsgroup, Baym explored the social organization of, and struggles over, meaning within an online cultural system. Borrowing from Bourdieu and others, she noted: "While in theory all participants in a Usenet group are equal, in fact group values make some forms of cultural capital more valuable than others and, hence, lend those with such capital greater status" (Baym 2000, 159). With her methodological approach she found that small-group interaction online was like many kinds of small-group interaction, and in this case her method was well suited because the phenomena of interest framed the internet itself as a social context. With this analytical frame, social norms evolve as a community grows, such that deviance can mean different things at different times, and the processes of entry, exit, and self-presentation can be different at different times. We must be conscious, however, that this analytical frame is different from one in which we study the social context of the internet, in which we are interested in the norms, rules, and patterns of behavior that evolve on- and offline. It is insufficient to immerse ourselves in an online field site if we want to answer broader questions and generate transportable theory about the role of hypermedia our system of political communication.

PROBLEMS AND PROSPECTS OF ETHNOGRAPHY

As a method, ethnography is useful in forcing a researcher to define a field site, but as a term, "ethnography" is generously. Ethnography is in favor once again as a method for studying organizational behavior and the social diffusion of new media technologies, but it is still a rigorous and demanding method in that the ethnographer has to give careful thought to the selection of field sites. Comparativists select some cases but not others, statisticians select some data samples and discard other data samples, and ethnographers have to identify who in their line of sight is of interest. Because ethnography is centered on specific actors, it has earned a reputation for rendering rich description – narratives with historical depth and contextual perspective that trace social processes within groups. For some scholars, the "good stuff" of ethnography is the way that it drops the reader into the social setting, reveals the mundane and everyday, and delivers both a point and a punch line (Bate 1997).

Ethnography allows the researcher to explore all the open-ended questions that cannot be asked in typical survey instruments, and it is these questions that allow the researcher to delve into the culture of a new community. By letting people tell stories about how they enter and experience the group, their images of the group, winning and losing, being injured or surviving, the researcher can discover culture and closely experience organizations (Fineman and Gabriel 1996). Moreover, communities are defined by symbols, social and physical boundaries, rituals, and self-awareness. Cohen writes:

> Whether or not its structural boundaries remain intact, the reality of community lies in its members' perception of the vitality of its culture. People construct community symbolically, making it a resource and repository of meaning, and a referent of their identity.
>
> (Cohen 1985, 45)

Ethnography is particularly useful in capturing and categorizing community symbols, since in-depth interviews and community membership allow a researcher to probe for meaning and watch symbolic communities interact and evolve. Along with symbols, keywords also give away culture, and their use during conferences and daily work can reveal shared understanding of social boundaries, roles, and responses

(Williams 1985). But as Morrill and Fine (1997) summarize, while ethnographic research may provide depth, multiple perspectives, and process, it sacrifices control, researcher objectivity, and generalizability.

Ethnography is about careful in-depth interviews, but it also is about observing small-group interaction. In my particular professional community, I could study group interaction in the workplace or at the special conferences and other professional events that occur throughout the year. The companies were spread out across the country (Boston, New York, San Francisco, Washington), but I could not reasonably do rigorous ethnography in all parts of the e-politics community (Radway 1988; Marcus 1995; Abu-Lughod 1997).

Ethnography often proceeds with a purposive sampling of people and situations worthy of close study and with combinations of variation, extreme, snowball, and theoretical sampling (Morrill and Fine 1997; Witte et al. 2000). Variation sampling identifies a discrete organization as a field site and tries to sample all relevant actors and contexts in the organization. Even though the e-politics community has some formal social organizations, many members are spread throughout the country and throughout different kinds of organizations: firms, political parties, sole proprietorships, and government agencies. Extreme sampling selects the most unusual cases precisely because they help define a norm by being so unusual. The e-politics community of practice is still small enough that extreme sampling is not necessary. Snowball sampling depends on individual informants to refer the researcher to other informants, introducing bias in the overall sample.

Theoretical sampling allows cases to be selected for their fit within categories of a model, but if no overall model exists, this method may not be useful. It is common for ethnographers to select informants either with theoretical sampling or by allowing informants to recommend other informants. Critics point out that, in either case, relying on informants or on researchers' models can result in inappropriate bias in sample selection. On its own, ethnography helps researchers to delve into the cultural dynamics of the hypermedia organization, but because it keeps them focused on individual attitudes and small group interaction, researchers still have to justify sample selection. This method does not equip researchers to set the community easily in a larger cultural context.

We trust ethnographers' processes of case selection when we know that they know their subjects' lives inside and out. When the primary means of interacting with subjects is the internet, we should be much less confident that researchers' observations have any offline context. Certainly from a researcher's standpoint it may be interesting to have subjects' text-based content and responses to explore, but the inability to make independent observations leaves researchers confined to content analyses of subjects' analytical frames. In other words, relying on subjects' interpretations of their social worlds will give researchers a rich but incomplete picture.

Ethnographers who depend on hypermedia technologies for their interactions with subjects may be uncertain about the time, location, and social context in which messages are generated, draining color about the real field site from researchers' observations (Daft and Lengel 1986). While they are in the field, researchers are also supposed to be immersed in the activities of the community, learning languages or jargon and engaging at as many levels as possible in the daily lives of the subjects. Fieldwork involves conducting in-depth interviews, observing casual and formal interactions, making photographic records of icons and events, collecting community stories from different perspectives, and collating information on how subjects view the world. But for some researchers claiming to do ethnography online, going into the field is little more than a state of mind because there is so little convergence between their lives and the subjects' lives; there is no physical entry into or exit from the community. There is no territorially based field site, and the social cues that are available are unbundled from much of the context in which the content was produced.

PROBLEMS AND PROSPECTS OF SOCIAL NETWORK ANALYSIS

Proponents of social network analysis have been vocal about presenting their method as suitable for studying any social relationship, especially those mediated by the new communications technologies. In practice, few researchers rely exclusively on social network analysis, but some rely on it so heavily that it is worthwhile to give the method a friendly critique so that we can be aware of its strengths and weaknesses. Social network analysis is good at making personal relationships comparable, defining core and group membership and expanding the number of social observations (in terms of subjects and relationships between subjects) possible in traditional ethnography (Scott 2000). Thus, it has been especially useful in studying ideational communities created when an organization such as a firm or nonprofit or government agency permits the formal and legitimate peripheral participation of its staff with other organizations; researchers can observe organizational learning and the diffusion of ideas and innovation across these communities (Brown and Duguid 1991). The method exposes routes of communication and the width of the road, but data on the content of communication or relationships are highly reduced and often unsuitable for the comprehensive study of organizational culture. In this sense, social network analysis is like other quantitative methods that are valued for testing generalized theories but criticized for their positivist and unreflexive treatment of subjects and relationships. Social network analysis identifies the relative positioning of members and the partitioning of subgroups, but it does not reveal why those positions and partitions are socially significant. In this sense, social network analysis alone is particularly unsuitable for theorizing about organizational culture, and when researchers conducting this type of analysis claim to deepen their work with participant observation, they usually only highlight its inadequacy. Social network analysis frequently uses close-ended questions – questions that limit the range of descriptive possibility – to map out the strength of association among individuals and among groups. The diagrams yielded by such analysis can reveal a group core and a periphery, the strength of external attachments, and obligatory points of passage between communities. Moreover, they can identify high-density personal networks in the hypermedia organization, which are important in making up for the physical isolation and organizational alienation that some members may express at the outset. Thus, an understanding of the social network can help researchers to understand both their own positions and their informants' positions relative to the rest of the observable community.

Although ethnography will generate rich data about particular interactions, only a large relational database reveals egocentric and sociocentric overlapping networks and the density and directionality of ties, allowing the researcher to put the events and people of interest into a richer context (Scott 2000). Social network analysis identifies core and peripheral members and more comprehensively charts entry into and exit from the group. For example, it reveals that suppliers and manufacturers may rely heavily on personal connections among staff to sort out small disagreements in the interpretation of contracts and on the threat of ostracism from the network as a means of enforcing them (Uzzi 1996).

In a sense, every social study is a study of the network of relationships between individuals and groups. Social network analysis may be an excellent means of testing the expanse of cultural norms, but not of uncovering and identifying culture in the first place. Social network analysis is a method that often assigns ordinal values to norms of trust and reciprocity enveloping social actors. These values are determined with close-ended questions that ultimately reduce social relationships to mutually commensurate values.

On its own, social network analysis misses much of the rich information that the researcher can obtain by participating in the workplace and observing small-group interaction. As a method, it can bring perspective to complexly layered social networks, but it may make employment, peer, and personal networks falsely congruent. More important, social network analysis has limited use in revealing stories of mobility within communities. Narratives about how people enter and leave a network or about how people move from periphery to core and back are difficult to reduce to comparative values.

Social network analysis needs to be assessed critically before it is applied, especially in the study of new organizations and new media. The method is based on transactional measurement, and therefore is only as good as the quality of the content exchanged. Since computer-mediated communication consists of text, modest graphics, or limited audio or video images, the method is best for distilling evidence that a communication or transaction occurred, not for assessing its particular content or significance. Moreover, social network analysis may allow community members to see new aspects of their organization, and only intimate familiarity with group dynamics will allow the researcher to assess the effects of their research critically. Again, few social network analysts conduct their work without some kind of ground-truthing. But casual interviews or participant observation alone are not ethnography, and ground-truthing by interview or participant observation is not as good as going into the field as an ethnographer.

Network Ethnography

Network ethnography is the process of using ethnographic field methods on cases and field sites selected using social network analysis. Active or passive observation, extended immersion, or in-depth interviews are conducted at multiple sites or with interesting subgroups that have been purposively sampled after comparison through social network analysis. Although this strategy may sound like a straightforward marriage of two traditional methods, in fact it makes several important conceptual advances possible.

First, the meaning of "field sites" evolves, and instead of choosing territorial field sites, the researcher has to choose a perceived community and select the important nodes in the social network as field sites. Indeed, the field site may not be a socially significant physical place at all, but may be more ephemeral. For example, a sequence of conferences or trade shows occurring in sterile hotels can still represent key events full of important social interactions. Other field site nodes might include the loft of a start-up e-commerce business, the foundation headquarters in Rockefeller Plaza, the newsroom of a trade magazine, or the somber brown-bag lecture-luncheon series at a small think-tank. Compared with selecting a single field site, identifying several nodal events or physical locations does not dilute the evidence because the important material – the social interaction of community members – remains constant. Whatever the case, thinking of the community as having constituent parts forces researchers to be aware of the shared and unique features of different organizations that are home to members of an extended ideational family. This can make for richer contextual detail.

Second, the researcher can manage sample bias that might appear in selecting informants with an extreme, snowball, or other sampling method. Whereas snowball sampling does not allow the researcher to control the direction of sample growth, social network analysis will identify some of the most significant informants in the network, but may also bring to light other members and roughly illustrate their relationship to the rest of the community. In this sense, network ethnography permits more rigorous theoretical sampling.

Third, the researcher can dynamically use the initial ethnographic and social network analysis to improve subsequent inquiry. Simultaneously, the researcher can avoid banal data with the rich detail of in-depth interviews and participant observation of central informants, events, and crucial field sites. Herein lies another advantage to network ethnography: It may help the researcher manage entrance into communities of practice. To enter a community, the researcher takes advantage of bonds of trust between members, but member affinities over an informal social network may be stronger than their affinities within a formal organization's hierarchy. It may be more important to have the confidence of key community members (as identified by network analysis) than it is to have official blessings from an organization's managers. In-depth interviews that collect basic stories about community history will help in the design of survey questions suitable for social network analysis. The social network analysis will identify key organizations, events, and people worth discussing in in-depth interviews.

Finally, the researcher can more accurately chart community change over time and track the passage of ideas. Regardless of the label the researcher wants to apply, when working with a knowledge-based community, it is important to know who knew what and when. Network ethnography, unlike snowball sampling, allows researchers to conduct theoretical sampling from a large population while managing the direction of the sample. After defining research questions, it is crucial to define and justify the selection of evidential cases, an exercise that requires researchers to imagine the universe of cases so as to rationalize the choice of particular cases (e.g., why should we be interested in your grandmother?). Network ethnography allows qualitative researchers to think strategically about the selection of cases by empowering them to define the universe of cases themselves. This is an epistemological exercise, however, so the researcher still needs to construct good arguments about why the range of attributes and properties may be interesting.

NETWORK ETHNOGRAPHY APPLIED

One example of a hypermedia community is the network of political campaign consultants who specialize in taking ideologies online. This e-politics community is a trans-organizational system that extends from the major political parties to activist networks, telecommunications and computing professionals, and journalists. In line with the classic definition of a trans-organizational system, the community is an expanded network of stakeholders who are motivated to interact because they are dependent on the same limited pool of foundation and political money, committed to enhancing the quality of communication between citizens and political leaders, and have integrating mechanisms that allow for leadership, the exchange of ideas, and mutual support (Cummings 1984). But there are also clear norms of performance that establish guidelines for conduct and broad collective goals that help to define good and bad players, insiders and outsiders.

This community is interesting, because it is weaving new communications technologies into many aspects of political life by designing Web sites and integrating new technologies into campaign structure and culture. Early in my search for a field site, one fixer told me:

There's a mini Constitutional Congress going on right now. Whatever American democracy looks like in fifteen or twenty years, it will have been designed by us.

Who was the "us"? What was their project? Informants often expressed their opinions on political events through the cultural framework of a community of democratic warriors working with political hypermedia:

> All our experience in Florida this election shows that one single electoral result isn't possible with existing technology. Democracy has always operated with a margin of error, and it's our job to close that margin of error. Democracy isn't real yet – it is constrained by the limits of our ingenuity.

Often they referred to their network of thirty or forty people as the "e-politics community." My research questions concerned the social construction of the new forms of political communication that campaigns use to organize and communicate with the public. I needed a method that would allow me to interact with people in the environment of their own professional community, as they literally and figuratively constructed technology for other political actors.

Four particular challenges had to be overcome. First, the community of political campaign managers was structurally, functionally, and ideationally unique. Second, the research questions necessitated a level of analysis that was neither devoted to the behavior of macro-political institutions, such as political parties, the media, or the government, nor beholden to micro-level analysis of the particulars of voter learning and behavior. Third, the method had to allow an exploration of the multiple dimensions of contemporary work: formal employment relationships and professional obligations, and informal discourse about the broad democratic project in which many in the e-politics community feel engaged. Finally, the research method had to provide balanced evidence that did not prejudice findings toward either technological determinism or organizational determinism.

This field site was not a traditional professional community since multiple overlapping ties of very different kinds define it. Individuals in the community occupy different positions in several companies, non-governmental agencies, academic centers, government agencies, political parties, and news media. Some work in sole proprietorships or for politicians or firms on contract. Others work for some of the more traditional businesses – such as polling or public relations agencies – that are trying to add to the range of products and services that they currently offer the country's political leaders, political parties, and lobbyists. Many work for the few mid-sized firms that actually describe themselves as being in the business of e-politics. Members of the community have relatively complex formal, semiformal, and informal relationships that quickly become difficult to track because it is more of an occupational than organizational category. It becomes a group of people who consider themselves to be engaged in the same sort of work; who identify (more or less positively) with their work; who share a set of values, norms, and perspectives that apply to but extend beyond work-related matters; and whose social relationships meld the realms of work and leisure (Van Maanan and Barley 1984).

Although many members have the same occupation, many work for very different organizations. Moreover, many are not clear peers with equivalent or comparable organizational roles; rather, they constitute a knowledge-based group, a specific community of experts sharing a belief in a common set of cause-and-effect relationships as well as common values to which policies governing these relationships will be applied. Despite the diversity of formal, organizational affiliations, I believed that this group shared principle and causal beliefs, patterns of reasoning about how politics should and should not work, an understanding of the value of technology in politics and commitment to this marriage, and, consequently, a common policy agenda (Haas 1992). For many members, the project of digitizing democratic institutions was the primary basis of affiliation, not loyalty to the university-based academic centers, nongovernmental and, governmental agencies, political parties, and firms around the country within which they were formal members.

Second, I wanted to craft a research method that was not predisposed to generating theory for particular levels of analysis. For example, much of the theorizing about how democratic institutions change occurs either at the macro-structural level, where we examine elections, revolutions, or elite behavior – or at a micro-structural level, where we examine how voters learn, reach decisions, or respond to media. Those who study large-scale institutional change often do so either by studying the interaction of social groups, such as countries or political parties, or by examining aggregated databases about political trends. Those who study small-scale institutional change often do so with experiments or in-depth interviews. Since my analytical frame posited that both technology and democratic values are socially constructed and that they are not constructed in monthly or annual increments convenient for statistical analysis, I needed a method that would allow me to watch the dialogue of ideas within the community. Since this discrete community is an important part of the larger democratic process, I also needed a method that would allow me to set the evolving democratic discourse in the community within the larger context of electoral politics. I needed a method that would let me speak to the intermediate or meso-structural connections created by the small group interactions of a specific community that was powerful within the sphere of contemporary politics. I wanted to investigate how the actors themselves modeled political discourse and what they thought of their political masters and the voting public. The people building new political communication technologies are powerful in the sense that they influence how the largest political parties and interest groups in the country use information and organize themselves.

Third, I needed a way of distinguishing between formal organizational affiliations and actual power relationships in the creative process. In *Talking about Machines* (1996), Orr found two important parts to the definition of work. In this ethnography of a modern job, he found that work is both a series of employment relationships and what is actually being done day to day. Since I expected to find that work in the community of practice had these two components, I needed a method to help me study each of them. Moreover, I quickly discovered the importance of ideational work, or exchanging and debating ideas about democratic politics. In the e-politics community formal structures and actual work are often distinct. I could not always predict the nature of a respondent's day-to-day work from the apparent employment relationship. The exchange of ideas that propels many people does not always occur along the lines of employment or with immediate colleagues. The ideational work community comes from extended social networks. Moreover, much of the literature on professionalization describes how information is monopolized and expertise is bounded. The opposite seemed to occur in this group. Even though many firms, charities, schools, pollsters, parties, and consultants would take different positions on many policy questions, their IT people collaborated, sharing strategies, content, and data.

Fourth, method choice would have clear implications for the quality of evidence gathered to answer these research questions, especially vis-à-vis organizational or technological determinism. Scholars have long noted the cultural pervasiveness of technological determinism, finding that people often provide their own accounts of history in language laden with it (Smith and Marx 1994). Moreover, there is a definite tradition of describing the form and shape of democratic institutions as a consequence of the technical prowess of a polity in collating public opinion

(Winner 1980); it has been argued, for example, that the telegraph made politicians more accountable at the turn of the century (Blondheim 1994). On first contact, some members of the community will announce that the logical, if not inevitable, application of hypermedia technology is in political life, where it makes democracy more direct and more deliberative. A kind of soft determinism is at work here in which the community believes that, even though citizens must step up and use the technology, using the internet for politics is unavoidable.

In sum, social network analysis alone probably would have revealed that I did not have much of a community to study, that its individual actors are not bounded by a formal organization or physical proximity but are merely a collection of individuals with common professional interests in technology and politics. Ethnography alone probably would have revealed that there is a strong community bond between some members, but it would not have rendered a broader portrait of the size of the community, revealed distant members, or exposed widely held norms, rules, and patterns of behavior. Network ethnography, however, produced rich cultural data about ideational work in a wired community practice. It was data I could situate between the contexts of micro-level group interaction and the large-scale machinations of political elites and historical voting trends, with little risk of producing technologically or organizationally deterministic results.

AN EXAMPLE: CONFIRMING FIELD OBSERVATIONS

Table A.1 (p. 229) reveals the diversity of organizations participating in this work. The table lists all of the organizations sampled in this study, through social network analysis, organizational survey, informant interviews, or ethnographic observation. After only a few weeks of fieldwork, I had collected a number of observations about how members of the community were concerned about the dominant role that private, for-profit commercial enterprises had taken in producing political hypermedia. These concerns were difficult to substantiate beyond the observations of several informants, however. To help understand the relationships between formal organizations and the informal community, I created a data set based on conference panel interaction. In the five years preceding the 2000 elections, there were thirty-five professional conferences on themes of digital democracy and politics online. I used the programs and transcripts for all of the conferences – the universe of cases – to build a database of who sat with whom and what was discussed. Network analysis of attendance, topics, and changing affiliations helped me to understand social relationships and idea formation, as well as the diffusion from the group of twenty who attended the early meetings to the hundreds who attended the Politics Online 2000 Conference. Moreover, the panel transcripts and recorded debates were an important source for linguistic and content analysis in my search for the talking ideology.

In all, 765 different people registered for at least one conference about politics online during the five-year period, but that participation was unevenly distributed. For example, nine people attended five panels between 1995 and 2000. Over the same period, 753 people sat in the audience or appeared in five panels at most, and twenty-one people sat on at least five panels over the same period. A quarter of those who participated in one of the conferences attended only as audience members, and four-fifths of those who participated either attended or joined in only one panel discussion. Since panel participation was usually by invitation, and speakers were expected to share stories of triumph and failure (usually triumph), those who spoke on panels framed the debate and discussion about e-politics. About 150 people spoke on at least two panels, about sixty people spoke on at least three panels, and a core group of about thirty people spoke on at least four panels. This core group appeared to dominate dialogue about the social construction of political life online, and they were clearly people I needed to observe.

Private firms and political consultants dominated dialogue during this period about how technology could be applied in political life. In total, there were 151 instances of a dyadic relationship involving a representative of a dot-com; these represented over 60 percent of all the dyadic interactions. These relationships are graphically represented in Figure A.1, where the value of each tie is the number of times its members participated on a panel with members from other subgroups. Moreover, analysis of the network of conference panel interaction revealed patterns in how the same people changed formal organizational affiliations over the years, exposing how many individual people moved between formal employment in government and private industry while maintaining informal membership in the e-politics community. It also quantitatively confirmed field observations that people working for civic groups felt frustrated by limited access to granting agencies and felt more camaraderie with private firms than with foundation staff. This analysis identified individuals who were core members of the community, several of whom I had not met in my field site but were clearly important subjects.

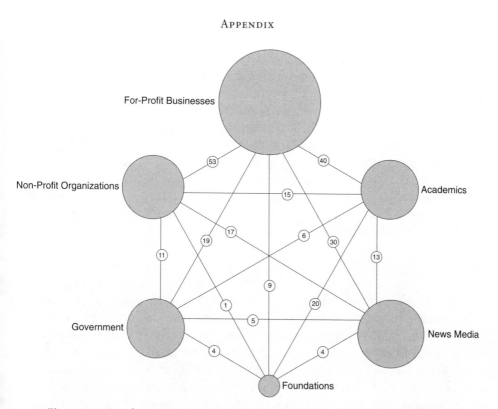

Figure A.1: Panel participation at e-politics conferences, by organizational subgroups, 1995–2000.

Of course, I knew I had to spend time with certain people who had not been pointed out to me through social network analysis. Several of the chief organizers were rarely also panelists, and so social network analysis alone would not have revealed their centrality. Some of the acknowledged experts actually liked to heckle from the sidelines. Analyzing the conferences this way helped me to re-enter the field more purposively because I could sample individuals, projects, and organizations on the basis of several features: their core or peripheral positions and ideological platform, their duration in the universe of cases, and their entry or exit trajectory.

As a multimethod approach, network ethnography has several disadvantages. For the researcher, an important part of ethnography is actually the formation of genuine friendships within the community, and the urge to do a comprehensive study can get in the way of maintaining regular contact with a small group of informants and fixers. The more decentralized the community, the more costly is travel. More important are the epistemological and research implications of defining a community that has not been through the exercise of examining itself in depth. Researchers want to study networked communities in their nascent form, and mapping a community will elucidate its fragments. And as in traditional ethnography, being associated with certain core or periphery groups in a large network will affect the researcher's ability to enter other parts of the community. True, face-to-face ethnography may help a researcher to manage this risk better than online ethnography, because information signals about social stigma can be inadvertently transmitted through personal contact, but mediated contact allows subjects to manage and control such signals.

CONCLUSION

The benefit of network ethnography is that it strikes a balance between macro-structure and technological or organizational determinism, on the one hand, and micro-agency of the social construction of culture, on the other. The qualitative researcher need *not* sacrifice control, objectivity, and generalizability. It also forces researchers to justify the choice of field sites and individuals in a way that some might otherwise not, especially inexperienced ethnographers or ethnographers faced with the challenges of studying a hypermedia organization. An old sociological wisdom holds that qualitative methods tend to be best for generating theory, and quantitative methods tend to be best for testing theory. Network ethnography helped to generate theories about how democratic ideals are infused into technological design, and to test how technological design perpetuates those ideas in broader social contexts.

I provided a friendly critique of both ethnography and social network methods and argued that a synthesized technique of network ethnography helps to accomplish research goals in spite of the problems inherent in hypermedia field sites. Network ethnography is a distinct research method – not just social network analysis with some interviews tossed in to casually specified relations in the network, and not just ethnography with a network spider diagram generated by some software. Network ethnography has allowed construction of a grounded theory without encountering some of the sample-bias issues of which other grounded-theory research has been accused, allowing a systematic sample, with considerable depth, of the relations in a community.

In choosing to study a physically disparate community, I did not develop the many deep friendships that some ethnographers find are the lasting reward of good ethnography, and the travel costs of keeping up with a multisited community were significant. But the method did overcome several of the particular challenges: the unusual community structure, the need for context within micro- and macro-political processes, the ideational nature of community work, and my search for kinds of evidence that would not prejudice observations toward either social or technological determinism. Moreover, I did not want to fabricate a community by creating a sample of cases selected on the basis of shared norms and values; network ethnography revealed core and peripheral members, outsiders traveling in the same policy circles, and "bad" members of the community. If I had deliberately selected people based on shared norms about technology and politics, my sample would have suffered from elective affinity.

Network ethnography allows the researcher to strategize over multiple points of entry into a community, avoiding the less manageable cascading or snowball sampling methods of traditional ethnography. Through the analysis of attendance records at professional meetings, or through surveys of trust and reciprocity, social network analysis helps to confirm the centrality or periphery of community members. The method allows the researcher to give special attention to the qualitative social boundaries that can demarcate a community, boundaries that are unbundled from territorial space. Obviously, researchers should adapt this method as they see fit, but, generally, an application of network ethnography would occur in stages. First, researchers would research, select, and enter a field site until they have a rough sense of community boundaries. This is necessary to identify a sample population, select the criteria for survey questions on centrality, and ultimately, ground-truth the results of social network analysis. Second, the researcher would conduct a social network analysis on as many members of the community as possible, especially with members who may have more (unobserved) contact with other members than they have had with the researcher. Third, the researcher would use the findings of social network analysis to identify subgroups and clusters worthy of close study, previously unsuspected points of entry for further fieldwork, and subsequent methodological strategies such as purposive sampling for in-depth interviews according to core membership, periphery isolation, membership duration, or other individual attributes.

Several scholars of organizational behavior have charted the rise of different kinds of networked organizations, networked communities, or networked professions (Castells 1996). Network ethnography is particularly useful for the in-depth study of key contemporary professions and communities of practice, such as those in the sphere of e-commerce and political campaigns. This synergistic method helped to define community boundaries and core groups in a distributed social network and to organize different kinds of observations about the social construction of political hypermedia. Network ethnography is an amalgam of traditional ethnography and social network analysis. The sample is generated purposefully but informed by network analysis. As a method, it reveals the complex fabric of associations between members with very different roles in very different organizations, while also exposing their deeply shared ideational commonalities. It is similar to theoretical sampling, but it allows for more strategy in selecting events, respondents, and organizations for in-depth analysis from the universe of cases.

As workplaces and professions become increasingly wired, physical proximity becomes strategically less important for social organization. Employers and employees may be less inclined to flock to areas of the country or areas within a city where their industry has a professional presence and finds prestige in place. If this displacement happens to other professional communities and they become as decentralized as the community in this study, scholars of work and organizational behavior will be faced with unprecedented research challenges in studying communities of practice that might appear elusive because they are not centered in the way autoworkers are associated with Detroit, traders are associated with Wall Street, or IT workers are associated with Silicon Valley. As a synthesized method, network ethnography may help scholars to face contemporary research challenges in the wired community networks – professional and otherwise – that are proliferating in modern political life.

Table A.1: *Network Ethnography Sampling: Conferences, Organizations, and Projects, 1996–2004*

Academics

American University, School of Law[a]

California Institute of Technology[a]

California State University Northridge[a]

Colby College[a]

Columbia University, School of Journalism[a]

George Mason University, Department of Public and International Affairs[a]

George Washington University, Computer Science Department[a]

George Washington University, Graduate School for Political Management[a–c]

Georgetown University[a]

Georgia Institute of Technology[a]

Harvard University, John F. Kennedy School of Government[a,c]

Massachusetts Institute of Technology[a]

Northern Arizona University[a]

Northwestern University[a]

Pennsylvania State University[a]

Princeton University[a]

Rutgers University, School of Communication, Information and Library Sciences[a]

San Francisco State University[a]

Stanford University[a]

Univeristy of Twente, Netherlands[a]

University of British Columbia[a]

University of California, Berkeley[a]

University of California, San Diego[a]

University of California, Santa Barbara[a,c]

University of Cincinnati[a]

University of Georgia, Carl Vinson Institute of Government[a]

University of Illinois, Champaign Urbana[a]

University of Illinois, Chicago[a]

University of Maryland, Baltimore County[a]

University of Maryland[a]

University of Michigan[a]

University of Pennsylvania, Annenberg Public Policy Center[a,b]

University of Pennsylvania, Annenberg School of Communication[a]

University of Pennsylvania, Moore School of Electrical Engineering[a]

University of Pennsylvania, Wharton School of Business[a]

University of Rochester[a]

University of Texas, Austin[a]

University of Washington, Seattle[a]

Wellesley College[a]

Yale University[a]

Conferences

Advertising and Marketing on the Internet, Alexandria, Virginia, April 2000[a]

Aspen Institute: Campaigns and Elections in Cyberspace, Queenstown, Maryland, October 1999[a]

CampaignNet 2K.1, Washington, D.C., March 2000[a]

Communications and Policy Technology Network Council, Washington, D.C., multiple[a,d]

(*continued*)

Table A.1 *(continued)*

Conferences *(continued)*

Communications and Policy Technology Network Table, Washington, D.C., multiple[a,d]

Caught in the Web II, Philadelphia, April 2000[a]

Cyberpolitics 2000, Part II: The Internet and American Democracy, San Francisco, October 2000[a]

Cyberpolitics 2000, Part III: The Industry Plays Politics, San Francisco, November 2000[a]

Democracy Online Project: In Search of Democracy's Domain in a Wired City (#3), Austin, Texas, June 2000[a]

Democratic National Convention, Internet Avenue, Los Angeles, California, August 2000[b,c,d]

Heritage Foundation: Government and New Economy: Facilitator or Threat, Washington, D.C., November 2000[a]

In Search of Democracy's Domain in a Dot-Com World, Public Testimony, Session I, Washington, D.C., April 2000[a]

In Search of Democracy's Domain in a Dot-Com World, Public Testimony, Session II, Washington, D.C., May 2000[a]

Internet Policy Institute: e-Voting Workshop, Washington, D.C., October 2000[a,d]

National Civic League, Arlington, Virginia, November 2000[a,d]

Neglection 2000, Washington, D.C., December 2000[a,d]

Online Political Advertising and Communications Seminar Program, Washington, D.C., October 1999[a,d]

Politics Online 1996, San Francisco, December 1996[a]

Politics Online 1996, Washington, D.C., November 1996[a]

Politics Online 1997, Washington, D.C., June 1997[a]

Politics Online 1998, Washington, D.C., December 1998[a]

Politics Online 1999, Washington, D.C., December 1999[a,d]

Politics Online 2000, Washington, D.C., December 2000[a]

Republican National Convention, Internet Alley, Philadelphia, Pennsylvania, July 2000[b,c,d]

VIP Voting Integrity, Washington, D.C., March 2000[a,d]

White House Conference on the New Economy, Washington, D.C., April 2000[a]

For-Profit Businesses

Advanced Consulting[a]
Advertising Age[a]
AffinityOnline.com[b]
Allied Minds Inc., Actionize.com[b]
Amazing Media[a]
Andersen Consulting[a]
AOL[a]

AOL, Election Guide[a]
AOL, President Match[a]
AOL, Straw Poll[a]
APCO[a,c]
AppNet Designs[a,b]
Aristotle Publishing[a–c]
Arlen Communications[a]

For-Profit Businesses (*continued*)

Aspen Software[a]
AT&T Labs[a]
A2S2 Digital Projects, Inc.,
    IntellectualCapital.com[a]
BitWrench Incorporated[a]
Bivings Woodell[a]
Bonner and Associates[a]
Booz, Allen and Hamilton[a]
Campaign Advantage[a,c]
Capitol Advantage[a–c]
Carol Trevelyn Strategy Group[a,c]
Casey/Dorin Internet Productions[a,c]
Compaq[a]
Computers and Publishing, Inc.[a]
Connecticut Business and Industry
    Association[a]
Context-Based Research Group[a]
Creators Syndicate[a]
CyberCash[a]
Dan Carol & Company[a,c]
D-Code[a]
Democrats.com[a–c]
Digex Incorporated[a]
Dimension Enterprises
    Incorporated[a]
Dittus Group[a]
DLW Internet Consultants[a]
Dynamic Logic, Incorporated[a]
Eadventure Holdings
Eadventure Holdings, Release 1.0[a]
e-Advocates[a–c]
Eastman Kodak[a]
eballot.net[b]
eContributor.com[a,b]
Edesigns-graphics.com[b]
Election.com[a–c]
Election Systems and Software[a]
Engage Technologies[a]
E. Politics[a]
E-Strategy.com[b]

Evolutionary Technologies
    International[a]
FantasyElections.com[b]
FAQvoter.com/Broad Daylight, Inc.[b]
Fenn King Communications[a]
FG Squared[a]
Flycast[a]
Flying Kite Communications[a,c]
Foreman, Heidepriem & Mager[a]
Forrester Research[a,c]
FreeDevelopers[a]
Gill Consulitng[a]
Global Business Network[a]
Global Strategies[a]
Goddard Claussen Strategic
    Advocacy[a]
Government Technology,
    GovTech.net[b]
GovWorks.com[a–c]
Grassroots.com[a–c]
Greitzer & Locks[a]
Grunwald Associates[a]
HarrisInteractive[a,c]
Hogan & Hartson, LLP[a]
Hokaday Donatelli Campaign
    Solutions[a–c]
Horizon Trading[a]
IBM[a]
IDEV.com[b]
Imaging Solutions
Imagitas[a]
Intellectual.com[a]
IntellectualCapital.com[b]
InterActivate[a]
Interactive Applications Group[b]
Interpublic[a]
IntraActive[a]
I-Politics.com[a,b]
iProgress[a]
Issue Dynamics, Incorporated[a,c,d]

(*continued*)

Table A.1 *(continued)*

For-Profit Businesses *(continued)*

Juno.com, Juno Advocacy Network[a,c]
Koening & Dorsey[a]
Lake, Snell, Perry and Associates[a,c]
LaPorte Communication Services[a]
Litton Industries[a]
LobbyForMe, L4M, Inc.[a,b]
Lucent Technologies[a]
MadScience.com[b]
ManyMedia[a]
Mascott Communications[a]
Master-Soft.com[b]
Microsoft[a]
Microvote[a]
Mindshare[a–c]
Mindwave Research[a]
MSN[a]
National Alliance of Business[a]
National Petroleum and Refiners Association[a]
Net.Capitol[a]
NETCampaign[a,b]
Netivation[a–d]
Net Politics Group[a–c]
Netscape-AOL[a]
New Media Associates[a]
New Media Communications[a]
New York Life Insurance Company[a]
Nielsen / Netratings[a]
NMP Consulting[a]
Notable Software[a]
Oglivy, Adams & Rinehart[a]
One Economy Corporation[a]
PC Data, Inc.[a]
Phil Noble & Associates[a,b]
Piper and Marbury[a]
Playing2Win[a]
Policast.com[b]
Political Insider, PoliticalInsider.com[b]
PoliticalJunkie.com[b]

PoliticallyBlack.com[a,b]
Politicallylatino.com[b]
Politics.com[a,b]
PoliticsOnline[a,b]
Polling Company, PollingCompany.com[b]
Polling Company[a]
Presage Internet Campaigns[a,c]
Princeton Survey Research Associates[a]
Proctor and Gamble[a]
Proxicom[a]
PSI and the Iowa 2000 Project[a]
PSI Net Consulting Solutions[a]
Publicus.net[b]
PurePolitics.com[b]
RadicalMail[a]
Right Side of Web[a]
RSA Security[a]
Sandler, Reiff & Young, PC[a]
Sawyer Miller Advertising
SAXoTECH, publicus.com[a]
Sherpa Consulting[a]
Soft Edge, Inc.[a]
Soza & Co.[a]
SpeakOut.com[a,b]
Stand for Children[a]
State Net[a]
Stone Media[a]
Sullivan & Mitchell PLLC[a]
Tarrance Group[a,c]
TechCentralStation.com[a]
Telediplomacy Incorporated[a]
This Nation, ThisNation.com[b]
Torso.com[a]
Town Hall, Incorporated[a]
Trippi, McMahon and Squier[a]
True Ballot, Inc[a,b]
Turtleback Interactive[a,c]
24/7 Media[a]

For-Profit Businesses (*continued*)

UNICAST[a]
UP Inc.[a]
US Newswire[a]
UST Public Affairs[a]
VirtualTownHall.net[a]
VirtualWorkroom[a]
VoteAction.com[b]
Vote.com[a–c]
Votehere.net[a,b]

Votenet-FEC Info[a,b]
Voter.com[a,c]
VoxCap.com[b]
Washington WebWorks[a]
WhoWhere?[a]
Wiley, Rein and Fielding[a]
Winston Strategic Information[a]
Wired Strategies[a,c]
Yahoo[a]

Foundations

Benton Foundation[a]
Carnegie Foundation[a]
DebateAmerica.org[b]
Freedom Forum[a]
Fund for the City of New York[a]
Heritage Foundation[a]
Kettering Foundation[a]

Libraries and Public Access to Information, Bill and Melinda Gates Foundation[a]
Markle Foundation[a–c]
Open Society Institute[a]
Pew Charitable Trusts[a,d]
Pew Internet and American Life Project[a]
Rockefeller Foundation[a]

Government

Connecticut Secretary of State[a]
Elections Canada[a]
Embassy of Switzerland[a]
Fannie Mae[a]
Federal Communications Commission, Office of the Chief Technologist[a,c]
Federal Communications Commission[a]
Federal Election Commission[a]
Federal Election Commission, Office of the General Counsel[a]
Federal Voter Assistance Program[a]
Iowa State Division of Elections[a]
Maryland State Board of Elections[a]
National Republican Senatorial Committee
National Science Foundation[a]

National Security Agency[a]
Office of Elections, Okaloosa County, Florida[a]
Office of Georgia Governor Sonny Perdue[a]
Office of Representative Anna Eschoo, U.S. House (D-CA-14th)[a]
Office of Representative Charles Norwood (R-GA)[a]
Office of Representative Julia Carson (D-IN)[a]
Office of Representative Marty Meehan (D-MA)[a]
Office of Representative Richard Gephardt (D-MO)[a]
Office of Representative Thomas Delay (R-TX)[a]
Office of Senator Conrad Burns (R-MT)[a]

(*continued*)

Table A.1 *(continued)*

Government *(continued)*

Office of Senator Patrick Leahy (D-VT)[a]

Office of the California Secretary of State[a]

Office of the Committee on House Administration[a]

Office of the Division of Elections, Florida State[a]

Office of the House Democratic Policy Committee[a,c]

Office of the House Republican Conference[a,c]

Office of the Senate Democratic Policy Committee[a]

Office of the Senate Democratic Technology and Communications[a,c]

Office of the Senate Republican Conference[a,c]

Office of the Senate Republicans Systems Administrator[a,c]

Office of the Speaker of the House[a,c]

Office of the United States Department of Commerce[a]

Royal Danish Embassy[a]

Smithsonian Institution[a]

United Nations[a]

United States Department of Commerce[a]

Washington State Division of Elections[a]

White House[a,c]

Wisconsin State Elections Board[a]

News Media

ABCNews.com[a,c]

Associated Press[a]

BushOnGuns.com[b]

Cable News Network (CNN)[a]

Cable News Network (CNN), All Politics[a,c]

California Journal[a]

Campaigns and Elections[a,c]

CBS[a]

Congressional Quarterly[a]

Congressional Quarterly, Governing Magazine[a]

Election2000.aol.com[b]

Fox.com[a]

Fox News[a]

Freedom Channel.com[a]

GalleryWatcher.com[b]

Hotline[a]

Indianapolis Star and News[a]

Industry Standard[a]

Internet Newsroom[a]

Japan Economic Review[a]

Knight Ridder[a]

Lexis-Nexis[a]

Los Angeles Times[a]

MSNBC[a]

Multimedia Daily[a]

National Journal, Cloakroom[a]

National Journal, PoliticsNow[a]

National Journal, Technology Daily[a,c]

National Public Radio, Technology Nation[a]

Newsday / LA Times[a]

Newsweek[a]

New York Times[a,c]

New York Times, Cybertimes[a]

OnlineDemocracy.com[b]

Policy News and Information Service, Policy.com[b]

Political Pulse[a]

Privacy Times[a]

News Media (*continued*)

Real Clear Markets,
    RealClearMarkets.com[b]
Real Clear Politics,
    RealClearPolitics.com[b]
Roll Call[a]
San Francisco Chronicle[a]
San Jose Mercury News[a]
Slate Magazine[a]

Time Magazine, Netly News[a]
USA Today[a]
Washington Post[a]
WashingtonPost.com[a]
Washington Post, Digital Ink[a]
Wired Magazine, Hotwired/Netizen[a]
Wired[a]
WPNI[a]

Nonprofit Organizations

Alliance for Better Campaigns,
    bettercampaigns.org[b]
American Association of Advertising
    Agencies[a]
American Association of Colleges[a]
American Association of Political
    Consultants[a]
American Association of Retired
    Persons[a]
American Council of Life
    Insurance[a]
American Planning Association[a]
American Political Network[a]
America's Community Bankers[a]
Americans for Tax Reform[a]
America's Future Foundation[a]
AmeriCorps VISTA[a]
Amnesty International[a]
Archdiocese of Philadelphia[a]
Association for Computing
    Machinery[a]
Association of Online Professionals[a]
Athena Alliance[a]
Austin Entrepreneurs Foundation[a]
Austin FreeNet[a]
Banking Industry Technology
    Secretariat[a]
BBBOnline Privacy Program[a]
Bighorn Center for Public Policy,
    BighornCenter.org[b]
Bionomics Institute[a]

BiPAC[a]
Black America's PAC[a]
Brookings Institute[a]
California Voter Foundation[a–d]
Campaign to Elect Clinton-Gore,
    1996[a–c]
Campaign to Elect Dole-Kemp,
    1996[a,c]
Campaign to Elect Gore-Lieberman,
    2000[a,c]
Campaign to Elect Jeb Bush for
    Governor, Florida, 1998[a]
Campaign to Elect Jesse Ventura for
    Governor, Minnesota, 1998[a,c]
Campaign to Elect Lois Capps to
    House of Representatives (D-23),
    1998[a]
Campaign to Elect Perot-Choate for
    President, 1996[a,c]
Campaign to Elect Peter Vallone for
    Governor, New York, 1998[a]
Campiagn to Elect Nader-LaDuke,
    2000[d]
Campaign to Nominate Bill Bradley
    for President, 2000[a]
Campaign to Nominate John McCain
    for President, 2000[a,c]
Campaign to Re-Elect Senator
    Barbara Boxer (D-CA), 1998[a]
Campaign to Re-Elect Senator John
    Kerry (D-MA), 1996[a,c]

(*continued*)

Table A.1 *(continued)*

Nonprofit Organizations *(continued)*

Capnet.org[b]

Center for Democracy and Technology[a,c]

Center for Governmental Studies[a,b]

Center for Media Education[a]

Center for Public Integrity, PublicIntegrity.org[b]

Christian Coalition[a]

Citizens for Better Medicare[a–c]

CitySkills.org[a]

Civil Rights Forum on Communications Policy[a]

civilrights.org, Technology Project[a]

Commission on Public Debates, Debates.org[b]

Common Cause[a,c]

Communications and Policy Technology Network[a]

Community Technology Centers' Network[a]

Community Technology Foundation of California[a]

Consumers Union[a]

Corporation for Public Broadcasting, CPB.org[b]

Council for Excellence in Government[a]

Cyberspace Law Institute[a]

DC Watch[a]

DebateAmerica.org[b]

Democracy in Action[a]

DemocracyNet (DNet)[a,b]

Democracy Online Project[a–c]

Democracy Project, DemocracyProject.org[b]

Democratic Congressional Campaign Committee[a]

Democratic National Committee, Bush-Cheney.net[b]

Democratic National Committee, MillionairesForBush.com[b]

Democratic National Committee[a]

E-Democracy.org[a]

Election Center[a]

EMILY'S List[a]

E-Voter Institute[a,c]

Freedom Channel, FreedomChannel.com[b]

Freedom Forum, FreedomForum.org[b]

Generations United[a]

George Washington University, Graduate School of Political Management, Committee for the Study of the American Electorate[a]

GreedyTV.org[b]

Half the Planet[a]

Handgun Control, Inc., BushandGuns.com[b]

Highway1[a]

Human Rights Campaign[a]

Independent Bankers Association of America[a]

Information Technology Association of America[a]

Institute for Global Communication[a]

Institute for Policy Innovation[a]

Institute for the Study of Civic Values[a]

Internet Alliance[a,b]

Internet Policy Institute[a–c]

Internet Political Report[a]

Internet Voter's Guide[b]

KQED Digital Content Strategy Project[a]

Lawyers' Committee for Civil Rights under Law[a]

LDScitizen.com[b]

Nonprofit Organizations (*continued*)

League of Conservative Voters, LCV.org[b]

League of Women Voters[a,b]

Libertarian Party[a]

Mainstreat USA, MomsForTheMainstream.com[b]

MajorleagueAsshole.com[b]

Minnesota E-Democracy[a–c]

Miretek Systems[a]

Morino Institute[a]

MoveOn.org[a–c]

National Academy of Social Insurance[a]

National Association of Secretaries of State[a,c]

National Association of State Election Directors[a]

National Civic League[a]

National Coalition on Black Civic Participation[a]

National Commission on Federal Election Reform[a]

National Conference of State Legislature, NCSL.org[b]

National Education Association[a]

National Low Income Housing Coalition[a]

National Republican Congressional Committee[a,c]

National Research Council, Computer Science & Telecommunications Board[a]

Net Elections, NetElections.org[b]

NetAction[a]

New Democratic Leadership Council, NDOL.org[b]

OMB Watch[a,c]

OnlineDemocracy.com[b]

Pacific Research Institute[a]

Pennsylvania Chemical Industry Council[a]

Pennsylvania State Employees Retirement System[a]

Philadelphia Two / Direct Democracy[a]

PolicyLink[a]

PoliticalInformation.com[b]

Politics1.com[b]

PollingReport.com[b]

PowerUP Inc.[a]

Progressive Policy Institute, PPIOnline.org[a,b]

Project Vote Smart[a]

Proposition 211[a]

Public Broadcasting Service, Horizons Cable Network[a]

Public Broadcasting Service, NewsHour Online[a]

Public Relations Society of America

Public Relations Society of America, Silicon Valley Chapter[a]

publicus.net

Quorum.org[a,b]

Republican National Committee, Goreline.com[b]

Republican National Committee, GoreReinventionConvention.com[b]

Republican National Committee[a]

Rock the Vote[a]

Service Employees International Union[a]

Smart Voter, SmartVoter.org[b]

Surdna Foundation[a]

Syracuse MetroNet[a]

Taxpayers for Common Sense, Taxpayer.net[b]

TechNet[a]

Techno Democracy Project[a]

Technology for All Americans[a]

TechRocks[a,c,d]

(*continued*)

Table A.1 *(continued)*

Nonprofit Organizations *(continued)*	
Third Millenium[a]	WomenVote.com[b]
ThreeStory.com[b]	x-pac[a-c]
Tobacco Free Kids[a]	YoungImpact.org[b]
Voters Telecom Watch[a]	Young Republican National
Voting Integrity Project[a]	Federation, Inc., Yrock.com[b]
Web White and Blue[a,b]	Youngrepuglicans.com[a]
Wisconsin Manufacturers and Commerce, WMC.org[b]	Youth Vote 2000, YouthVote.org[a,b]

Note: For the most part, these organizational names here are as reported by study participants. I have classified the organizations as primarily academic, for profit, nonprofit, governmental, foundation or news media because these are the groupings revealed by analysis of social networks in all conferences about politics and technology between 1995 and 2000. However, I have not provided details about the legal or tax status of each organization. This list includes a wide range of limited liability partnerships, political action committees, nonprofits, for-profits, charities, incorporated businesses, unicorporated businesses, limited charters, professional associations, sole proprietorships, political campaigns, and branded hypermedia projects.

[a] Sampled in social network analysis.
[b] Sampled in organizational survey.
[c] Sampled in interview.
[d] Sampled in ethnography.

Glossary

An *avatar* is the virtual representation of a real person. Political avatars appear in audio or graphic form, often on the internet or over the telephone. They encourage citizens to vote and promote themselves, other candidates, or issue positions. Avatars can seem interactive. For example, avatars have been programmed to listen in on a group's discussion board and to respond to arguments with counter-arguments or with links to issue-specific Web sites.

As a noun, *blog* is short for Web log. A blog is a Web page that serves as a publicly accessible personal journal for an individual. Typically updated daily, blogs often reflect the personality of the author. Blog can also be used as a verb, "to author a Web log."

Chat is real-time communication between two users via computer. Once a chat has been initiated, either user can enter text by typing on the keyboard and the entered text will appear on the other user's monitor. Most networks and online services offer a chat feature.

A *cookie* is a message given to a Web browser by a Web server. The browser stores the message in a text file. The message is then sent back to the server each time the browser requests a page from the server. The main purpose of cookies is to identify users and possibly prepare customized Web pages for them. When you enter a Web site using cookies, you may be asked to fill out a form providing such information as your name and interests. This information is packaged into a cookie and sent to your Web browser which stores it for later use. The next time you go to the same Web site, your browser will send the cookie to the Web server. The server can use this information to present you with custom Web pages.

So, for example, instead of seeing just a generic welcome page at a political party's website, you might se a welcome page with some headlines related to those you were researching the last time you visited. Cookies last for a particular browsing session, or until the user deliberately clears them out. Some share information with the server that places them on your computer; others are meant to be read by other servers as you visit other websites.

A *flashmob* is a sudden gathering of people, often for a peculiar political or cultural exercise. People in flash mobs are given short notice about location and time, perform according to a written script, and disperse quickly.

A *flash program* is a bandwidth friendly and browser independent vector-graphic animation technology. As long as different browsers are equipped with the necessary plug-ins, Flash animations will look the same. With Flash, users can draw their own animations or import other vector-based images.

Formed by combining hack with activism, *hacktivism* is the act of hacking into a Web site or computer system in order to communicate a politi-cally or socially motivated message. Unlike a malicious hacker, who may disrupt a system for financial gain or out of a desire to cause harm, the hacktivist performs the same kinds of disruptive actions in order to draw attention to a political cause. For the hacktivist, it is an internet-enabled way to practice civil disobedience and protest.

An *impression* is an advertisement's appearance on an accessed Web page. For example, if the page you're on shows three ads, that's three impres-sions. Advertisers use impressions to measure the number of views their ads receive, and publishers often sell ad space according to impressions. It can be tough to know, though, whether an impression really means a visitor saw the ad, since they could be browsing without graphics or might not have scrolled down far enough. Impressions are tracked in a log maintained by a site server and are often sold on a cost per thousand basis.

Internet Relay Chat (IRC), is a chat system developed by Jarkko Oikarinen in Finland in the late 1980s. IRC has become very popular as more people get connected to the internet because it enables people connected anywhere on the internet to join in live discussions. Unlike older chat systems, IRC is not limited to just two participants. To join an IRC discussion, you need an IRC client and internet access. The IRC client is a program that runs on your computer and sends and receives messages to and from an IRC server. The IRC server, in turn, is responsible for making sure that all messages are broadcast to everyone participating in a discussion. There can be many discussions going on at once; each one is assigned a unique channel.

Opposition research is the deliberate investigation of one campaign's history by a competing campaign. The opposition researcher will look through both a public and private history of a candidate, lobby group, or issue-group in the hope of finding scandalous information about the opponent.

A *page view* is a unit of measured exposure, when a web page has been viewed by one visitor. Page views are often used in online advertising, where advertisers use the number of page views a site receives to determine where and how to advertise.

A *portal* is a website or service that offers a broad array of resources and services, such as e-mail, forums, search engines, and on-line shopping malls. The first web portals were online services, such as AOL, that provided access to the web, but by now most of the traditional search engines have transformed themselves into web portals to attract and keep a larger audience. A web portal is commonly referred to as simply a *portal*.

Spam is electronic junk mail or junk newsgroup postings. Some people define spam even more generally as any unsolicited e-mail. However, if a long-lost brother finds your e-mail address and sends you a message, this could hardly be called spam, even though it's unsolicited. Real spam is generally e-mail advertising for some product sent to a mailing list or newsgroup. In addition to wasting people's time with unwanted e-mail, spam also eats up a lot of network bandwidth. Consequently, there are many organizations, as well as individuals, who have taken it upon themselves to fight spam with a variety of techniques. But because the internet is public, there is really little that can be done to prevent spam, just as it is impossible to prevent junk mail. However, some online services have instituted policies to prevent spammers from spamming their subscribers. There is some debate about the source of the term, but the generally accepted version is that it comes from the Monty Python song, "Spam spam spam spam, spam spam spam spam, lovely spam, wonderful spam..." Like the song, spam is an endless repetition of worthless text. Another school of thought maintains that it comes from the computer group lab at the University of Southern California who gave it the name because it has many of the same characteristics as the lunchmeat Spam: Nobody wants it or ever asks for it. No one ever eats it; it is the first item to be pushed to the side when eating the entree. Sometimes it is actually tasty, like the 1% of junk mail that is really useful to some people.

A *spider program* automatically fetches web pages. Spiders are used to feed pages to search engines. It's called a spider because it crawls over the web. Another term for these programs is webcrawler. Because most web pages contain links to other pages, a spider can start almost anywhere. As soon as it sees a link to another page, it goes off and fetches it. Large search engines, like Alta Vista, have many spiders working in parallel.

Spyware, also called adware, is any software that covertly gathers user information through the user's internet connection without his or her knowledge, usually for advertising purposes. Spyware applications are typically bundled as a hidden component of freeware or shareware programs that can be downloaded from the internet. Once installed, the spyware monitors user activity on the internet and transmits that information in the background to someone else. Spyware can also gather information about e-mail addresses and even passwords and credit card numbers. Spyware is similar to a Trojan horse, in that users unwittingly install the product when they install something else. A common way to become a victim of spyware is to download certain peer-to-peer file swapping products that are available today. Aside from the questions of ethics and privacy, spyware steals from the user by using the computer's memory resources and also by eating bandwidth as it sends information back to the spyware's home base via the user's internet connection. Because spyware is using memory and system resources, the applications running in the background can lead to system crashes or general system instability. Because spyware exists as independent executable programs, it has the ability to monitor keystrokes, scan files on the hard drive, snoop other applications, such as chat programs or word processors, install other spyware programs, read cookies, and change the default home page on the Web browser, consistently relaying this information back to the spyware author who will either use it for advertising/marketing purposes or sell the information to another party. Licensing agreements that accompany software downloads sometimes warn the user that a spyware program will be installed along with the requested software, but the licensing agreements may not always be read completely because the notice of a spyware installation is often couched in obtuse, hard-to-read legal disclaimers.

Usenet is a worldwide bulletin board system that can be accessed through the Internet or through many online services. The Usenet contains more than 14,000 forums, called newsgroups, that cover every imaginable interest group. It is used daily by millions of people around the world.

A *webring* is a series of Web sites linked together in a ring that by clicking through all of the sites in the ring the visitor will eventually come back to the originating site. All of the sites within the ring share a similar topic or purpose. There are Web rings on topics such as computer games and technology, hobbies such as quilting or stamp collecting, sports, traveling, pop culture, music, cars, etc. Web rings are a way for sites to generate more traffic by encouraging users to visit the other sites within the ring. Sites in the ring typically have an icon or graphic that indicates that it is part of a specific Web ring and visitors have the option of choosing the "next" or "previous" site in the ring.

References

Abbott, A. D. 1988. *The System of Professions: An Essay on the Division of Expert Labor.* Chicago: University of Chicago Press.

Abercrombie, N. 1991. "The Privilege of the Producer." In *Enterprise Culture*, ed. R. Keat and N. Abercrombie. London, Routledge.

Abu-Lughod, L. 1997. "The Interpretation of Culture(s) after Television." *Representations* 59: 109–134.

Accenture. 2001. *Egovernment Leadership: Rhetoric vs. Reality – Closing the Gap.* Chicago: Accenture. Working Paper 17.

Adler, P., and P. Adler, eds. 1987. *Membership Roles in Field Research.* Qualitative Research Methods Series. Newbury Park: Sage.

Alexander, C. J., and L. A. Pal. 1998. *Digital Democracy: Policy and Politics in the Wired World.* Toronto: Oxford University Press.

Almond, G., and S. Verba. 1963. *The Civic Culture: Political Attitudes and Democracy in Five Nations.* Thousand Oaks, Calif.: Sage.

Althaus, S. L., and D. Tewksbury. 2000. "Patterns of Internet and Traditional News Media Use in a Networked Community." *Political Communication* 17(1): 21–45.

Anderson, B. 1991. *Imagined Communities: Reflections on the Origin and Spread of Nationalism.* London and New York: Verso.

Arterton, F. C. 1987. *Teledemocracy: Can Technology Protect Democracy?* Newbury Park, Calif. [Washington, D.C.]: Sage; Roosevelt Center for American Policy Studies.

Bainbridge, W. 2003. "The Future of Internet: Cultural and Individual Conceptions." In *Society Online: The Internet in Context*, ed. P. N. Howard and S. Jones. Thousand Oaks, Calif.: Sage.

Barley, S. 1986. "Technology as an Occasion for Structuring: Evidence from Observations of CT Scanners and the Social Order of Radiology Departments." *Administrative Sciences Quarterly* 31: 78–108.

Barley, S. 1996. "Technicians in the Workplace: Ethnographic Evidence for Bringing Work into Organization Studies." *Administrative Sciences Quarterly* 41: 404–441.

Barley, S. 1997. *Between Craft and Science: Technical Work in U.S. Settings.* Ithaca: Cornell University Press.

Barney, D. 2000. *Prometheus Wired: The Hope for Democracy in the Age of Network Technology.* Chicago: University of Chicago Press.

Barrett, M., and G. Walsham. 1999. "Electronic Trading and Work Transformation in the London Insurance Market." *Information Systems Research* **10**(1).

Bartels, L. 1996. "Uninformed Votes: Information Effects in Presidential Elections." *American Journal of Political Science* **40**(1): 194–230.

Bate, J. 1997. "Whatever Happened to Organizational Anthropology? A Review of the Field of Organizational Ethnography and Anthropological Studies." *Human Relations* **50**(9): 1147–1175.

Batt, R., et al. 2001. Net-Working, Work Patterns and Workforce Policies for the New Media Industry. Washington, D.C.: Economic Policy Institute.

Baudrillard, J. 1978. *Critique of the Political Economy of the Sign.* St. Louis: Telos.

Baym, N. K. 2000. *Tune in, Log On: Soaps, Fandom, and Online Community.* Thousand Oaks, Calif.: Sage.

Behr, R., and S. Iyengar. 1985. "Television News, Real World Cues, and Changes in the Public Agenda." *Public Opinion Quarterly* **49**(1): 38–57.

Beniger, J. 1990. "Conceptualizing Information Technology as Organization, and Vice Versa." In *Organizations and Communication Technology*, ed. J. Fulk and C. Steinfield. Thousand Oaks, Calif.: Sage: 29–45.

Bennett, D., and P. Fielding. 1999. *The Net Effect: How Cyberadvocacy Is Changing the Political Landscape.* Washington, D.C.: Capitol Advantage.

Benoit, W., and P. Benoit. 2000. "The Virtual Campaign: Presidential Primary Websites in Campaign 2000." *American Communication Journal* **3**(3).

Berger, P., and T. Luckmann. 1967. *The Social Construction of Reality.* New York: Doubleday.

Berman, J., and D. Weitzner. 1995. "Abundance and User Control: Renewing the Democratic Heart of the First Amendment in the Age of Interactive Media." *Yale Law Journal* **104**(7): 1619–1637.

Bijker, W. E., and J. Law. 1992. *Shaping Technology/Building Society: Studies in Sociotechnical Change.* Cambridge, Mass.: MIT Press.

Bijker, W. E., et al. 1987. *The Social Construction of Technological Systems: New Directions in the Sociology and History of Technology.* Cambridge, Mass.: MIT Press.

Bimber, B. 1998a. "The Internet and Political Mobilization: Research Note on the 1996 Election Season." *Social Science Computer Review* **16**(4): 391–401.

Bimber, B. 1998b. "The Internet and Political Transformation: Populism, Community, and Accelerated Pluralism." *Polity* **31**(1): 133–160.

The Bivings Report. 2002. "Viral Marketing: How to Infect the World." London: The Bivings Group. Working Paper, April.

Blondheim, M. 1994. *News over the Wires: The Telegraph and the Flow of Public Information in America, 1844–1897.* Cambridge, Mass.: Harvard University Press.

Blumenthal, S. 1982. *The Permanent Campaign.* New York: Simon and Schuster.

Boczkowski, P. 2004. *Digitizing the News: Innovation in Online Newspapers.* Cambridge: MIT Press.

Borsook, P. 2000. *Cyberselfish: A Critical Romp through the Terribly Libertarian Culture of High Tech.* New York: Public Affairs.

Bourdieu, P. 1990. "Structure, Habitus, Practices." In *The Logic of Practice.* Palo Alto: Stanford University Press: 52–65.

Bourdieu, P. 1993. *The Field of Cultural Production.* New York, Columbia University Press.

Bowker, G. C., and S. L. Star. 1999. *Sorting Things Out: Classification and Its Consequences.* Cambridge, Mass.: MIT Press.

Brants, K., et al. 1996. "The New Canals of Amsterdam: An Exercise in Local Electronic Democracy." *Media, Culture and Society* **18**: 233–47.

Bronson, P. 2000a. *The First $20,000,000 Are Always the Hardest.* New York: HarperPerennial.

Bronson, P. 2000b. *The Nudist on the Late Shift.* New York: Broadway Books.

Brown, J. S. 2000. *The Social Life of Information.* Boston: Harvard Business School Press.

Brown, J. S., and P. Duguid. 1991. "Organizational Learning and Communities of Practise." *Organizational Science* **2**: 40–57.

Browning, G. 1996. *Electronic Democracy: Using the Internet to Influence American Politics.* Wilton, Conn.: Pemberton Press.

Budge, I. 1997. *The New Challenge of Direct Democracy.* Cambridge, U.K.: Polity Press.

Burbank, M. 1997. "Explaining Contextual Effects on Vote Choice." *Political Behavior.* **19**(2): 113–32.

Calhoun, C. 1998. "Community without Propinquity Revisited: Communications Technology and the Transformation of the Urban Public Sphere." *Sociological Inquiry* **68**(3): 373–397.

Canter, L. A., and M. S. Siegel. 1994. *How to Make a Fortune on the Information Superhighway: Everyone's Guerrilla Guide to Marketing on the Internet and Other on-Line Services.* New York: HarperCollins.

Cappella, J., V. Price, and L. Nir. 2002. "Argument Repertoire as a Reliable and Valid Measure of Opinion Quality: Electronic Dialogue during Campaign 2000." *Political Communication* **19**(1): 73–93.

Carmel, E. 1997. "American Hegemony in Packaged Software Trade and the 'Culture of Software.'" *Information Society* **13**: 125–142.

Casey, C. 1996. *The Hill on the Net: Congress Enters the Information Age.* Boston: AP Professional.

Casey, C. 2002. Interview, Washington, D.C.

Castells, M. 1996. *The Rise of the Network Society.* New York: Blackwell.

Clemens, E. S. 1997. *The People's Lobby: Organizational Innovation and the Rise of Interest Group Politics in the United States, 1890–1925.* Chicago: University of Chicago Press.

Clift, S. 2000. Interview, Los Angeles.

Cohen, A. P. 1985. *The Symbolic Construction of Community.* London: E. Horwood; Tavistock.

Congressional Quarterly. 2003. 105th Congress, 1995–1996 Election Results.

Constant, D., and L. Sproull. 1994. "What's Mine Is Ours, or Is It? A Study of Attitudes about Information Sharing." *Information Systems Research* **5**(4): 400–421.

Constant, D., et al. 1996. "The Kindness of Strangers: The Usefulness of Electronic Weak Ties for Technical Advice." *Organizational Science* **7**(2): 119–135.

Contractor, N., and E. Eisenberg. 1990. "Communication Networks and New Media in Organizations." In *Organizations and Communication Technology*, ed. J. Fulk and C. W. Steinfield. Newbury Park: Sage: 143–172.

Contractor, N., and P. Monge. 2004. *Theories of Communication Networks.* Oxford: Oxford University Press.

Converse, P. 1964. "The Nature of Belief Systems in Mass Public." In *Ideology and Discontent*, ed. D. Apter. New York: Free Press.

Converse, P. 1987. "Changing Conceptions of Public-Opinion in the Political-Process." *Public Opinion Quarterly* **51**(4): S12–S24.

Cornfield, M. 2000. Interview, Washington, D.C.

Correll, S. 1995. "The Ethnography of an Electronic Bar: The Lesbian Cafe." *Journal of Contemporary Ethnography* **24**(3): 270–298.

Cummings, T. 1984. "Transorganizational Development." *Research in Organizational Behavior* **6**: 367–422.

D'Alessio, D. 1997. "Use of the World Wide Web in the 1996 U.S. Election." *Electoral Studies* **16**(4): 489–500.

D'Alessio, D. 2000. "Adoption of the World Wide Web by American Political Candidates, 1996–1998." *Journal of Broadcasting & Electronic Media* **44**(4).

Daft, R., and R. Lengel. 1986. "Organizational Information Requirements, Media Richness and Structural Design." *Management Science* **32**(5): 554–571.

Dahl, R. A. 1956. *A Preface to Democratic Theory.* Chicago: University of Chicago Press.

Dahl, R. A. 1989. *Democracy and Its Critics.* New Haven: Yale University Press.

Davis, R., and D. Owen. 1998. *New Media and American Politics.* New York: Oxford: University Press.

Delli Carpini, M. 2000. "Gen.com: Youth, Civic Engagement, and the New Information Environment." *Political Communication* **17**(4): 341–349.

Delli Carpini, M. X., and S. Keeter. 1996. *What Americans Know about Politics and Why It Matters.* New Haven: Yale University Press.

Dewey, J. 1954. *The Public and Its Problems.* Athens: Ohio University Press.

Diamond, E., et al. 1993. "Pop Goes Politics: New Media, Interactive Formats, and the 1992 Campaign." *American Behavioral Scientist* **37**(2): 257–261.

Dibbell, J. 1993. "How an Evil Clown, a Haitian Trickster Spirit, Two Wizards, and a Cast of Dozens Turned a Database into a Society." *Village Voice*, December 21, pp. 36–42.

Dijk, J. v., and K. L. Hacker. 2000. *Digital Democracy: Issues of Theory and Practice.* London: Sage.

DiMaggio, P. 1997. "Culture and Cognition." *Annual Review of Sociology* **23**: 263–87.

DiMaggio, P., et al. 2001. "Social Implications of the Internet." *Annual Review of Sociology* **27**(1): 307–36.

Dinkin, R. 1989. *Campaigning in America: A History of Election Practices.* Westport, Conn.: Greenwood.

Doppelt, J. 1999. *Nonvoters: America's No-Shows.* Thousand Oaks, Calif.: Sage.

Dove, L. 2001. Interview, Washington, D.C.

Downing, J. 1989. "Computers for Political Change: Peacenet and Public Data Access." *Journal of Communication* **39**: 154–162.

Downing, J. 1991. *Computers for Social Change and Community Organizing.* New York: Haworth.

Drinkard, J. 1999. "E-Politics: How the Internet Is Transforming Grassroots Campaigns." *USA Today*, August 31, p. 1.

Dulio, D., et al. 1999. "Untangled Web: Internet Use during the 1998 Election." *PS: Political Science & Politics* **32**(1): 53–59.

Dutton, W., and K. L. Kraemer. 1985. *Modeling as Negotiating: The Political Dynamics of Computer Models in the Policy Process.* Norwood, N.J.: Ablex.

Eliasoph, N. 1998. *Avoiding Politics: How Americans Produce Apathy in Everyday Life.* Cambridge, U.K., and New York: Cambridge University Press.

Elmer, G. 2004. *Profiling Machines: Mapping the Personal Information Economy.* Cambridge: MIT Press.

Emirbayer, M., and J. Goodwin. 1994. "Network Analysis, Culture and the Problem of Agency." *American Journal of Sociology* **99**(6): 1411–1454.

Entman, R. M. 1989. *Democracy without Citizens: Media and the Decay of American Politics.* New York: Oxford University Press.

Etzioni, A. 2000. "Debating the Societal Effects of the Internet: Connecting with the World." *Public Perspective* **11**(3): 43–43.

Everard, J. 2000. *Virtual States: The Internet and the Boundaries of the Nation-State.* London: Routledge.

Fallows, J. M. 1996. *Breaking the News: How the Media Undermine American Democracy.* New York: Pantheon.

Faucheux, R. 1998. "How Campaigns Are Using the Internet: An Exclusive Nationwide Survey." *Campaigns and Elections* **19**(9): 22–25.

Ferdinand, P., ed. 2001. *The Internet, Democracy and Democratization.* London: Frank Cass.

Ferejohn, J. A., and J. H. Kuklinski. 1990. *Information and Democratic Processes.* Urbana: University of Illinois Press.

Fineman, S., and Y. Gabriel. 1996. *Experiencing Organizations.* London and Thousand Oaks, Calif.: Sage.

Foot, K., and S. Schneider. 2002. "2002 Campaign Web Sphere Analysis." Pew Charitable Trusts, PoliticalWeb.Info. Http://politicalweb.info, accessed November 27, 2004.

Foucault, M. 1977. *Discipline and Punish: The Birth of the Prison.* New York: Pantheon.

Foucault, M. 1991. "Governmentality." In *The Foucault Effect: Studies in Governmentality,* ed. C. G. Graham Burchill and Peter Miller. Chicago: University of Chicago Press.

Foucault, M. 1999. "Power as Knowledge." In *Social Theory, the Multicultural and Classic Readings,* ed. C. Lemert. Boulder: Westview: 475–81.

Frantzich, S. 1982. *Computers in Congress: The Politics of Information.* Thousand Oaks, Calif.: Sage.

Friedenberg, R. 1997. *Communication Consultants in Political Campaigns.* Westport, Conn.: Praeger.

Friedland, L. 1996. "Electronic Democracy and the New Citizenship." *Media, Culture and Society* **18**: 185–212.

Ganly, G. 1991. "Power to the People via Personal Electronic Media." *Washington Quarterly, Spring,* pp. 5–22.

Garton, L., et al. 1997. "Studying Online Social Networks." *Journal of Computer Mediated Communication* **3**(1): Online at http://www.ascusc.org/jcmc/vol3/issue1/garton.html.

Gerhards, J., and D. Rucht. 1992. "Mesomobilization: Organizing and Framing Two Protest Campaigns in West Germany." *American Journal of Sociology* **96**: 555–596.

Giddens, A. 1987. *Social Theory and Modern Sociology.* Stanford, Calif.: Stanford University Press.

Giddens, A. 1990. *The Consequences of Modernity.* Stanford, Calif.: Stanford University Press.

Giddens, A. 1991. *Modernity and Self Identity: Self and Society in the Late Modern Age.* Stanford Calif.: Stanford University Press.

Glass, A. 1996. "On-Line Elections: The Internet's Impact on the Political Process." *Harvard International Journal of Press/Politics* **1**(4): 140–146.

Goldstein, M. L. 2003. *Guide to the 2004 Presidential Election.* Washington, D.C.: Congressional Quarterly Press.

Gould, R. 1995. *Insurgent Identities; Class, Community and Protest in Paris from 1848 to the Commune.* Chicago: University of Chicago Press.

Graber, D. A. 1996. "The 'New' Media and Politics: What Does the Future Hold?" *PS: Political Science & Politics* **29**(1): 157–68.

Grabher, G. 2001. "Ecologies of Creativity: The Village, the Group, and the Heterarchic Organization of the British Advertising Agency." *Environment and Planning A* **33**: 351–374.

Grabher, G. 2002. "Fragile Sector, Robust Practice: Project Ecologies in New Media." *Environment and Planning A* **34**(11): 1903–2092.

Gray, C. H. 2001. *Cyborg Citizen: Politics in the Posthuman Age.* New York and London: Routledge.

Groper, R. 1996. "Electronic Mail and the Reinvogoration of American Democracy." *Social Science Computer Review* **14**(2): 157–68.

Grossman, L. 1996. *The Electronic Republic: Reshaping Democracy in the Information Age.* New York: Penguin.

Gutstein, D. 1999. *E.Con.* Toronto: Stoddart.

Haas, P. M. 1990. *Saving the Mediterranean: The Politics of International Environmental Cooperation.* New York: Columbia University Press.

Haas, P. M. 1992. "Introduction: Epistemic Communities and International Policy Coordination." *International Organization* **46**(1): 147–286.

Habermas, J. 1970. *Toward a Rational Society; Student Protest, Science, and Politics.* Trans. Jeremy J. Shapiro. Boston: Beacon.

Habermas, J. 1991. *The Structural Transformation of the Public Sphere.* Cambridge: MIT University Press.

Hacker, K. 1996. "Missing Links: The Evolution of Electronic Democratization." *Media, Culture and Society* **18**(2): 213–232.

Hacker, K., et al. 1996. "Uses of Computer-Mediated Political Communication in the 1992 Presidential Campaign: A Content Analysis of the Bush, Clinton and Perot Computer Lists." *Communication Research Reports* **13**(2): 138–146.

Hagel, J., et al. 1997. *Net Gain: Expanding Markets through Virtual Communities.* Boston: Harvard Business School Press.

Hague, B. N., and B. Loader. 1999. *Digital Democracy: Discourse and Decision Making in the Information Age.* London and New York: Routledge.

Hakken, D. 1999. *Cyborgs@Cyberspace: An Ethnographer Looks to the Future.* New York: Routledge.

Hardesty, R. 1976. "The Computer's Role in Getting out the Vote." In *The New Style in Election Campaigns,* ed. R. Agranoff. Boston: Holbrook.

Hardy, B. W., and D. A. Scheufele. 2005. "Examining Differential Gains from Internet Use: Comparing the Moderating Role of Talk and Online Interactions." *Journal of Communication* **55**(1): 71–84.

Hargittai, E. 2003. "Serving Citizens' Needs: Minimizing Online Hurdles to Accessing Government Information." *IT & Society* **1**(3): 27–41.

Harrison, L. E., and S. P. Huntington. 2000. *Culture Matters: How Values Shape Human Progress.* New York: Basic Books.

Hauben, M. 1997. *Netizens.* Los Alamitos, Calif.: IEEE Computer Society Press.

Hayward, A. 2000. *Sam's Teach Yourself E-Democracy Today.* Indianapolis: Sams.

Heclo, H. 1999. "Hyperdemocracy." *Wilson Quarterly* **24**(1): 62–71.

Herbst, S. 1998. *Reading Public Opinion: How Political Actors View the Democratic Process.* Chicago: University of Chicago Press.

Herrnson, P. S. 1992. "Campaign Professionalism and Fundraising in Congressional Elections." *Journal of Politics* **54**(3): 859–870.

Hilgartner, S., and C. Bosk. 1988. "The Rise and Fall of Social Problems: A Public Arenas Model." *American Journal of Sociology* **94**(1): 53–78.

Hill, K. 1998. *Cyberpolitics: Citizen Activism in the Age of the Internet.* Lanham, Md: Rowan & Littlefield.

Hill, S., and J. G. Hughes. 1997. "Computer Mediated Political Communication: The Usenet and Political Communities." *Political Communication* **14**(1): 3–27.

Hine, C. 2000. *Virtual Ethnography.* London and Thousand Oaks, Calif.: Sage.

Hirsch, P. 1972. "Processing Fads and Fashions: An Organization-Set Analysis of Cultural Industry Systems." *American Journal of Sociology* **77**(4): 639–659.

Horkheimer, M., and T. W. Adorno. 1972. *Dialectic of Enlightenment.* New York: Herder and Herder.

Howard, P. N. 2003. "Digitizing the Social Contract: Producing American Political Culture in the Age of New Media." *Communication Review* **6**(3): 213–245.

Howard, P. N. 2005. "Deep Democracy, Thin Citizenship: The Impact of Digital Media in Political Campaign Strategy." *Annals of the American Academy of Political and Social Science* **597**(1): 153–170.

Howard, P. N., and T. J. Milstein. 2003. "Spiders, Spam, and Spyware: New Media and the Market for Political Information." In *Internet Studies 1.0,* ed. M. Consalvo. New York: Peter Lang.

Howard, P. N., et al. 2001. "Days and Nights on the Internet: The Impact of a Diffusing Technology." *American Behavioral Scientist* **45**(3): 382–404.

Huckfeldt, R. 1995. *Citizens, Politics and Social Communication: Information and Influence in an Election Campaign.* New York: Cambridge University Press.

Huff, C., et al. 1989. "Computer Communication and Organizational Commitment: Tracing the Relationship in a City Government." *Journal of Applied Social Psychology* **19**: 1371–1391.

Huntington, S. P. 1996. *The Clash of Civilizations and the Remaking of World Order.* New York: Simon & Schuster.

Hurwitz, R. 1999. "Who Needs Politics? Who Needs People? The Ironies of Democracy in Cyberspace." *Contemporary Sociology* **28**(6): 655–661.

Innis, H. 1991. *The Bias of Communication.* Toronto: University of Toronto Press.

Innis, H. A., and M. Innis. 1972. *Empire and Communications.* Toronto: University of Toronto Press.

Introna, L., and H. Nissenbum. 2000. "Shaping the Web: Why the Politics of Search Engines Matters." *Information Society* **16**(3): 1–17.

Ireland, E., and P. T. Nash. 2001. *Winning Campaigns Online: Strategies for Candidates and Causes.* Bethesda, Md.: Science Writers Press.

Jackall, R. 1988. *Moral Mazes: The World of Corporate Managers.* Oxford: Oxford University Press.

Jagoda, K. 2000. *E-Voter Study 2000: Measuring the Effectiveness of the Internet in Election 2000.* Washington, D.C.: E-Voter Institute.

Jagoda, K., and N. Nyhan. 1999. *E-Voter 98: Measuring the Impact of Online Advertising for a Political Candidate.* Washington, D.C.: Westhill Partners.

Jennings, K., and V. Zeitner. 2003. "Internet Use and Civic Engagement." *Public Opinion Quarterly* **67**(3): 311–334.

Johnson, T., et al. 1999. "Doing the Traditional Media Sidestep: Comparing the Effects of the Internet and Other Nontraditional Media with Traditional Media in the 1996 Presidential Campaign." *Journalism and Mass Communication Quarterly* **76**(1): 99–123.

Johnson-Cartee, K. S., and G. A. Copeland. 1997. *Inside Political Campaigns: Theory and Practise.* Westport, Conn.: Praeger.

Kamarck, E. C. 1999. "Campaigning on the Internet in the Elections of 1998." In *Democracy.Com?: Governance in the Network World,* ed. E. C. Kamarck and J. S. Nye. Hollis, N.H.: Hollis.

Kamarck, E. C. 2002. "Political Campaigning on the Internet: Business as Usual?" In *Governance.Com: Democracy in the Information Age,* ed. J. S. Nye. Washington, D.C.: Brooking Institution Press.

Kamarck, E. C., and J. S. Nye, eds. 1999. *Democracy.Com?: Governance in the Network World.* Hollis, N.H.: Hollis.

Kamarck, E. C., and J. S. Nye.2002. *Governance.Com: Democracy in the Information Age.* Washington, D.C.: Brookings Institution Press.

Katz, E. 1987. "Communications Research since Lazarsfeld." *Public Opinion Quarterly* **51**(Special): S25–S45.

Katz, E. 1992. "On Parenting a Paradigm: Gabriel Tarde's Agenda for Opinion and Communication Research." *International Journal of Public Opinion Research* **4**(1): 80–85.

Kernell, S., and M. McDonald. 1999. "Congress and America's Political Development: The Transformation of the Post Office from Patronage to Service." *American Journal of Political Science* **43**(3): 792–811.

Kiesler, S., and L. Sproull. 1988. *Technological and Social Change in Organizational Communication Environments.* Pittsburgh, Pa.: Carnegie Mellon University Press.

Kiesler, S., and L. Sproull. 1992. "Group Decision Making and Communication Technology." *Organizational Behavior and Human Decision Processes* **52**(1): 96–123.

Kirp, D. 1992. "Two Cheers for the Electronic Town Hall: Or Ross Perot, Meet Alexis de Tocqueville." *The Responsive Community* **2**(4): 48–53.

Klein, H. 1999. "Tocqueville in Cyberspace: Using the Internet for Citizen Associations." *Information Society* **15**(4): 213–220.

Klinenberg, E., and A. Perrin. 2000. "Symbolic Politics in the Information Age: The 1996 Republican Presidential Campaigns in Cyberspace." *Information, Communication and Society* **3**(1): 17–38.

Kling, R. 1996. "Being Read in Cyberspace: Boutique and Mass Media Markets, Intermediation, and the Costs of on-Line Services." *Communication Review* 1(3).

Klotz, R. 1998a. "Discussion of Women's Issues in the 1996 Internet Campaign." *Woman & Politics*, **19**(4): 67–86.

Klotz, R. 1998b. "Virtual Criticism: Negative Advertising on the Internet in the 1996 Senate Race." *Political Communication* 15: 347–365.

Knack, S. 1995. "Does Moter-Voter Work? Evidence from State-Level Data." *Journal of Politics* 57(3): 796–811.

Knack, S., and J. White. 1998. "Did States' Moter Voter Programs Help the Democrats?" *American Politics Quarterly* **26**(3): 344–366.

Knorr-Cetina, K. 1999. *Epistemic Cultures: How the Sciences Make Knowledge.* Cambridge, Mass.: Harvard University Press.

Koehler, J. 1998. *The Human Side of Intranets: Content, Style and Politics.* Boca Raton, Fla.: Saint Lucie Press.

Kohut, A., and L. Rainie. 2003. *Modest Increase in Internet Use for Campaign 2002.* Washington, D.C.: Pew Research for the People and the Press, Pew Internet and American Life Project: 24.

Kraut, R., et al. 1998. "Internet Paradox – a Social Technology That Reduces Social Involvement and Psychological Well-Being?" *American Psychologist* **53**(9): 1017–1031.

Krosnick, J., and S. Telhami. 1995. "Public Attitudes toward Israel: A Study of the Attentive and Issue Publics." *International Studies Quarterly* **39**(4): 535–54.

Ku, G., L. L. Kaid, and M. Pfau. 2003. "The Impact of Web Site Campaigning on Traditional News Media and Public Information Processing." *Journalism and Mass Communication Quarterly* **80**(3): 528–547.

Kunda, G. 1992. *Engineering Culture: Control and Commitment in a High-Tech Corporation.* Philadelphia: Temple University Press.

Kush, C. 2000. *Cybercitizen: How to Use Your Computer to Fight for All the Issues You Care About.* New York: St. Martin's Griffin.

Kush, C. 2004. *The One-Hour Activist: The 15 Most Powerful Actions You Can Take to Fight for the Issues and Candidates You Care About.* San Francisco: Jossey-Bass.

Lane, F. S. 2001. *Obscene Profits: The Entrepreneurs of Pornography in the Cyber Age.* New York: Routledge.

Latour, B. 1981. "Unscrewing the Big Leviathan: How Actors Macrostructure Reality and How Sociologists Help Them Do It." *In Advances in Social Theory and Methodology: Towards an Integration of Micro and Macro Sociologies,* ed. K. Knorr-Cetina and Cicourel. Boston: Routledge: 277–303.

Lazarsfeld, P., and R. Merton. 1948. "Mass-Communication, Popular Taste, and Organized Social Action." In *The Communication of Ideas,* ed. L. Bryson. New York: Harper & Brothers: 95–118.

Lessard, B., and S. Baldwin. 2003. *Net-Slaves 2.0: Tales of "Surviving" the Great Tech Gold Rush.* New York: Allworth.

Lessig, L. 1999. *Code and Other Laws of Cyberspace.* New York: Basic Books.

Lewis, M. 2000. "Knowledge Networks: The Two-Bucks-a-Minute Democracy." *New York Times Magazine,* November 5, pp. 64–67.

Lippmann, W. 1991. *Public Opinion.* New Brunswick, N.J.: Transaction.

Luntz, F. 1988. *Candidates, Consultants and Campaigns: The Style and Substance of American Electioneering.* Oxford, U.K.: Blackwell.

Lupia, A. 1994. "Short Cuts versus Encyclopedias: Information and Voting Behavior in California Insurance Reform Elections." *American Political Science Review* **88**(3): 63–76.

Lupia, A. 1998. *The Democratic Dilemma: Can Citizens Learn What They Really Need to Know?* New York: Cambridge University Press.

Macauley, S. 1963. "Non-Contractual Relations in Business: A Preliminary Study." *American Sociological Review* 28: 55–67.

Mann, C., and F. Steward. 2000. *Internet Communication and Qualitative Research Online: A Handbook for Researching Online.* London: Sage.

Mansbridge, J. 1983. *Beyond Adversary Democracy.* Chicago: University of Chicago Press.

Marcus, G. 1995. "Ethnography in/of the World System: The Emergence of Multi-sited Ethnography." *Annual Review of Anthropology* **24**: 95–117.

Margolis, M. 2000. *Politics as Usual: The Cyberspace Revolution.* Walnut Creek, Calif.: AltaMira.

Margolis, M., et al. 1997. "Campaigning on the Internet: Parties and Candidates on the World Wide Web in the 1996 Primary Season." *Harvard International Journal of Press/Politics* **2**(1): 59–78.

Markham, A. 1998. *Life Online: Researching Real Experience in Virtual Space.* Walnut Creek, Calif.: AltaMira.

Massey, D. S., and N. A. Denton. 1993. *American Apartheid: Segregation and the Making of the Underclass.* Cambridge, Mass.: Harvard University Press.

Mauser, G. 1983. *Political Marketing: An Approach to Campaign Strategy.* New York: Praeger.

McAdam, D. 1982. *Political Process and the Development of Black Insurgency, 1930–1970.* Chicago: University of Chicago Press.

McGrath, M. 2000. "Wired for Civic Engagement: Using New Technology to Build Community." *National Civic Review* **89**(3): 193–202.

McLean, I. 1989. *Democracy and New Technology.* Cambridge, U.K.: Polity.

McLuhan, M. 1994. *Understanding Media: The Extensions of Man.* Cambridge: MIT University Press.

McNulty, W., and H. Truslow. 2002. How It Looked Inside the Booth. *New York Times,* November 6, p. B9.

Mele, C. 1999. "Cyberspace and Disadvantaged Communities: The Internet as a Tool for Collective Action." In *Communities in Cyberspace,* ed. M. A. Smith and P. Kollock. London: Routledge: 290–310.

Merton, R. K., et al. 1946. *Mass Persuasion: The Social Psychology of a War Bond Drive.* New York: Harper.

Milbank, D. 1999. "Virtual Politics: Candidates' Consultants Create the Customized Campaign." *New Republic,* July 5, pp. 22–27.

Miles, S. 2001. *How to Hack a Party Line: The Democrats and Silicon Valley.* New York: Farrar, Straus and Giroux.

Miller, D., and D. Slater. 2000. *The Internet: An Ethnographic Approach.* Oxford and New York: Berg.

Moll, M., and L. Shade, eds. 2001. *E-Commerce vs. E-Commons: Communications in the Public Interest*. Ottawa: Canadian Centre for Policy Alternatives.

Morrill, C., and G. Fine. 1997. "Ethnographic Contributions to Organizational Sociology." *Sociological Methods and Research* 25(4): 424–451.

Morris, D. 1999. *Vote.Com*. Los Angeles: Renaissance Books.

Morris, D. 2000. Interview, New York, N.Y.

Mutz, D. 1995. "Effects of Horse-Race Coverage on Campaign Coffers: Strategic Contributing in Presidential Primaries." *Journal of Politics* 57(4): 1015–1042.

Myers, D. D. 1993. "New Technology and the 1992 Clinton Presidential Campaign." *American Behavioral Scientist* 37(2): 181–187.

Neff, G. 2005. *Venture Labor: Work and the Burden of Risk in New York's Internet Industry*.

Neff, G., and D. Stark. 2004. "Permanently Beta: Responsive Organization in the Internet Era." In *Society Online: The Internet in Context*, ed. P. N. Howard and S. Jones. Thousand Oaks, Calif.: Sage.

Nie, N., and L. Erbring. 2000. "Our Shrinking Social Universe." *Public Perspective* 11(3): 44–45.

Noble, P. 2000. Interview, Los Angeles.

Norman, D. 1989. *The Design of Everyday Things*. New York: Basic Books.

Norris, P. 2000a. *A Virtuous Circle: Political Communications in Postindustrial Societies*. Cambridge and New York: Cambridge University Press.

Norris, P. 2000b. "The Internet and U.S. Elections, 1992–2000." In *Governance.Com: Democracy in the Information Age*, ed. E. C. Kamarck and J. S. Nye. Cambridge, Mass., and Washington, D.C.: Visions of Governance in the 21st Century, Brookings Institution Press: 59–77.

Ogburn, W. 1937. "The Influence of Inventions on American Social Institutions in the Future." *American Journal of Sociology* 43(3): 365–376.

Orlikowski, W. 1995. *Evolving with Notes: Organizational Change around Groupware Technology*. Cambridge: Sloan School Working Paper 186.

Orlikowski, W., and S. Barley. 2001. "Technology and Institutions: What Can Research on Information Technology and Research on Organizations Learn from Each Other?" *MIS Quarterly* 25(2): 145–165.

Ornstein, N. J., and T. E. Mann. 2000. *The Permanent Campaign and Its Future*. Washington, D.C.: American Enterprise Institute; Brookings Institution.

Orr, J. 1996. *Talking about Machines: An Ethnography of a Modern Job*. Ithaca, N.Y.: IRL Press.

Paccagnella, L. 1997. "Getting the Seats of Your Pants Dirty: Strategies for Ethnographic Research on Virtual Communities." *Journal of Computer Mediated Communication* 3(1): http://www.ascusc.org/jcmc/vol3/issue1/paccagnella.html.

Palast, G. 2003. "Winner Takes All." *The Big Issue*, June 16–22, pp. 10–11.

Parsons, T. 1969. *Politics and Social Structure*. New York: Free Press.

Patterson, O. 1997. *The Ordeal of Integration: Progress and Resentment in America's "Racial" Crisis*. Washington, D.C.: Counterpoint.

Pellow, D. N., A. Weinberg, and A. Schnaiberg. 1995. "Pragmatic Corporate Cultures: Insights from a Recycling Enterprise." *Greener Management International* 12: 95–110.

Perrow, C. 1999. *Normal Accidents*. Princeton, N.J.: Princeton University Press.

Phillips, J. 2000. Interview, Washington, D.C.

Pickering, J., and J. King. 1995. "Hardwiring Weak Ties: Interorganizational Computer-Mediated Communication, Occupational Communities, and Organizational Change." *Organizational Science* **6**(4): 479–486.

Podolny, J., and K. Page. 1998. "Network Forms of Organization." *Annual Review of Sociology* **24**: 57–76.

Poster, M. 1990. *The Mode of Information*. Cambridge, U.K.: Polity.

Poster, M. 1995. *The Second Media Age*. Cambridge, U.K.: Polity.

Postman, N. 1993. *Technopoly: The Surrender of Culture to Technology*. New York: Vintage.

Pratt, A. 2002. "Hot Jobs in Cool Places: The Material Cultures of New Media Product Spaces; the Case of the South of the Market, San Francisco." *Information, Communication and Society* **5**(1): 27–50.

Project Vote Smart. 2005. "Vote Smart Web Yellow Pages." Project Vote Smart. http://www.vote-smart.org, accessed May 2005.

Puopolo, S. 2001. "The Web and U.S. Senatorial Campaigns 2000." *American Behavioral Scientist* **44**(12): 2030–2047.

Putnam, R. D. 2000. *Bowling Alone: The Collapse and Revival of American Community*. New York: Simon & Schuster.

Putnam, R. D., et al. 1993. *Making Democracy Work: Civic Traditions in Modern Italy*. Princeton, N.J.: Princeton University Press.

Radway, J. 1988. "Reception Study: Ethnography and the Problem of Dispersed Audiences and Nomadic Subjects." *Cultural Studies* **2**(3): 359–376.

Rainie, L. 2000. *Trust and Privacy Online: Why Americans Want to Rewrite the Rules*. Washington, D.C.: Pew Internet and American Life Project.

Ransell, E. 1999. "Democracy Is an Interactive Form of Government: Tracey Western." *Fast Company*, Issue 30, December, p. 302.

Rash, W. 1997. *Politics on the Nets: Wiring the Political Process*. New York: W. H. Freeman.

Redd, L. 1988. "Telecommunications, Economics and Black Families in America." *Journal of Black Studies* **19**(1): 111–23.

Reed, L. 2001. Interview, Washington, D.C.

Rheingold, H. 1993. *Virtual Community: Homesteading on the Electronic Frontier*. Reading, Mass.: Addison-Wesley.

Rheingold, H. 2002. *Smart Mobs: The Next Social Revolution*. Cambridge, Mass.: Perseus.

Rice, R., and J. Katz 2003. "The Internet and Political Involvement in 1996 and 2000." In *Society Online: The Internet in Context*, ed. S. Jones. Thousand Oaks, Calif.: Sage.

Ronfeldt, D. 1992. *Cyberocracy Is Coming*. New York: Taylor and Francis.

Rosen, E. 2000. *The Anatomy of Buzz: How to Create Word-of-Mouth Marketing*. New York: Doubleday/Currency.

Sabato, L. 1981. *The Rise of Political Consultants: New Ways of Winning Elections*. New York: Basic Books.

Sabato, L. 1988. *Magic – or Blue Smoke and Mirrors? Reflections on New Technologies and Trends in the Political Consultant Trade*. Washington, D.C.: Annenberg Washington Program, Communications Policy Studies, Northwestern University.

Sabel, C. F. 1990. "Moebius-Strip Organizations and Open Labor Markets: Some Consequences of the Reintegration of Conception and Execution in a Volatile Economy." In *Social Theory for a Changing Society*, ed. J. Coleman. Boulder: Westview: 23–54.

Sabel, C. F. 1992. "Studied Trust: Building New Forms of Co-operation in a Volatile Economy." In *Industrial Districts and Local Economic Regeneration*, ed. B. Pyke and W. Sengenberger. Geneva, Switzerland: Institute for Labour Studies: 215–250.

Sachs, H. 1995. "Computer Networks and the Formation of Public Opinion." *Media, Culture and Society* 17(1): 81–99.

Sassen, S. 2004. "Sited Materialities with Global Span." In *Society Online: The Internet in Context*, ed. P. N. Howard and S. Jones. Thousand Oaks, Calif.: Sage: 295–306.

Saxenian, A. 1994. *Regional Advantage: Culture and Competition in Silicon Valley and Route 128*. Cambridge, Mass.: Harvard University Press.

Scammell, M. 2000. "The Internet and Civic Engagement: The Age of the Citizen-Consumer." *Political Communication* 17(4): 351–355.

Schier, S. E. 2000. *By Invitation Only: The Rise of Exclusive Politics in the United States*. Pittsburgh: University of Pittsburgh Press.

Schneider, S. M. 2001. "Congressional Candidate Web Sites in Campaign 2000: What Web Enthusiasts Wanted, What Candidates Provided." Net-Election.org. Http://web.archive.org/web/20010602192820/netelection.org/research/jan10report.pdf, Accessed August 23, 2004.

Schudson, M. 1998. *The Good Citizen: A History of American Civic Life*. New York: Martin Kessler.

Schwartz, E. 1996. *Netactivism: How Citizens Use the Internet*. Sebastopol, Calif.: Songline Studies.

Scott, J. C. 1985. *Weapons of the Weak: Everyday Forms of Peasant Resistance*. New Haven and London: Yale University Press.

Scott, J. C. 1998. *Seeing like a State: How Certain Schemes to Improve the Human Condition Have Failed*. New Haven: Yale University Press.

Scott, J. 2000. *Social Network Analysis: A Handbook*. Thousand Oaks, Calif.: Sage.

Selnow, G. 1994. *High-Tech Campaigns: Computer Technology in Political Communication*. Westport, Conn.: Praeger.

Selnow, G. 1998. *Electronic Whistle-Stops: The Impact of the Internet on American Politics*. Westport, Conn.: Praeger.

Sewell, W. 1992. "A Theory of Structure, Duality, Agency, and Transformation." *American Journal of Sociology* 98(1): 1–29.

Shah, D. V., N. Kwak, and R. L. Holbert. 2001. ""Connecting" and "Disconnecting" with Civic Life: Patterns of Internet Use and the Production of Social Capital." *Political Communication* 18(2): 141–162.

Shapiro, C., and H. Varvian. 1999. *Information Rules: A Strategic Guide to the Network Economy*. Boston: Harvard Business School Press.

Shenk, D. 1997. *Data Smog: Surviving the Information Glut*. San Francisco: Harper Edge.

Silver, D. 2000. "Margins in the Wires: Looking for Race, Gender, and Sexuality in the Blacksburg Electronic Village." In *Race in Cyberspace*, ed. B. Kolko, L. Nakamura, and G. B. Rodman. Boston: Routledge: 133–150.

Silver, M., and D. Geller. 1978. "On the Irrelevance of Evil: The Organization and Individual Action." *Journal of Social Issues* 34(4): 125–35.

Simmel, G., and K. H. Wolff. 1950. *The Sociology of Georg Simmel*. Glencoe, Ill.: Free Press.

Smith, M. R., and L. Marx. 1994. *Does Technology Drive History?: The Dilemma of Technological Determinism.* Cambridge: MIT Press.

Spears, R., and M. Lea. 1994. "Panacea or Panopticon? The Hidden Power in Computer-Mediated Communication." *Communication Research* 21(4): 428–459.

Sproull, L. 1992. *Connections: New Ways of Working in the Networked Organization.* Cambridge: MIT Press.

Sproull, L., and S. Kiesler. 1986. "Reducing Social Context Cues: Electronic Mail in Organizational Communication." *Management Science* 32(11): 1492–1512.

Stark, D. 1999. "Heterarchy: Distributing Intelligence and Organizing Diversity." In *The Biology of Business: Decoding the Natural Laws of Enterprise*, ed. J. Clippinger. San Francisco: Jossey-Bass: 153–179.

Starke-Meyerring, D., et al. 2004. "American Internet Users and Privacy: A Safe Harbor of Their Own?" In *Society Online: The Internet in Context*, ed. P. N. Howard and S. Jones. Thousand Oaks, Calif.: Sage.

Stimson, J. A. 2004. *Tides of Consent: How Opinion Movements Shape American Politics.* New York: Cambridge University Press.

Stromer-Galley, J. 2000. "Online Interaction and Why Candidates Avoid It." *Journal of Communication* 50(4): 111–132.

Stromer-Galley, J. 2003. "Will Internet Voting Increase Turnout? An Analysis of Vote Preference." In *Society Online: The Internet in Context*, ed. S. Jones. Thousand Oaks, Calif.: Sage.

Suchman, L. A. 1987. *Plans and Situated Actions: The Problem of Human-Machine Communication.* Cambridge and New York: Cambridge University Press.

Sunstein, C. R. 2001. *Republic.com.* Princeton, N.J.: Princeton University Press.

Swidler, A. 1986. "Culture in Action: Symbols and Strategies." *American Sociological Review* 51: 273–286.

Tambini, D. 1999. "New Media and Democracy: The Civic Networking Movement." *New Media & Society* 1(3): 305–29.

Tarde, G. 1898. *Opinion and Conversation: L'opinion et la foule.* Paris: Alcan.

Tarrow, S. 2003. "Rooted Cosmopolitans: Transnational Activists in a World of States." Cornell University. Workshop on Transnational Contention. *Working Paper:* 2001–2003. March 19.

Taylor, H. 2000. "Does Internet Research Work?" *International Journal of Market Research* 42(1): 51–63.

Tedesco, J. C., et al. 1998. "Presidential Campaigning on the Information Superhighway: An Exploration of Content and Form." In *The Electronic Election: Perspectives on the 1996 Campaign Communication*, ed. L. L. Kaid and D. G. Bystrom. Mahwah, N.J.: Lawrence Erlbaum.

Tehranian, M. 1990. *Technologies of Power: Information Machines and Democratic Prospects.* Norwood, N.J.: Ablex.

Tewksbury, D., and S. Althaus. 2000. "Differences in Knowledge Acquisition among Readers of the Paper and Online Versions of a National Newspaper." *Journalism and Mass Communication Quarterly* 77(3): 457–479.

Tewksbury, D., A. Weaver, and B. Maddex. 2001. "Accidentally Informed: Incidental News Exposure on the World Wide Web." *Journalism and Mass Communication Quarterly* 78(3): 533–554.

Toffler, A. 1985. *The Adaptive Corporation.* New York: McGraw-Hill.

REFERENCES

Toffler, A. 1990. *Powershift: Knowledge, Wealth, and Violence at the Edge of the 21st Century.* New York: Bantam.

Toffler, A., and H. Toffler. 1995. *Creating a New Civilization: The Politics of the Third Wave.* Atlanta: Turner.

Tsagarousianou, R., et al. 1998. *Cyberdemocracy: Technology, Cities, and Civic Networks.* London and New York: Routledge.

Turkle, S. 1995. *Life on the Screen: Identity in the Age of the Internet.* New York: Touchstone.

Uzzi, B. 1996. "The Sources and Consequences of Embeddedness for the Economic Performance of Organizations: The Network Effect." *American Sociological Review* 61: 674–698.

Uzzi, B. 1997. "Social Structure and Competition in Interfirm Networks: The Paradox of Embeddedness." *Administrative Sciences Quarterly* 42(3): 35–67.

Van Maanan, J., and S. Barley. 1984. "Occupational Communities: Culture and Control in Organizations." *Research in Organizational Behavior* 6: 287–365.

Vaughan, D. 1996. *The Challenger Launch Decision: Risky Technology, Culture, and Deviance at Nasa.* Chicago: University of Chicago Press.

Walch, J. 1999. *In the Net: An Internet Guide for Activists.* London: Zed Books.

Walker, J. 1991. *Mobilizing Interest Groups in America: Patrons, Professions, and Social Movements.* Ann Arbor: University of Michigan Press.

Warner, M. 2003. Machine Politics in the Digital Age. *New York Times*, November 9.

Warnick, B., and D. Endres. 2004. "Text-Based Interactivity in Candidate Campaign Web Sites: A Case Study from the 2002 Elections." *Western Journal of Communication* 68(3): 322–342.

Webster, F. 1995. *Theories of the Information Society.* London: Routledge.

Webster, J., and S. Lin. 2002. "The Internet Audience: Web Use as Mass Behavior." *Journal of Broadcasting & Electronic Media* 46(1): 1–12.

Wenger, E. 1998. *Communities of Practice: Learning, Meaning and Identity.* New York: Cambridge University Press.

West, D. 1993. *Air Wars: Television Advertising in Election Campaigns, 1952–1992.* Washington, D.C.: Congressional Quarterly Press.

Wicks, R., and B. Souley. 2003. "Going Negative: Candidate Usage of Internet Web Sites during the 200 Presidential Campaign." *Journalism and Mass Communication Quarterly* 80(1).

Wilhelm, A. 2000. *Democracy in the Digital Age: Challenges to Political Life in Cyberspace.* New York: Routledge.

Williams, R. 1985. *Keywords: A Vocabulary of Culture and Society.* New York: Oxford University Press.

Williams, R., and E. Williams. 2003. *Television: Technology and Cultural Form.* London and New York: Routledge.

Willock, R. 1998. "Digital Democracy: The 96 Presidential Campaign On-Line." In *The 1996 Presidential Campaign: A Communication Perspective*, ed. R. Denton. Westport, Conn.: Praeger: 179–197.

Winner, L. 1980. "Do Artifacts Have Politics?" *Daedalus* 109(1): 121–136.

Witte, J., and P. N. Howard. 2002. "The Future of Polling: Relational Inference and the Development of Internet Survey Instruments." In *Navigating Public Opinion: Polls, Policy and the Future of American Democracy*, ed. J. Manza, F. L. Cook, and B. I. Page. New York: Oxford University Press: 272–289.

Witte, J., et al. 2000. "Method and Representation in Internet-Based Survey Tools: Mobility, Community, and Cultural Identity in Survey 2000." *Social Science Computer Review* **18**(2): 179–195.

Wittig, M., and J. Schmitz. 1996. "Electronic Grassroots Organizing." *Journal of Social Issues* **52**(1): 53–69.

Wright, R. 1995. Hyperdemocracy. *Time Magazine,* January 23, pp. 15–21.

Xenos, M. A., and K. A. Foot. 2005. "Politics as Usual, or Politics Unusual? Position Taking and Dialogue on Campaign Websites in the 2002 U.S. Elections." *Journal of Communication* **55**(1): 169–185.

Yates, J. 1993. *Control through Communication: The Rise of System in American Management.* Baltimore: Johns Hopkins University Press.

Young, O. 1991. "Political Leadership and Regime Formation: On the Development of Institutions in International Society." *International Organization* **43**(4): 349–375.

Zaller, J., and S. Feldman. 1992. "A Simple Theory of the Survey Response – Answering Questions versus Revealing Preferences." *American Journal of Political Science* **36**(3): 579–616.

Zerubavel, E. 1992. *Terra Cognita: The Mental Discovery of America.* New Brunswick: Rutgers University Press.

Index

261

Mansbridge, Jane, 42, 102, 149, 207

mass media campaigns, 3, 107, 145–147; information processes, 152; organizational behavior, 160; source of content, 161; structure, 160

McLuhan, Marshall, 67

media effects: negative effects of new media, 64–65; neutral effects of new media, 65–66; positive effects of new media, 62–63; technology and politics, 5, 62

memory, 55, 59, 208

MeetUp.com, 14, 17

Merton, Robert, 61, 135, 183, 193

MessageTester, DataBank.com, 81

methods, 42, 60; and sampling, 218, 229. *See also* cultural frame; media effects; network ethnography; polling; social network analysis

MoveOn.org, 14, 167

narrowcasting, 37, 82, 87, 92, 148, 154, 159, 171, 180, 181, 183, 189, 191; defined, 8

National Association for the Advancement of Colored People (NAACP), 137

National Education Association (NEA), 88

National Organization for Women (NOW), 29

National Rifle Association (NRA), 15, 29, 137, 138, 194

network ethnography, 40–42, 219–223

Nielsen ratings, 5, 95

nonvoters, 131, 133, 147, 197

NPHaHo, 166

objects, 54, 55

OpinionBot, Voting.com, 106

opposition research, 5, 44, 148, 157, 168, 241

organizational behavior. *See* information management; management

page view, 241

Paris Commune, 141

PeaceNet, 12

Plato, 102

political consultants, 43–44; authority of IT specialists, 168; community identity, 48–51; as a cultural industry, 2, 133, 166, 169; goals, 44–48; industry conferences, 2, 35, 166, 223–226; power and status, 158; shared ideology, 51–54

political culture: defined, 71; defined by campaign managers, 54–60; hard determinism and free will, 68–69; soft determinism, 71

polling: direct and indirect inference, 127; push poll, 87, 116, 157, 174; random digit dial surveys, 98, 107, 116

portal, 241

privacy, 128; deciding to violate, 176; informed consent, 76, 80, 117, 132, 178, 187, 199; privacy policy, 110, 113; in survey research, 110

presidential campaigns: to elect Bush-Cheney, 2000, 45, 48, 49, 96; to elect Bush-Cheney, 2004, 17; to elect Bush-Quale, 1992, 8; to elect Clinton-Gore, 1992, 8; to elect Clinton-Gore, 1996, 10; to elect Gore-Lieberman, 2000, 138, 153; to elect Kerry-Edwards, 2004, 17, 138; to elect Nader-LaDuke, 2000, 13; to elect Perot-Stockdale, 1992, 8; to nominate Bradley, 2000, 13, 108, 121, 153; to nominate Dean,